THE ENERGY AND ENVIRONMENT CHECKLIST

An Annotated Bibliography of Resources

Prepared by
BETTY WARREN

FRIENDS OF THE EARTH · SAN FRANCISCO

Library of Congress Catalog Number 79-56912
ISBN: 0-913890-37-5

Distributed by Friends of the Earth Books
          124 Spear Street
          San Francisco 94105

Cover by Bill Oetinger

Abbreviations

The following abbreviations are used in this bibliography:
  AEC—Atomic Energy Commission (defunct)
  CEP—Citizens' Energy Project
  DOE—Department of Energy
  EARS—Environmental Action Reprint Service
  EPA—Environmental Protection Agency
  ERDA—Energy Research and Development Administration (defunct)
  FEA—Federal Energy Administration (defunct)
  FOE—Friends of the Earth
  FTC—Federal Trade Commission
  HEW—Department of Health, Education, and Welfare
  HUD—Department of Housing and Urban Development
  NASA—National Aeronautics and Space Administration
  NRC—Nuclear Regulatory Commission
  NSF—National Science Foundation
  NTIS—National Technical Information Service
  OECD—Organization for Economic Cooperation and Development
  OPEC—Ogranization of Petroleum Exporting Countries
  OSHA—Occupational Safety and Health Act
  S.A.S.E.—Self-addressed stamped envelope
  UCS—Union of Concerned Scientists
  TEA—Total Environmental Action
  TIC—Technical Information Center
  UNESCO—United Nations Educational, Scientific, and Cultural
    Organization
  UNIPUB—United Nations Publications
  USGPO—United States Government Printing Office

CONTENTS

INTRODUCTION

THIS BIBLIOGRAPHY, in the tradition of all Friends of the Earth publications, has been compiled with the aim of furthering the understanding of the ecological imperatives: everything is connected to everything else, and there is no such thing as a free lunch.

Most of the entries are concerned with energy and its impact upon society and the environment. The emphasis is on resources for the Soft Energy Path; however, important works representing other viewpoints are included in order to make this a well-rounded reference. The annotations are, for the most part, descriptive rather than critical; inclusion of a work does not constitute endorsement. We have not attempted to include the vast technical literature published by government agencies, universities, and research organizations, which is available in major libraries, or can be obtained through resources listed in this bibliography. The 1980 edition of the *Energy and Environment Checklist* has been completely revised, expanded, and reorganized. We hope that you will find it a useful tool.

We are most grateful to the many individuals and organizations that have helped in providing this information. Although too numerous to list here, their names and good works appear throughout this volume.

Ordering Materials

In this rapidly advancing field it is not possible to keep up with every change in price, date, and edition, and additions and deletions. These data can only be considered approximate. The prices quoted are for the least expensive edition located, usually a paperback. Some organizations have a sliding price scale, for example. $5 to individuals and non-profit groups, but $10.00 to business; this will be indicated as $5/$10.

To purchase materials listed in the bibliography and not available locally, it is advisable to send for publication lists and catalogs to confirm current availability, price, and shipping charges. Even if the requested item is no longer in stock, there may be revisions or additional material of interest. A large, self-addressed, stamped envelope (S.A.S.E.) would be appreciated by non-profit organizations. The ORGANIZATIONS section includes the addresses of many of these sources; additional information may be found in ORGANIZATIONS: REFERENCES, and in the publishers' section of *Books in Print* at your library reference desk.

In this bibliography, several major sources of material are indicated by abbreviations in parentheses after the citations:

(FOE)—Friends of the Earth, 124 Spear St., San Francisco, CA 94105.
A booklist describes many publications on energy, the environment, and the Earth's Wild Places. We do recommend these books!

(CEP)—Citizens' Energy Project, 1110 Sixth St., Suite #300, Washington, DC 20001.
Catalog includes many books and articles on energy issues for the general reader and the student. Accurate, informative, and inexpensive.

(EARS)—Environmental Action Reprint Service, Box 545, La Veta, CO 81055.
This mail-order bookstore is an excellent source of carefully selected, readable, and useful books, both technical and non-technical, as well as articles, plans, posters, pins, stickers, and T-shirts. Send for the free *Energy* and *Nuclear* catalogs.

(ReSource)—Re-Source, Inc., P.O. Box 127, Astor Station, Boston, MA 02123.
Resources for the nuclear activist, including books, literature, and paraphernalia. A catalog is available.

(TEA)—Total Environmental Action, Inc., 24 Church Hill, Harrisville, NH 03450.
A reliable source of information on solar energy, with books, slides, plans, and consulting services.

(NTIS)—National Technical Information Service, U.S. Department of Commerce, 5285 Port Royal Road, Springfield, VA 22161.
The central source for U.S. government research publications.

(UNIPUB)—United Nations Publications, 345 Park Ave. South, New York, NY 10010.
Publishers and distributors of United Nations and other international scientific studies.

(USGPO)—Superintendent of Documents, U.S. Government Printing Office, Washington, DC 20402.
Subject bibliographies describe the wide range of publications available. See U.S. GOVERNMENT.

ENERGY AND THE ENVIRONMENT

References

Barnouw, Dorothy Beach, and Dickinson, Irene Power. *Energy Bibliography. Annotated.* Washington, D.C.: National Intervenors, 1978. 60 pp. $2.00. (CEP)
This resource contains in-depth reviews of over 200 selected books on nuclear power and solar energy, as well as listing over 200 journals and organizations concerned with safe energy.

Considine, Douglas M., ed. *Energy Technology Handbook.* New York, N.Y.: McGraw-Hill, 1977. 1857 pp. $58.50.
This complete one-volume reference work is for scientists, engineers, industry, educators, and concerned citizens was prepared by experts from government, industry, universities, and research organizations. It sets forth the fundamentals of major energy sources, with emphasis on the more promising new technologies.

Crabbe, David, and McBride, Richard. *The World Energy Book: An A-Z Atlas and Statistical Source Book.* Cambridge, Mass.: Massachusetts Institute of Technology Press, 1978. 259 pp. $12.50.
This comprehensive reference includes an A-Z section with approximately 1500 terms, definitions, and illustrations related to energy technology, economics, production, and utilization. An atlas of 35 maps illustrates the distribution of energy resources and consumption, while the statistical section provides additional data.

Ehrlich, Paul R., Ehrlich, Anne H., and Holdren, John P. *Ecoscience: Population, Resources, Environment.* San Francisco, Calif., Freeman, 1977. 1052 pp. $19.95.
Here is the environmentalist's all purpose reference book: a staggeringly comprehensive work on biology, physics, energy economics, population dynamics, agriculture, and more. The authors look at everything through ecological glasses, stressing interdependencies. Each section is followed by an annotated bibliography.

Environment Information Center, Inc., 292 Madison Ave., New York, NY 10017
This is one of the world's largest independent clearinghouses for energy and environment information. Services include computer tapes; microfiche libraries; document data banks; contract research; information on laws, films, organizations, people, and publications; and publications which are updated monthly, bi-monthly, or annually such as:

Energy Information Abstracts.	*Environment Information Abstracts.*
Energy Information Locator.	*Environment Regulation Handbook.*
Energy Directory Update.	*Environment Index.*

Toxic Substances Handbook.
Land Use Planning Abstracts.

Solar Energy Update.
Energy Index.

These comprehensive (and expensive) volumes may be located in DOE, EPA, or university libraries.

Environment Information Center, Inc. *The Energy Index.* New York, N.Y.: Environment Information Center, Inc. Updated annually.

Provides access to all types of energy information: reviews major energy events of the year, legislation, conferences, publications, films, statistics. Abstracts from the literature are indexed by subject, author, and region.

Government Institutes, Inc. *Energy Reference Handbook.* Government Institutes, Inc., 4733 Bethesda Ave., NW, Washington, DC 20014. 286 pp. $14.95.

A glossary of over 3000 key words and abbreviations frequently used in the field of energy, plus conversion tables and data.

Hammond, Kenneth A.; Macinko, George; and Fairchild, Wilma B., eds. *Sourcebook on the Environment: A Guide to the Literature.* Association of American Geographers. Chicago, Ill.: University of Chicago Press, 1978. 613 pp.

The major elements and issues relating to the environment are all considered here. Each section includes an overview and cites extensive references; lists of organizations and periodicals are included, as well as a review of federal environmental legislation. In the Energy and Environment Section, author Earl Cook finds that energy use and the maintenance of environmental quality are in fundamental conflict in a growth-oriented society.

Hunt, V. Daniel. *Energy Dictionary.* New York, N.Y.: Van Nostrand Reinhold, 1979. 518 pp. $22.50.

An overview of the field of energy is followed by definitions and explanations of more than 4000 terms used today; many are illustrated. Conversion factors, acronyms, and other useful features are also included.

McGraw-Hill. *Encyclopedia of Energy.* New York, N.Y.: McGraw-Hill, 1976. 785 pp. $24.50.

A reference for scientists, engineers, educators, and the lay reader, with information on all aspects of energy, including economic, political, environmental, and technological topics, drawn largely from government and industry sources. Well organized and conveniently indexed.

Research and Education Association. *Modern Energy Technology.* Research and Education Association, 342 Madison Ave., New York, N.Y.: 10017. 1975. Vols. I & II, approx. 1800 pp.

A compendium of technical information on all aspects of conventional and alternative energy technologies.

U.S. Department of Energy. Energy Information Administration. *EIA Publications Directory.* Washington, D.C., January, 1979. S/N 061-000-0027704. 59 pp. $2.40. Also, *Supplement.* July 1979. S/N 061-000-00348-7. (USGPO)

A guide to DOE/EIA reports, with summaries and ordering information; a major source of statistical information on all aspects of energy supply and demand, reserves, world prices, production, transportation, and utilities.

U.S. Department of Energy/Technical Information Center. *Selected DOE Headquarters Publications.* DOE/AD-0010/4. 1979. Free from DOE/TIC, P.O. Box 62, Oak Ridge, TN 37830.

A guide to recent DOE publications available to the general public, with information for ordering.

U.S. Energy Research and Development Administration. *Magnetohydrodynamics. Power Generation and Theory: A Bibliography.* TID-3356. ERDA, Office of Public Affairs/Technical Information Center, 1975. 875 pp. $13.60.
Magnetohydrodynamic generators promise to provide a more efficient method for conversion of thermal energy to electric power than conventional power plants. Includes 8539 citations, foreign and domestic, in categories and cross-indexed.

World Energy Conference. *Directory of Energy Information Centers in the World.* Paris, 1976. 299 pp.
Provides an outline of the services available at each location.

World Priorities, Inc. *World Energy Survey.* World Priorities, Inc., Box 1003, Leesburg, VA 22075. 1979. 34 pp. $3.50.
Many graphs and charts clarify data on energy use, future energy options, resource availability, and environmental and health effects.

Overviews and Issues.

Ames, Mary E. *Outcome Uncertain: Science and the Political Process.* Communications Press Inc., 1346 Connecticut Ave. NW, Washington, DC 20036. 1978. $7.95.
Traces the interaction of government, science, and industry in four case studies: the SST; the North Anna Nuclear Plant; the saccharin ban; and DNA research.

Aronowitz, Stanley. *Food, Shelter, and the American Dream.* New York, N.Y.: Seabury Press, 1974. 188 pp. $5.95.
Assesses the causes and implications of the food and energy shortages. Points out the economic, political and social consequences of government manipulation of resources as an instrument of policy.

Ashley, Holt; Rudman, Richard L.; and Whipple, Christopher. *Energy and the Environment: A Risk/Benefit Approach.* New York, N.Y.: Pergamon, 1976. 305 pp. $20.00.
Stanford University's Institute for Energy Studies and industry's Electric Power Research Institute. cooperated on this series of seminars on the problems involved in allocating limited national resources among future energy options, using risk/benefit methodology to help decide major issues.

Bailey, James E., ed. *Energy Systems: An Analysis for Engineers and Policy Makers.* New York, N.Y.: Marcel Dekker, 1978. 163 pp. $19.50.
An interdisciplinary collection of seminar papers that describe the various economic, political, and technological constraints on solutions to the energy crisis.

Barney, Gerald O., ed. *The Unfinished Agenda: The Citizen's Policy Guide to Environmental Issues.* New York, N.Y.: Crowell, 1977. 184 pp. $3.95.
This report, sponsored by the Rockefeller Brothers Fund, outlines the major problems and makes specific recommendations in the areas of population, food, energy, natural resources, pollution, land use, DNA, and the role of society in decision-making.

Bergman, Elihu; Bethe, Hans A.; and Marshak, Robert, eds. *American Energy*

Choices Before the Year 2000. Lexington, Mass.: Lexington Books, 1978. 160 pp. $14.50.

This discussion of short term policy alternatives focuses on conservation, coal, uranium fission, the plutonium breeder reactor, and fusion.

Boyd, Waldo T. *The World of Energy Storage.* New York, N.Y.: Putnam, 1977. 159 pp. $5.29.

Here is a seldom considered aspect of energy management: the ways in which energy can be stored, as in elevated water, food, fuels, and by mechanical, electrochemical and thermal means. We must expend energy to store energy; and it is never possible to extract all of the energy from a given storage medium. A very readable, non-technical account. (Education)

Brown, Lester R. *Redefining National Security.* Washington, D.C.: Worldwatch Institute, 1977. 46 pp. $2.00 (FOE)

National security is broadly defined to include not only foreign military threats, but the unbalancing of the ecosystem by factors such as overpopulation; the depletion of forests, croplands, grazing lands, fisheries, and non-renewable energy sources; and by inadvertent climate modification.

Brown, Lester R. *Resource Trends and Population Policy: A Time for Reassessment.* Washington, D.C.: Worldwatch Institute, 1979. 55 pp. $2.00. (FOE) (EARS)

Population growth is causing increasing pressure on the earth's basic biological resources and supplies of fossil fuels.

Brown, Theodore L. *Energy and the Environment.* Columbus, Ohio: Charles Merrill Publishing Co., 1971. 141 pp.

Presents evidence which sets limits on man's consumption of energy due to thermal and air pollution, and world climate effects.

Brubaker, Sterling. *In Command of Tomorrow: Resource and Environmental Strategies for Americans:* A Resources for the Future Study. Baltimore, Md.: Johns Hopkins University Press, 1975. 177 pp. $7.95.

Advocates a future mode of living based on population restraint, restricted land use, a shift to inexhaustible energy sources, and greater use of common materials and renewable resources.

Brubaker, Sterling. *To Live on Earth: Man and His Environment in Perspective:* A Resources for the Future Study. Baltimore, Md.: John Hopkins University Press, 1972. 193 pp. $8.95.

Cites the major threats to the environment: man's effect on global climate, radioactivity, and the problems of energy, food, waste, and use of space.

Clark, Wilson. *Energy for Survival: The Alternative to Extinction.* New York, N.Y.: Doubleday, 1975. 652 pp. $4.95 (EARS) (TEA)

One of the best overall analyses of the socio-economic and environmental aspects of energy. Includes up-to-date energy information on a non-technical level, and extensive references.

Clarke, Robin. *Notes for the Future: An Alternative History of the Past Decade.* New York, N.Y.: Universe, 1976. 238 pp. $4.50. (EARS)

This collection of 27 essays on the beginnings of the post-industrial revolution includes the works of Barry Commoner, Paul Ehrlich, Garrett Hardin, Theodore Roszak, E.F. Schumacher, George Wald, M. Bookchin and many others.

Cockburn Alexander, and Ridgeway, James, eds. *Political Ecology: An Activists Reader on Energy, Land, Food, Technology, Health, and the Economics and Politics of Social Change.* New York, N.Y.: Times Books, 1979. 422 pp. $17.50.

The term "political ecology" describes the radical movements which struggle for the preservation of the environment and against nuclear power in the United States and advanced industrial countries. Contributors include E.F. Schumacher, Ralph Nader, Ivan Illich, Barry Commoner, George McGovern, Thorsten Veblen, Amory Lovins, and other innovative thinkers.

Common Cause. *Open for Business Only?* Issue Development Office, Common Cause, 2030 M St. NW, Washington, DC 20036. 1979. 100 pp. $3.00.

This study of openness and accountability within the U.S. Department of Energy finds that industry and business wield far greater influence than the general public.

Commoner, Barry. *The Closing Circle: Nature, Man, and Technology.* New York, N.Y.: Bantam Books, 1971 327 pp. $2.25 (EARS)

The roots of our environmental crisis lie in the means by which we produce wealth. Ecological survival requires the adoption of technologies appropriate to the natural world.

Commoner, Barry. *The Politics of Energy.* New York, N.Y.: Knopf, 1979. 101 pp. $4.95. (EARS)

Dr. Commoner analyzes the National Energy Plan and the politics behind it, and finds that it will not work. Energy prices will continue to rise, adding to inflationary pressures. The real costs and risks of dependence upon coal and nuclear power are prohibitive. The only alternative is to develop renewable energy sources now, and make the solar transition.

Commoner, Barry. *The Poverty of Power.* New York, N.Y.: Knopf, Inc., 1976. 314 pp. $2.75 (EARS) (TEA)

In-depth analysis of energy problems, the economic crisis, and social implications. Examines the powerful links between the ways we use and misuse energy, capital and labor, and predicts that huge energy conglomerates will topple of their own weight.

Commoner, Barry, et al., eds. *Energy and Human Welfare - A Critical Analysis. Vol. I: The Social Costs of Power Production.* New York, N.Y.: Macmillan Information, 1975. 217 pp. $14.95. Prepared for the Scientists' Institute for Public Information.

The environmental effects of thermal and air pollution, mining, oil spills, radioactivity, reactor safety, and the storage of radioactive wastes must be considered as costs of power production.

Commoner, Barry, ed al., eds. *Energy and Human Welfare Vol. II: Alternative Technologies for Power Production.* New York, N.Y.: Macmillan Information 1975. 213 pp. $14.95. Prepared for the Scientists' Institute for Public Information.

The outlook for fuel resources, new energy technologies and the environmental consequences of various energy technologies are analyzed in this study.

Commoner, Barry, et al., eds. *Energy and Human Welfare, Vol. III: The End Use for Power.* New York, N.Y.: Macmillan Information, 1975, 185 pp. $14.95. Prepared for the Scientists' Institute for Public Information.

Addresses, essays, and lectures on energy consumption in the United States make up this volume.

Cook, Earl. *Man, Energy, Society*. San Francisco, Calif.: W.H. Freeman, 1976. 478 pp. $7.95

Here is a geographical and historical view of energy that will provide the background necessary for an understanding of contemporary problems. Presents the physical, biological and social costs of present energy use, and points out the necessity of using renewable energy sources and moving toward a society of "affluent scarcity".

Critical Mass Journal. *Decentralized Energy Systems*. Critical Mass Journal, P.O. Box 1538, Washington, DC 20013.1977. $1.00.

Decentralized energy is more efficient and economical than massive energy systems, according to this comprehensive review.

Day, John A.; Fost, Frederic F.; and Rose, Peter. *Dimensions of the Environmental Crisis*. New York, N.Y.: Wiley, 1971. 212 pp.

Studies the roots of our environmental crisis, the population explosion, global aspects, ecosystem science, conservation, environmental law, pollution problems, and how to find realistic solutions to these dilemmas.

Darmstadter, Joel; Dunkerley, Joy; and Alterman, Jack. *How Industrial Societies Use Energy: A Comparative Analysis*. Resources for the Future. Baltimore, Md.: Johns Hopkins University Press, 1977. 298 pp. $16.95.

The purpose of this study is to analyze variations in energy consumption among highly industrialized countries, based on 1972 data. Factors considered include fuel and power prices, passenger mile volume, fuel economy, housing unit size, energy intensiveness of the industrial sector, and the degree of self-sufficiency in energy supplies.

DeBell, Garrett, ed. *The New Environmental Handbook*. San Francisco, Calif.: Friends of the Earth, 1980. 168 pp. $4.95. (FOE)

In the spirit of the book that kicked off the original Earth Day movement, a new team of writers and specialists looks at the environmental gains made in the last ten years, and at the emerging challenges and opportunities. Issues such as energy, wilderness, pollution, transportation, conservation, and health are brought into focus, with ideas on how you can take part in the action.

DiCerto, Joseph J. *The Electric Wishing Well: The Solution to the Energy Crisis*. New York, N.Y.: Collier, 1976. 317 pp. $3.95.

We can no longer depend upon disappearing fossil fuels and hazardous nuclear energy, but must turn to the vast untapped natural forces that could provide clean, safe, and abundant energy.

Doolittle, Jesse S. *Energy: A Crisis — A Dilemma — Or Just Another Problem?* Matrix Publishers, 207 Kenyon Rd., Champaign, IL 61802. 1977. 310 pp. $12.95.

A text for non-technical college students and the general reader which surveys the uses of conventional and emerging technologies, and considers the interactions between energy production and the environment.

Dorf, Richard C. *Energy, Resources, and Policy*. Reading, Mass.: Addison-Wesley, 1978. 486 pp. $16.95. Instructor's Guide, $2.50.

This introductory college text covers the uses of energy, fossil fuels, nuclear power, alternative energy sources, the economics of energy conservation, and policy alternatives for the United States and the world.

Ehrlich, Paul R., and Ehrlich, Anne H. *The End of Affluence*. New York, N.Y.: Ballantine Books, 1974. 307 pp. $1.95.

The era of unlimited growth is ending, and will soon be followed by disastrous shortages of food, energy, and material resources. Discusses the energy crisis, nuclear hazards, and alternative energy sources. Offers practical steps for the individual to take.

Encyclopedia Britannica, eds. *Energy, the Fuel of Life*. New York, N.Y.: Bantam/Britannica, 1979. 281 pp. $2.50.

This excellent reader provides background material on the origins of the universe, the sun as the source of all of earth's energy, energy in life processes, energy stored in the earth, and the renewable flows of energy in wind and water, powered by the sun. The environmental effects of energy use and the energy crisis are also examined.

Eppen, Gary, ed. *Energy: The Policy Issues*. Chicago, Ill.: University of Chicago Press, 1975. 121 pp. $2.95.

A wide range of contributors discusses energy economics, the environment, the social and economic impact of conservation measures, international implications, and government regulation.

Fabricant, Neil, and Hallman, Robert M. *Toward a Rational Power Policy: Energy, Politics, and Pollution*. New York, N.Y.: George Brazillier, 1971. 291 pp. $8.95.

A report by the Environmental Protection Agency of the City of New York advocating the establishment of a state commission on energy needs, the public interest, and the environment. It also recommends the repeal of the Price-Anderson Act.

Farmer, Gary. *Unready Kilowatts*. La Salle, Ill.: Open Court., 1975. 333 pp. $15.00.

An examination of energy and the environment, with discussions of the energy industry, the nuclear controversy, legislative issues, environmental activists, and alternate resource potentials.

Environmental Education Group. *Energy Options*. Environmental Education Group, 18014 Sherman Way, #169, Reseda, CA 91335. 75 pp. $1.50.

All global energy options are examined, with an assessment of their availability, longevity, and environmental impact. Hydrogen, often overlooked in other works as an energy source, is treated at length.

Ferrar, Terry A; Clemente, Frank; and Uhler, Robert. *Electric Energy Policy Issues*. Ann Arbor, Mich.: Ann Arbor Science Publishers, 1979. 140 pp. $27.00.

Energy facility development is examined from the perspective of market and public institution decision-making. Policy issues and the social trade-offs involved are assessed. For administrators, social scientists, and concerned citizens.

Fowler, John M. *Energy and the Environment*. New York, N.Y.: McGraw-Hill, 1975. 496 pp. $8.50.

Power resources, pollution, energy conversion, the mixed blessings of nuclear energy, energy from the sun and sea, and conservation are subjected to careful scrutiny.

Freeman, S. David. *Energy: The New Era*. New York, N.Y.: Walker, 1974. 386 pp. $2.45.

The problems of a high energy civilization must be solved through new policies of energy conservation and by tapping the eternal energy sources.

Freeman, S. David, et al. *A Time to Choose: America's Energy Future*. Ford Foundation Energy Policy Project. Cambridge, Mass.: Ballinger, 1974. 528 pp. $8.95.

Plausible energy scenarios for the future are drawn from data on U.S. energy policy, resources, and environmental and nuclear risks. Growth in energy consumption can be slowed or stopped without a calamitous effect on the economy or on the quality of our life. Recommendations include redirecting research toward conservation, diversity of energy supplies, environmental protection, and public health and safety.

Gabel, Medard. *Energy, Earth, and Everyone: A Global Energy Strategy For Spaceship Earth.* San Francisco, Calif.: Straight Arrow, 1975. 160 pp. $4.95.

The World Game Workshop treats the whole earth and all of its energy needs as one functional unit as it considers the problems of energy production, distribution, and conversion in the context of humanity, its total history, and its needs. Unusual charts and illustrations.

Gilliland, Martha W. ed. *Energy Analysis: A New Public Policy Tool.* American Association for the Advancement of Science, Boulder, Colo.: Westview Press, 1978. 110 pp. $13.50.

The contributors to this volume represent diverse viewpoint on the methods of energy analysis and the factors to be considered, such as fuel consumption, physical laws, labor, environment, economics, and policy impacts.

Gordon, Howard, and Meador, Roy. *Perspectives on the Energy Crisis.* Ann Arbor, Mich.: Ann Arbor Science Publishers, 1977. Vol. 1, 517 pp. $30.00. Vol. 2, 533 pp. $30.00.

Volume 1 contains 23 reports on the technical, regulatory, environmental, and economic aspects of the energy crisis, and world energy and mineral resources. Volume 2 contains 36 reports on resources of fossil fuels, solar and nuclear energy.

Halacy, D.S. Jr. *The Energy Trap.* New York, N.Y.: Four Winds Press, 1975. 143 pp. $6.95.

A consideration of the energy crisis, its link to the Gross National Product, nuclear hazards, and alternative fuel resources leads to the conclusion that man must turn to solar energy, a simpler life style, and a restricted population.

Hammond, A.L.; Metz, W.D.; and Maugh, T.H. *Energy and the Future.* Washington, D.C.: American Association for the Advancement of Science, 1973. 184 pp. $4.95.

An assessment of the technologies and research developments that will form the basis of the future energy policies.

Hanley, Wayne, and Mitchell, John, eds. *The Energy Book: A Look at the Death Throes of One Energy Era and the Birth Pangs of Another.* Massachusetts Audubon Society. Brattleboro, Vt.: Stephen Greene, 1980. 186 pp. $11.95.

The history of man's use of energy brings us up to the present and the end of the age of cheap fossil fuels. Nuclear energy is beset by many problems, but a renaissance of conservation and solar solutions is in sight. Photo essays contrast the fossil fuel economy with an alternative landscape and lifestyle.

Hayes, Denis. *Pollution, the Neglected Dimension.* Washington, D.C.: Worldwatch Institute, 1979. 32 pp. $2.00. (FOE) (EARS)

The problems caused by increased carbon dioxide in the atmosphere, toxic substances in the environment, and the accumulation of nuclear wastes can no longer be neglected.

Hayes, Denis. *Rays of Hope: The Transition to a Post-Petroleum World.* New York, N.Y.:

Norton, 1977. 240 pp. $3.95 (EARS)

Hayes finds hope for the future in the wide range of possible applications of solar and other alternative energy sources. He examines the technological, economic, and social problems associated with fossil fuels and nuclear power,

Hemdal, John F. *The Energy Center*. Ann Arbor, Mich.: Ann Arbor Science Publishers, 1978. 272 pp. $30.00.

Will Energy Centers be the cities of the future? Hemdal explores the advantages and the pitfalls of locating power generation facilities and large consumers together with transportation lines, labor pools, and raw materials.

Herman, Stewart W., and Cannon, James S., with Malefatto, Alfred J. *Energy Futures: Industry and the New Technologies*. Inform, Inc. Cambridge, Mass.: Ballinger, 1976. 684 pp. $30.00. Abridged edition, 320 pp. $10.95.

Based upon over 200 research projects of American corporations, this comprehensive study describes new energy conversion technologies for solar, wind, hydrogen, nuclear fusion, trash-to-energy, geothermal, oil shale, coal gasification and liquefaction, fuel cells, and breeder reactors.

Holdren, John P., and Herrera, Philip. *Energy*. San Francisco, Calif.: Sierra Club, 1971. 252 pp. $2.75.

This classic text is worth looking for. It explores the dilemma of America's appetite for energy - particularly electric power - and the increasing environmental costs of nuclear power plants and fossil fuel consumption. Also included are case studies of citizen challenges to the utilities over nuclear power plant siting and operation.

Hollander, Jack, ed. *Annual Review of Energy*. Palo Alto, Calif: Annual Reviews, Inc. Vol. 1, 1976, 793 pp.; Vol. 2, 1977, 519pp.; Vol. 3, 1978, 544 pp. $17.00 each.

Scholarly articles review energy resources, technologies, and policies, from national and international perspectives. Topics covered include conventional and alternative options, conservation, economics, and the impacts upon health, safety, and the environment.

Hollander, Jack, ed. *Annual Review of Energy*. Palo Alto, Calif.: Annual Reviews, Inc. Vol. 4, 1979, 559 pp. $17.00.

In addition to other articles on energy options, problems, and policies, this volume includes a 71-page summary of the National Academy of Sciences study by the Committee on Nuclear and Alternative Energy Systems (CONAES), written by Harvey Brooks and Jack Hollander. See National Academy of Sciences, *Energy in Transition*.

Holloman, John H., and Grenon, Michel. *Energy Research and Development*. Cambridge, Mass.: Ballinger, 1975. 272 pp. $22.50.

Survey status of energy technologies in the U.S. and other major industrialized nations.

House, Peter W. *Trading Off Environment, Economics, and Energy: EPA's Strategic Environmental Assessment System*. Lexington, Mass.: Lexington Books, 1977. 160 pp. $16.50.

A description of the Environmental Protection Agency's computer-based system (SEAS) for creating comprehensive long-range policy impact statements.

Kalter, Robert J., and Vogely, William A., eds. *Energy Supply and Government Policy*. Ithaca, N.Y.: Cornell University Press, 1976. 356 pp. $5.95.

Energy experts from leading universities and government agencies explore energy policies from an environmental perspective, and address such issues as fossil and nuclear energy, the role of the public in energy research and development, the failure of the U.S. energy policy, and options for the future. Recommendations are made for more realistic energy policies.

Kash, Don E. et al. *Our Energy Future: The Role of Research, Development, and Demonstration in Reaching a National Consensus on Energy Supply.* Norman, Okla.: University of Oklahoma Press, 1976. 486 pp. $5.95
Delineates constraints on increasing energy supplies from domestic resources, and calls for broader social participation in decision-making. Emphasis is on conventional energy sources and electricity.

Landsberg, Hans, Chairman. *Energy: The Next Twenty Years.* Study Group Report, Ford Foundation/Resources for the Future. Cambridge Mass.: Ballinger, 1979. 656 pp. $9.95.
The authors conclude that with proper policy and planning, and a willingness to pay the costs, energy can be produced to meet any reasonable projection of demand. Unconventional energy sources are to be considered as long-term resources, and for the present we cannot do without nuclear power.

Lawrence, Robert, ed. *New Dimensions to Energy Policy.* A Policy Studies Organization Book. Lexington, Mass.: Lexington Books, 1979. 256 pp. $21.95.
New approaches to energy policy are presented from political, economic, and sociological perspectives.

League of Women Voters Education Fund. *Energy Dilemmas: An Overview of U.S. Energy Problems and Issues.* League of Women Voters, 1730 M St. NW, Washington, DC 20036. 1977. 39 pp. $1.00, plus $.50 handling per order.
A thorough analysis of the political, social, and economic issues relating to energy supply and demand.

League of Women Voters Education Fund. *Energy Options: Examining Sources and Defining Government's Role.* League of Women Voters, 1730 M St. NW, Washington, DC 20036. 1977. 55 pp. $1.00, plus $.50 handling per order.
A concise yet comprehensive inventory of energy sources and the major problems associated with each. Political implications are explored, and questions are raised regarding government policies.

Lindberg, Leon N., ed. *The Energy Syndrome: Comparing National Responses to the Energy Crisis.* Lexington, Mass.: Lexington Books, 1977. 382 pp. $16.00.
The energy syndrome is a group of symptoms that describe a system malfunction: practices that require steady increases in the energy supply; public policies dominated by energy producers; and institutional obstacles to the search for alternatives. Energy prices rise, and resources are depleted. The energy policies of the United States are compared with those of other countries.

Lovins, Amory B. *Energy Strategy: The Road Not Taken?* San Francisco, Calif.: Friends of the Earth, 1976. 12 pp. $.50. (FOE) (EARS).
Lovins examines the direction of U.S. energy policies, and offers an alternative course of soft energy technologies.

Lovins, Amory B. *Soft Energy Paths: Toward a Durable Peace.* New York, N.Y.: Harper and Row, 1977. 231 pp. $3.95. (FOE) (EARS) (TEA)
This seminal work presents the consequences of choosing between a soft

technology path (renewable energy sources) and the hard technologies (nuclear and fossil fuels) for our energy future. It compares the capital costs of available technologies, and studies the related problems of socio-politics, values, and nuclear proliferation.

Lovins, Amory B. *World Energy Strategies - Facts, Issues, Options.* New York, N.Y.: Friends of the Earth, 1975. 131 pp. $6.95 (FOE) (EARS)
     Factual analysis of energy supply and demand; the problems of fossil, nuclear, and geothermal energy and their environmental impact; energy income technologies; conservation; and the issues that must affect our choice of energy strategies.

Lovins, Amory B. and Price, John. *Non-Nuclear Futures: The Case for an Ethical Energy Strategy.* Cambridge, Mass.: Ballinger Publishing Co., 1975. 223 pp. $6.95.
     The authors explore the economics and ethics of energy, and find that the amount of capital needed for the nuclear dream is ridiculously unattainable.

Lovins, Amory B. and his Critics. *The Energy Controversy.* San Francisco, Calif.: Friends of the Earth, 1979. 450 pp. $6.95. (FOE) (EARS)
     Lovins and his critics testify before the Senate Select Committee on Small Business. Set in the form of dialogues, this discussion raises fundamental questions regarding the nature of the energy problem, and the feasibility of the "soft path" solution.

McMullan, J.T.; Morgan, R.; and Murray, R.B. *Energy Resources.* Resource and Environmental Sciences Series. New York, N.Y.: Wiley, 1977. 177 pp. $7.95.
     Energy technologies and resources are outlined in this presentation for the non-specialist reader. Topics include natural energy sources, fossil and nuclear energy, and energy from waste.

Mead, Walter J. and Utton, Albert E., eds. *U.S. Energy Policy: Errors of the Past, Proposals for the Future.* Cambridge, Mass.: Ballinger, 1979. 200 pp. $17.50.
     Twelve essays on public policy implications examine the areas of international oil economics, federal energy policy, controls, taxes and subsidies, coal and oil shale, energy conservation, effects of higher prices, stripmining costs, nuclear waste problems, and clean air provisions.

Meador, Roy. *Future Energy Alternatives: Energy Problems and Prospects.* Ann Arbor, Mich.: Ann Arbor Science Publishers, 1978. 198 pp. $9.95.
     The potential of a variety of alternate energy sources is analyzed, with comparison of advantages, costs, risks, environmental impact, and expected availability. The nuclear power controversy is also discussed.

Metzger, Norman. *Energy: The Continuing Crisis.* New York, N.Y.: Crowell, 1977. 242 pp. $12.95.
     An examination of the gap between energy supplies and needs, demographic and geographic factors, environmental impact, government policies, and costs of energy options leads to the conclusion that society's future lies in renewable energy sources.

Miller, George T. *Energy and Environment: The Four Energy Crises.* Belmont, Calif.: Wadsworth, 1975. 122 pp.
     Power resources, energy policy, environmental policy, the laws of energy, the nuclear dilemma, energy alternatives, thermal pollution, and possible climate modification are among the factors contributing to the current crises.

Morgan M. Granger, ed. *Energy and Man: Technical and Social Aspects of Energy.* New

York, N.Y.: Institute of Electrical and Electronics Engineers, Inc., 1975. 515 pp. $21.95.

Various energy technologies and the social and environmental impacts of energy use are discussed in reprints from the technical literature.

Naill, Roger F. *Managing the Energy Transition: A System Dynamics Search for Alternatives to Oil and Gas.* Cambridge, Mass.: Ballinger. Vol. I, 1976, 284 pp. $22.50. Vol. II, 1979, 128 pp. $18.50.

Strategies to achieve independence from foreign sources of oil are analyzed with the aid of a mathematical model that interrelates energy demand, prices, capital, labor availability, new technologies, and environmental constraints.

National Academy of Sciences. *Energy and Climate.* National Academy of Sciences, 2101 Constitution Ave. NW, Washington, DC 20418. 1977. 158 pp. $9.50.

A report concerned with the combined effects over the next century or two, of a growing world population, an increasing per capita use of energy, and continued reliance on fossil fuels. The climatic questions raised are likely to become a major environmental issue of the next decade.

National Academy of Sciences. *Energy: Future Alternatives and Risks.* Cambridge, Mass.: Ballinger, 1974. 227 pp. $17.50.

A forum held in January, 1974 at the National Academy of Sciences, with representatives from industry, research institutes, and government, discusses alternatives of supply and demand, and the corresponding benefits and risks.

National Academy of Sciences. *Energy in Transition.* San Francisco, Calif.: W.H. Freeman, 1980. 608 pp. $11.95.

After three years of study, the Committee on Nuclear and Alternative Energy Systems (CONAES) of the National Academy of Sciences, composed of 16 experts representing a wide range of views, produced this comprehensive but inconclusive report. There was general agreement that the highest priority should be given to conservation and efficiency measures which could reduce energy demand by one half, while generating many jobs at little cost and with few risks. However, on other issues, the panelists could not reach consensus. Despite the acknowledge hazards and uncertainties associated with an accelerated program of electrification and synthetic fuels from coal and nuclear power, the study found no better near-term alternatives to the impending shortage of oil and gas. Most applications of solar energy were relegated to the next century, along with the breeder reactor and fusion. Evidently, in the absence of conclusive scientific data, major energy decisions will continue to be based largely on value judgments.

Norman, Colin. *Knowledge and Power: The Global Research and Development Budget.* Washington, D.C.: Worldwatch, 1979. 56 pp. $2.00. (FOE) (EARS)

Governments and corporations invest $150 billion in research and development annually to influence future events.

Norman, Colin. *Soft Technologies, Hard Choices.* Washington, D.C.: Worldwatch Institute, 1978. 48 pp. $2.00. (FOE) (EARS)

Norman summarizes the economic and ecological arguments for the soft path, and for a more equitable distribution of resources. However, there are many difficulties in devising the social mechanisms for the application of appropriate technology.

Odum, Howard T. *Environment, Power, and Society.* New York, N.Y.: Wiley-Inter-

Science, 1971. 317 pp. $6.50.

This classic explains the flow of energy in natural and manmade systems, how steady-state systems differ from growth systems, and how to make the transition.

Odum, Howard T., and Odum, Elisabeth C. *Energy Basis for Man and Nature.* New York, N.Y.: McGraw-Hill, 1976. 296 pp. $11.95. (EARS)

Outlines the basic principles of energy flows in ecological systems throughout the world, and tells how they shape human history and culture. A possibility for the future is a steady-state economy.

Penner, S.S., and Icerman, L. *Energy: Vol. I, Demands, Resources, Impact, Technology, and Policy.* Reading, Mass.: Addison-Wesley, 1974. 368 pp.

A thoroughly documented analysis of all energy resources is presented in these college lecture notes, with many illustrative charts and tables.

Penner, S.S. and Icerman, L. *Energy: Vol. II. Non-Nuclear Energy Technologies.* Reading, Mass.: Addison-Wesley, 1975. 673 pp. $16.50.

New developments are described in detail in this college text, including fossil and renewable energy technologies, energy storage systems, and electric power production. The scientific, technical, economic, and social problems involved in achieving energy independence are also discussed.

Phillips, Owen. *The Last Chance Energy Book.* Baltimore, Md.: Johns Hopkins University Press, 1979. 142 pp. $9.95.

We have squandered our supplies of fossil fuels; our increased dependence on coal and nuclear power poses grave risks to our health and the environment. However, there are exciting new possibilities for our energy future - we have only to make the choice.

Priest, Joseph. *Energy for a Technological Society: Principles, Problems, Alternatives.* Reading, Mass.: Addison-Wesley, Second Edition, 1979. 392 pp. $12.95.

This basic college text clearly explains the principles of utilizing fossil fuels; nuclear power, including the breeder reactor and fusion; solar and other energy alteratives; energy conservation; and the environmental and societal effects of the use of energy.

Reed, C.B. *Fuels, Minerals, and Human Survival.* Ann Arbor, Mich.: Ann Arbor Science Publishers, 1978. 200 pp. $12.50.

Our industrial society has a dim future because we are robbing the future for our present affluence. The discussion covers the energy shortage, pollution control, mineral resource depletion, nuclear problems, coal, and alternate energy systems.

Ridgeway, James. *The Last Play - The Struggle to Monopolize the World's Energy Resources.* New York, N.Y.: New American Library, 1973. 373 pp. $1.95.

Here is the story of the role of the energy monopolies in the energy crisis, and of the ways in which they control the world's energy resources, including not only fossil fuels, but uranium and future fuels as well.

Robinette, Gary. *Energy and the Environment.* Dubuque, Iowa: Kendall/Hunt Publishing Co., 1973. 302 pp. $9.95.

Detailed analysis of power generation, transmission, transformation, and distribution facilities, and their effects on the environment.

Rowland, Wade. *Fueling Canada's Future.* Toronto, Canada: Macmillan, 1974. 161 pp.

Considers the various sources of energy and their costs in economic, human, and ecological terms. Seeks ways of conserving resources and modifying government policies of unlimited growth. Applicable to the U.S. as well as the Canadian experience.

Ruedisili, Lon C., and Firebaugh, Morris M. *Perspectives on Energy.* New York, N.Y.: Oxford University Press, Revised 1978. 476 pp. $9.95.

Issues, ideas, and environmental dilemmas are covered in this collection of articles on fossil fuels, nuclear fission, alternative energy, energy conservation, and energy policy for the future.

Schneider, Stephen H. *The Genesis Strategy: Climate and Global Survival.* New York, N.Y.: Plenum Press, 1976. 419 pp. $4.95.

The intricate network of relationships between climate, food, population, technology, energy, pollution, and politics is outlined. Human activities, such as increased energy production, are drastically disturbing the delicate balance of the world climate system. Proposals are suggested for new institutions, agreements, and attitudes necessary for global survival.

Scheinman, Lawrence, ed. *North American Energy Policy.* Cambridge, Mass.: Ballinger, 1978. 192 pp. $15.00.

Academicians and public figures examine the economic, political, and technical dimensions of Canadian-American energy relations and cooperation.

Schurr, Sam H.; Darmstadter, Joel; Perry, Harry; Ramsay, William; and Russell, Milton. *Energy in America's Future: The Choices Before Us.* Resources for the Future. Baltimore, Md.: Johns Hopkins University Press, 1979. 555 pp. $11.00.

Among the questions addressed by this comprehensive study are how to cope with increasingly limited supplies of fossil fuels and higher energy prices, how to mitigate the adverse environmental, health, and safety impacts of some of the new technologies, and how to manage the transition to the abundant energy sources of the future. It finds that nuclear power will play a significant role in our energy future.

Shepard, Marion L., Chaddock, Jack B., Cocks, Franklin H., and Harman, Charles M. *Introduction to Energy Technology.* Ann Arbor, Mich.: Ann Arbor Science Publishers, 1977. 300 pp. $10.95.

This college text introduces the technology of energy conversion, discusses energy sources and uses, and planning for an energy future.

Singer, S. Fred. *Energy: Readings from Scientific American.* San Francisco, Calif: W.H. Freeman, 1979. 221 pp. $7.50.

Selected papers from *Scientific American* magazine from 1970 to 1979 treat topics of energy use, conversion, coal, nuclear energy, waste disposal, international stability, prospects of the breeder reactor and fusion, conservation, auto fuel consumption, and photovoltaics.

Stein, Charles, ed. *Critical Materials Problems in Energy Production.* New York, N.Y.: Academic Press, 1976. 916 pp. $34.50.

Identifies and concentrates on the most challenging materials problems in the production, distribution, and storage of all major energy sources.

Steinman, Michael, ed. *Energy and Environmental Issues: The Making and Implementation of Public Policy Issues.* Lexington, Mass.: Lexington Books, 1979.

An inquiry into the impacts of public policies in areas such as water quality planning, public utility pricing, solar energy, and pollution, from both local and national perspectives.

Stobaugh, Robert, and Yergin, Daniel, eds. *Energy Future: Report of the Energy Project at the Harvard Business School.* New York, N.Y.: Random House, 1979. 353 pp. $12.95. (TEA)

After a six-year study, this authoritative body of scholars finds that none of the conventional sources of domestic energy - oil, coal, natural gas, and nuclear - can supply much more energy than they do now. The proposed synthetic fuels program is based on uncertain technologies and risks; it would produce too little, too late, and at too great a cost to the economy and to the environment. Our only choice lies with either increased imports, or a serious move toward conservation and low technology solar sources. Although carefully researched the report avoids an overabundance of figures and charts, making it a very readable book.

Sullivan, Thomas F.P. ed. *Energy Law and Regulations.* Proceedings of the Energy Law Seminar. Government Institutes Inc., 4733 Bethesda Ave., NW, Washington, DC 20014. 1976. 142 pp.

An analysis of federal energy laws, FPC environmental considerations, FEA price and allocation regulations, coal and electricity use, conservation law, and federal assistance for energy shortages.

Szulc, Tad. *The Energy Crisis.* New York, N.Y.: Franklin Watts, revised edition, 1978. 152 pp. $6.90.

The focus is on the role of the oil industry in increasing America's dependence on foreign oil. The author calls for a strong national policy controlling domestic production of fuel, fuel imports, and allocation. Oil and gas reserves may be depleted by the year 2000; hence Americans must learn to conserve.

Tanzer, Michael. *The Energy Crisis: World Struggle for Power and Wealth.* New York, N.Y.: Monthly Review Press, 1974. 170 pp. $8.95.

The "energy crisis" is simply a reflection of far deeper underlying irrationalities of the world capitalist system..."the motive force of capitalism is not human needs but the drive for profits."

Taylor, Vince. *Energy: The Easy Path.* See ENERGY CONSERVATION: OVERVIEWS.

Teller, Edward. *Energy From Heaven and Earth.* San Francisco, Calif.: W.H. Freeman, 1979. 322 pp. $15.00.

Beginning with the cosmic origins of the sun's energy, and the biological origins of fuels, Dr. Teller outlines our various energy options. The world's critical energy problems can only be met by a proper combination of energy conservation, petroleum, coal, nuclear, geothermal, and solar. Nuclear problems will be solved, according to the author, and solar energy and fusion are prospects for the more distant future.

Thirring, Hans. *Energy for Man: From Windmills to Nuclear Power.* New York, N.Y.: Harper & Row, 1956, 1978. 409 pp. $5.95.

Thirring's classic survey of the world's energy resources was written with prescience of things to come. He describes present and future means of power generation, with their merits and drawbacks. A deep feeling for human welfare tempers his views on technology. He predicts increasing use of nuclear power, and warns of the peril of radioactive contamination.

Tuve, George L. *Energy Environment, Population, and Food: Our Four Interdependent Crises.*

New York, N.Y.: Wiley, 1976. 264 pp. $22.95.

A detailed summary of the past experience, present status, and future prospects in the areas of energy, environment, population, and food finds that unlimited growth and limited resources are incompatible, and urges a holistic approach to these problems.

Udall, Stewart; Conconi, Charles; and Osterhout, David. *The Energy Balloon.* New York, N.Y.: McGraw-Hill, 1974. 288 pp. $7.95. Penguin: $2.95.

Emphasizing the ethical as well as the practical dimensions of the energy crisis, Udall calls for a limited growth economy, the implementation of conservation and energy efficiency, and the development of a frugal national life-style.

U.S. Congress. *Energy: An Uncertain Future. An Analysis of U.S. and World Energy Projections Through 1990.* Washington, D.C., 1978. S/N 052-070-04774-7. 329 pp. $4.25. (USGPO)

Recent forecasts of national and international energy supply and demand are analyzed.

U.S. Congress. *The National Energy Act.* Washington, D.C., 1979. S/N 052-070-04794-1. 598 pp. $5.00 (USGPO)

The text of the National Energy Act of 1979.

U.S. Congress. *The National Energy Plan: Options Under Assumptions of a National Security Threat.* Washington, D.C., 1978. S/N 052-072-04482-9 403 pp. $4.50. (USGPO)

The energy problem is considered in the context of an assumed national security threat.

U.S. Energy Research and Development Administration. *A National Plan for Energy Research, Development, and Demonstration: Creating Energy Choices for the Future.* Washington, D.C.: Government Printing Office, 1976. #052-010-00478-6. 120 pp. $2.00. (USGPO)

Outlines the national energy problem and solutions; states goals, strategies, and priorities; discusses the FY 1977 budget and the status of the various energy technologies.

U.S. Executive Office of the President, Council on Environmental Quality. *Environmental Quality. The Ninth Annual Report.* Washington, D.C., December 1978. S/N 041-011-00040-8. 599pp. (USGPO)

This mine of information includes data on environmental laws, standards, enforcement, specific problems, the National Environmental Policy Act, energy, economics, and the global environment.

U.S. Executive Office of the President, Council on Environmental Quality. *The Good News About Energy.* Washington, D.C., 1979. S/N 041-011-00044-1. 55 pp. $2.30. (USGPO)

The United States can maintain a healthy economy without massive increases in energy use; growth in the gross national product can be achieved with low rates of growth in energy consumption. Energy should be priced at its replacement cost, with programs to cushion the impact on low-income people. Increases in the efficiency of energy use possible with today's technology would allow the U.S. economy to operate on 30-40 percent less energy, thus reducing the international, environmental, and social risks of energy production.

U.S. Environmental Protection Agency, Office of Research and Development,

Energy, Minerals, and Industry. *Energy/Environment II.* EPA-600/9-77-012. Washington, D.C., 1977. 563 pp. (NTIS)

The report of the Second National Conference on the Interagency Research and Development Program, which has the two-fold goal of having enough energy to maintain our way of life, and ensuring that our energy is used in environmentally sound ways. Includes risk assessment and control technologies.

U.S. Federal Energy Administration. *Nationl Energy Outlook.* Washington, D.C.: U.S. Government Printing Office, #041-018-0097-6. Feb. 1976. Approx. 500 pp. $7.30.

Evaluates policies and trends in the use of fossil, nuclear, and alternative energy sources as a basis for forecasting our energy future.

University of Oklahoma. *Energy Alternatives: A Comparative Analysis.* Science and Public Policy Program, University of Oklahoma. Washington, D.C., 1975. 636 pp. $7.45. (USGPO)

Prepared for the Council on Environmental Quality, this comprehensive work describes all energy resources, technologies, efficiencies, environmental and economic considerations, and energy consumption, with a methodology for making comparisons.

Utton, Albert E., and Mead, Walter J. *A Natural Resources Journal Symposium on Energy Policy.* Cambridge, Mass.: Ballinger, 1979. 96 pp. $13.50.

Energy specialists offer views on oil import dependence, gas and oil pricing, coal, oil shale, taxation, and energy conservation.

Vandeventer, Mary Lou, ed., with Friends of the Earth Staff. *Earthworks: Ten Years on the Environmental Front.* San Francisco, Calif.: Friends of the Earth, 1980. 224 pp. $8.95. (FOE)

Earthworks presents the best of *Not Man Apart,* including humor, poetry, think-pieces, and reports on the major environmental issues of the decade - an anthology of the literature and art that have given environmentalism the political force to improve people's lives.

Warkov, Seymour, ed. *Energy Policy in the United States.* New York, N.Y.: Praeger, 1978. 268 pp. $19.95.

Original research papers explore the social and behavioral aspects of energy consumption, public acceptance of alternate energy systems, regionalism, and the creation of an effective energy policy.

Wells, Malcolm. *Energy Essays.* Barrington, N.J.: Edmund Scientific Co. 1976. 70 pp. $5.95. (EARS)

A delightful, illustrated idea-pack on energy, air, food, water, and miracles.

Wilson, Carroll L., director. *Energy: Global Prospects, 1985-2000.* Report of the Workshop on Alternative Energy Strategies sponsored by Massachusetts Institute of Technology. New York, N.Y.: McGraw-Hill, 1977. 291 pp. $6.95.

Predicts energy shortages, but concentrates on increasing the energy supply rather than challenging the assumed continued growth in energy demand. Renewable energy sources are not expected to become significant before 2000; and little attention is given to environmental concerns.

Wilson, Kenneth D., ed. *Prospects for Growth: Changing Expectations for the Future.* New York, N.Y.: Praeger. 1977. 366 pp. $16.50.

Commissioned by the Edison Electric Institute, this collection of essays offers a wide range of views on the future of growth in the light of the realization that our resources have finite bounds.

Wilson, Richard, and Jones William. *Energy, Ecology, and the Environment.* New York, N.Y.: Academic Press, 1974. 353 pp. $6.95.

A technical text describing various methods of harnessing energy, and the resulting ecological damage. Topics include air and thermal pollution, radiation, accidents, waste disposal, and cost-benefit considerations.

Wilson, Richard, and Crouch, Edmund. *Risk-Benefit Analysis.* Cambridge, Mass.: Ballinger, 1979. 304 pp. $22.50.

The techniques of risk-benefit analysis can be used to evaluate the risks of air pollution, auto safety, radiation exposure, radiography, and mining, and draw implications for public health policies.

World Meteorological Organization. *Effects of Human Activity on Global Climate.* WMO, UN, 1978. 47 pp. $10.00. (UNIPUB)

Mankind affects global climate by fossil fuel consumption, which causes an increase in atmospheric carbon dioxide and a rise in global temperature. Aerosols and thermal pollution effects are also considered.

Economics

Alexander, Sidney S. *Paying for Energy.* Report of the Twentieth Century Fund Task Force on the International Oil Crisis. New York, N.Y.: McGraw-Hill, 1975. 136 pp. $3.95.

The Task Force, made up of oil experts, economists, bankers, and diplomats, discusses the energy crisis, the oil cartel, problems of pricing, and the world market.

Askin, A. Bradley, ed. *How Energy Affects the Economy.* Lexington, Mass.: Lexington Books, 1978. 160 pp. $15.50.

A dozen contributors tackle questions about the energy crisis, setting energy policy, changing consumption patterns, the impact of higher oil prices, and alternate energy scenarios.

Banks, Ferdinand E. *Scarcity, Energy, and Economic Progress.* Lexington, Mass.: Lexington Books, 1977. 224 pp. $18.50.

This text on environmental economics explores world energy supplies, pollution and recycling, economic growth, cartels, minerals, food, and population. The author considers nuclear power necessary to economic growth.

Brannon, Gerard M. *Energy Taxes and Subsidies.* A Report to the Energy Policy Project of the Ford Foundation. Cambridge, Mass.: Ballinger, 1974. 177 pp. $7.95.

Makes recommendations for market-oriented energy policies with specific taxes and subsidies which the author believes will make the markets more economically efficient allocators of society's scarce resources.

Buchsbaum, Steven, and Benson, James W. *Jobs and Energy: The Employment and Economic Impacts of Nuclear Power, Conservation, and Other Energy Options.* Council on Economic Priorities, 84 Fifth Ave., New York, NY 10011. 1979. 300 pp.

A detailed analysis of the economic and employment impact on Long Island of various energy options, including nuclear, present energy mix, and conservation/solar.

Critical Mass Journal. *Energy and Jobs.* Critical Mass Journal, P.O. Box 1538, Washington, DC 20013. 1976. $1.00.

A packet of materials illustrating that the development of solar energy and energy conservation would be a boost for employment, especially as compared to atomic energy.

Duchesneau, Thomas D. *Competition in the U.S. Energy Industry.* A report to the Energy Policy Project of the Ford Foundation. Cambridge, Mass.: Ballinger, 1976. 401 pp. $12.50.

Energy sources, market economy, public policy, and political influence are thoroughly investigated in this report.

Georgescu-Roegen, Nicholas. *The Entropy Law and the Economic Process.* Cambridge, Mass.: Harvard University Press, 1974. 457 pp. $5.95.

Explains the entropy law of biology and physics, and its relationship to the limits to economic growth.

Grossman, Richard, and Daneker, Gail. *Energy, Jobs, and the Economy.* Boston, Mass.: Alyson, 1979. 124 pp. $3.45.

The Environmentalists for Full Employment update and expand their 1977 monograph, *Jobs and Energy.* An energy-efficient economy based on renewable energy sources will provide more jobs as well as a more healthful environment. However, the U.S. Departments of Energy and Labor have made no serious effort to consider the employment consequences of energy policy. Essential reading for anyone concerned with bridging the gap between labor and the environmental movement.

Halvorsen, Robert. *Econometric Models of U.S. Energy Demand.* Lexington, Mass.: Lexington Books, 1978. 192 pp. $16.95.

Models are presented for determining the energy demands of various sectors and the responsiveness of demand to price. Electricity, oil, natural gas, and coal are considered, and substitutions among the different types of energy.

Hass, Jerome E., Mitchell, Edward J., and Stone, Bernell K. *Financing the Energy Industry.* A report to the Energy Policy of the Ford Foundation. Cambridge, Mass.: Ballinger, 1974. 138 pp. $7.95.

This report estimates the capital investment outlays of the energy industry, and examines financing problems that might seriously threaten the industry.

Henderson, Hazel. *Creating Alternative Futures: The End of Economics.* New York, N.Y.: Berkley Publishing Corporation, 1978. 403 pp. $4.95.

Henderson presents a challenge to traditional economics in this collection of essays, which covers a wide range of energy, economic, and societal issues. Our real job over the next ten years is to start recycling ourselves.

Hitch, Charles J., ed. *Modeling Energy-Economy Interactions: Five Approaches.* Washington, D.C.: Resources for the Future, 1977. 303 pp. $7.50.

Computer models found that energy and economic activity need not be closely linked. A lower energy future would bring a lower risk of catastrophic accidents and less damage to the environment and human health.

Hodson, H.V. *The Diseconomics of Growth.* London, England: Earth Island, 1973. 239 pp. $5.95. (EARS)

Hodson examines the pressures of population on resources and the environment, and demonstrates how little economic growth has to do with welfare, full employment, or business prosperity.

Kannan, Narasimhan P. *Energy, Economic Growth, and Equity in the United States.* The Mitre Corporation. New York, N.Y.: Praeger, 1979. 175 pp. $16.95.

Four computer simulation models were employed to study the growth of the U.S. Gross National Product. The results indicated that the most beneficial energy policy is accelerated conservation, because it provides the most stable economic growth, and reduces shortages and imports.

Maddala, G.S.; Chern, W.S.; and Chill, G.S. *Econometric Studies in Energy Demand and Supply.* New York, N.Y.: Praeger, 1978. 190 pp. $17.95.

After an examination of the problems of supply and demand for electricity and for fossil fuels, this study concludes that energy policy should rely on the price mechanism.

Miernyk, William A.; Giarratani, Frank; and Socher, Charles. *Regional Impacts of Rising Energy Prices.* Cambridge, Mass.: Ballingr, 1977. 160 pp. $16.50.

The new structure of energy prices will have differential regional impacts, with energy producing states gaining economically at the expense of energy consuming states.

Miller, Roger L. *The Economics of Energy - What Went Wrong?* New York, N.Y.: Morrow, 1974. 131 pp. $2.95.

Miller analyzes the energy crisis, the costs of energy use, and the resulting pollution, and points out that people must pay for the full social costs of their energy use.

Newland, Kathleen. *Global Employment and Economic Justice: The Policy Challenge.* Washington, D.C.: Worldwatch, 1979. 47 pp. $2.00. (FOE) (EARS)

A thorough reassessment of current economic policies must be undertaken to solve problems of unemployment.

Ross, Marc, and Williams, Robert. *Energy and Economic Growth.* Washington, D.C.: U.S. Government Printing Office, 1977. 66 pp. (USGPO)

The authors argue that the U.S. economy can continue to grow without any corresponding increase in energy consumption. Conservation and the improvement of energy use efficiency would also create many new job opportunities. The book does not, however, question the increasing generation of electricity, or the desirability of continuous economic growth.

Schumacher, E.F. *Good Work.* New York, N.Y.: Harper and Row, 1979. 223 pp. $9.95.

This post-humously published collection of lectures continues the themes of wiser use of natural resources, the economics of energy use, and the nature and control of organizations. "Good work" involves greater self-reliance and the production of goods and services which are more directly useful to society.

Schumacher, E.F. *Small is Beautiful: Economics As If People Mattered.* New York, N.Y.: Harper and Row, 1973. 290 pp. $2.95. (EARS)

Dr. Schumacher calls the assumptions of conventional economics into question in his human-centered approach to the solution of energy, resources, and manpower problems through labor-intensive intermediate technology.

Sonenblum, Sidney. *The Energy Connections: Between Energy and the Economy.* Cambridge, Mass.: Ballinger, 1978. 288 pp. $18.50.

The author examines the severity of the energy crisis, the desirability of economic growth, ways in which the future could differ from the past, and energy policy considerations.

Stokes, Bruce. *Worker Participation: Productivity and the Quality of Work Life.* Washington, D.C.: Worldwatch, 1978. 48 pp. $2.00. (FOE) (EARS)

Worker participation in the management and ownership of companies mobilizes previously untapped human resources and results in a better workplace and increased productivity.

The Human Dimension: Ethical, Social, and Health Implications

Anthropology Resource Center. *Native Americans and Energy Development.* Anthropology Resource Center, P.O. Box 90, Cambridge, MA 02138. 1978. $4.89.

This collection of well documented essays tells the tragic story of the exploitation of the Indians and their land by the large energy corporations. Indian Tribal Councils make decisions without adequate information on the value of their resources, or the health hazards, pollution, land disruption, and meager benefits which energy development will bring.

Berry, Wendell. *The Unsettling of America: Culture and Agriculture.* San Francisco, Calif.: Sierra Club, 1977. 228 pp. $4.95. (EARS)

This is the story of how Americans have become estranged from the land, and have abused it through agribusiness, petrochemical combines, and over-specialization, and are poisoning our foods and our bodies. Berry also explores the crises of ecology, energy, agriculture, and culture, and their interrelationships.

Brodeur, Paul. *The Zapping of America: Microwaves, Their Deadly Risk, and the Coverup.* New York, N.Y.: Norton, 1977. 343 pp. $11.95.

Brodeur details the many ways in which microwaves may damage human health. He finds that the effects may be cumulative, and related to increases in cancer deaths and other disorders—evidence which government and industry are anxious to cover up. Microwaves have become a vital part of our electronic systems for communications, medical instruments, microwave ovens and video games in the home, high voltage power lines overhead - and countless other devices with consequences as yet unknown.

Brown, Lester R. *The Twenty-Ninth Day: Accomodating Human Needs and Numbers to the Earth's Resources.* Worldwatch Institute. New York, N.Y.: Norton, 1978. 363 pp. $3.95. (EARS)

Is the global lilypond half full? Brown examines the interrelationships between the earth's biological, economic, and social systems, and warns that mounting population pressures will bring a crisis of vast proportions as we reach the limits of our planet's biological and energy resources.

Burby, Raymond J. III, and Bell, Fleming A. *Energy and the Community.* Cambridge, Mass.: Ballinger, 1978. 144 pp. $17.50.

This study explores the relationships between American lifestyles and energy use, how Americans can make more efficient use of energy resources, and how to bring about this transition. Considers problems of land use and transportation, and the impact of a nuclear power plant on the local community.

Cahn, Robert. *Footprints on the Planet: A Search for an Environmental Ethic.* New York,

N.Y.: Universe, 1978. 278 pp. $10.95.

Cahn finds evidence for the ethic in environmental test cases, in examples of socially responsible corporations, progressive States, and in communities testing new lifestyles that are more benign to the environment.

Finkel, Asher J. *Energy, the Environment, and Human Health.* The American Medical Association Congress on Environmental Health. Acton, Mass.: Publishing Sciences Group, 1974. 288 pp.

The American Medical Association considers the net balance between the harmful and beneficial results of the production and utilization of energy, including environmental impacts, human health hazards, and socio-economic implications, but does not come to any far-reaching conclusions.

Fritsch, Albert J., and The Science Action Coalition. *Environmental Ethics: Choices for Concerned Citizens.* Garden City, N.Y.: Anchor, 1979. 309 pp. $3.95.

The problems in four areas, endangered species, coal, nuclear energy, and chemical pollution are analyzed, together with their social implications. This provides an ethical framework and constructive alternatives for the establishment of an ecologically conscious life style.

Hessel, Dieter, ed. *Energy Ethics: A Christian Response.* National Council of Churches Energy Project, 475 Riverside Drive, New York, NY 10027. 1979. 150 pp. $3.95+ postage.

This treatise focuses on the relationship of energy to religion, ethics, society, politics, citizen action, and the environment.

Holdren, John P., et al. *Risk of Renewable Energy Sources: A Critique of the Inhaber Report.* ERG #79-3. Energy and Resources Group, University of California, Berkeley, CA 94720. June 1979. 232 pp. $7.00. (Reduced size version, $3.50).

The influential *Inhaber Report* from the Canadian Atomic Energy Control Board concluded that the health risks from the use of renewable energy sources were comparable to risks from fossil fuels, and greater than those from nuclear sources. (See Inhaber, Herbert. *Risk of Energy Production*) The University of California group found serious errors in Inhaber's calculations, methodology, and interpretation of data, and a bias against unconventional technologies. The corrected data lead to the opposite conclusion: that renewables entail much less risk to workers and to the public. (See also *Not Man Apart.* September 1979, p. 19

Inhaber, Herbert. *Risk of Energy Production.* Ottawa, Canada: Atomic Energy Control Board, Report AECB-1119, 1978. AECB, P.O. Box 1046, Ottawa, Canada, K1P 5S9.

The health hazards of deriving energy from wood, wind, and sunlight are comparable to those of using coal and oil, and much greater than those of using nuclear power, according to this controversial study which traces the risk factor from the production of basic materials through to the operation of the final product. A condensation of this study appeared in the February 23, 1979 issue of *Science* magazine.

See also: Holdren, John P. *Risk of Renewable Energy Sources: A Critique of the Inhaber Report;* and *Not Man Apart,* September, 1979, p. 19.

Landsberg, Hans H. et al. *Energy and the Social Sciences: An Examination of Research Needs.* Washington, D.C.: Resources for the Future, 1974. 778 pp. $10.00.

A National Science Foundation Study of power resources, research needs, and energy policy.

Mander, Jerry. *Four Arguments for the Elimination of Television*. New York, N.Y.: Morrow, 1978. 371 pp. $4.95.

Although this book may seem far removed from energy issues, it has relevance in explaining how the industrial-advertising-media menage can sell anything—including nuclear power—to the public. This fact has serious implications for movements of social change. Mander finds that TV may be hazardous to health and freedom, and cuts humans off from direct contact with and knowledge of their planet.

Murdock, Steve H., and Leistritz, F. Larry. *Energy Development in the Western United States: Impact on Rural Areas*. New York, N.Y.: Praeger, 1979. 424 pp. $23.95.

Energy development is having a profound socioeconomic impact, especially in the western states, as it brings rapid demographic and economic growth, increased demands on public and private services, and increasing rates of crime, drug abuse, divorce, and conflict over community control.

National Council of Churches. *Energy and Ethics: The Ethical Implications of Energy Production and Use*. National Council of Churches Energy Project, 475 Riverside Dr., New York, NY 10027. 1979. 50 pp. $1.00.

Questions are raised for study and discussion about the energy situation, ecological human choices, social justice, and appropriate action. See National Council of Churches of Christ under ORGANIZATIONS.

Newman, Dorothy K., and Day, Dawn. *The American Energy Consumer*. A report to the Energy Policy Project of the Ford Foundation. Cambridge, Mass.: Ballinger Publishing Co., 1975. 352 pp. $9.95.

An overview of energy lifestyles in America provides a basis for the design of energy policy alternatives, the improvement of energy use efficiency, and policies for people.

Ostheimer, John M., and Ritt, Leonard G. *Environment, Energy, and Black Americans*. Beverly Hills, Calif.: Sage, 1976. 38 pp. $3.00.

From surveys of black attitudes, and voting records of black Congressmen, this research paper concludes that environmentalists need to bridge the gap to the black community by emphasizing the human impact of environmental deterioration, and must work with the black leadership.

Perlman, Robert, and Warren, Roland L. *Families in the Energy Crisis: Impacts and Implications for Theory and Policy*. Cambridge, Mass., Ballinger, 1977. 256 pp. $17.50.

The effects of the energy crisis of the Seventies on 1440 families in metropolitan areas are observed in this study, which deals with issues of equity, relationships between attitudes and behavior, and family tasks affected. Impacts are more serious for lower income and minority families, and older people.

O'Toole, James, and the University of South Carolina Center for Futures Research. *Energy and Social Change*. Cambridge, Mass.: Massachusetts Institute of Technology Press, 1976. 185 pp. $4.95.

These technological, economic, and social forecasts predict higher energy prices and an increase in the use of electrical energy with the development of "super-batteries."

Reader, Mark, ed. *Energy: The Human Dimension*. A Conference sponsored by the Center for Environmental Studies, Arizona State University, The East Maricopa League of Women Voters, and the City of Scottsdale, Sept. 18-19,

1976. Tempe, Ariz.: Center for Environmental Studies, Research Paper No. 5, Arizona State University, 1977. 188 pp.

This is the report of an experiment in public discussion of the human dimensions of our energy choices in terms of ethical considerations, frontier and democratic values, alternative life-styles, and everyday life.

Sky, Alison, and Stone, Michelle. *On Site on Energy, Issue 5/6*. New York, N.Y.: Charles Scribner's Sons, 1974. 127 pp. $6.95.

Perceptive photographs and fresh concepts bring new insights into the impact of energy use on habitat and lifestyle, with implications for future planning and human survival.

Steinhart, Carol E., and Steinhart, John S. *Energy: Sources, Use, and Role in Human Affairs*. Mass.: Duxbury Press, 1974. 362 pp. $5.95.

A discussion of energy resources, energy use, and resulting social policies: the human side of the energy crisis.

Steinhart, Carol E., and Steinhart, John S. *The Fires of Culture: Energy Yesterday and Tomorrow*. Mass.: Duxbury Press, 1974. 273 pp. $4.95.

An analysis of energy sources and the environmental problems associated with increasing energy use in society, as well as the prospects for the future, and the role of energy in climate modification.

Stockholm Conference. *ECO I: The Human Environment Conference, June 1972*. San Francisco, Calif.: Friends of the Earth. 84 pp. $5.00. (FOE)

A book version of the daily newspapers published by Friends of the Earth and the British *Ecologist* during the historic United Nations' conference.

U.S. Energy Research and Development Administration. *The Impact of Energy Production on Human Health: An Evaluation of Means for Assessment*. Conf-751022. ERDA Office of Public Affairs/Technical Information Center, 1976. 144 pp. $6.75. (NTIS)

A study of techniques to determine potential effects of various energy producing industries on human health. It discusses the setting of standards for workers and the public as to radiation, carcinogens, and other toxic substances.

International Developments

Asian Productivity Organization. *Energy Management in Selected Asian Countries*. 1978. 150 pp. $8.00. (UNIPUB)

Information on energy utilization programs in eight oil-importing Asian countries, identifying major difficulties and measures for improvement.

Brookhaven National Laboratory Developing Countries Energy Program. *Energy Needs, Uses and Resources in Developing Countries*. Brookhaven National Laboratory Associated Universities, Inc., Upton, NY 11973. BNL 50784. TID 4500. 1978. 143 pp. $9.00. (NTIS)

Prepared for the Agency for International Development, this report identifies the energy needs, uses, and resources in developing countries of the world, and examines the energy options available for continued social and economic growth.

DeCarmoy, Guy. *Energy For Europe: Economic and Political Implications*. Washington, D.C.: American Enterprise Institute for Public Policy Research, 1977. 120 pp. $3.25.

This study examines the European energy predicament, and the constraints and opportunities influencing policy making in this area.

Dunkerley, Joy, ed. *International Comparisons of Energy Consumption*. Washington, D.C.: Resources for the Future, 1978. 252 pp. $7.50.
This volume contains the proceedings of a workshop on energy consumption sponsored by Resources for the Future and the Electric Power Research Institute.

Hayes, Denis. *Energy for Development: Third World Options*. Washington, D.C.: Worldwatch Institute, 1977. 44 pp. $2.00. (FOE) (EARS)
After a study of coal, petroleum, and nuclear power, the author concludes that conservation and renewable energy sources are the most advantageous choices for undeveloped countries.

Heisler, Martin O., and Lawrence, Robert M. *International Energy Policy*. A Policy Studies Organization Book. Lexington, Mass.: Lexington Books, 1979.
Energy policy is examined from a global perspective, including profiles of the Persian Gulf countries, Mexico, and China.

Hocking, Denis. *Energy Policy for New Zealand*. Friends of the Earth, Box 39-065, Auckland West, New Zealand. 91 pp. $2.50.
This balanced national energy analysis is based on a no- or slow-growth philosophy so far as energy- and capital-intensive industry is concerned. It recognizes social and economic values, as well as environmental considerations, and insists that energy sources must be carefully matched to end-use requirements. Its ideas are applicable to other countries as well.

International Energy Agency. *Annual Report on Energy Research, Development, and Demonstration Activities of the International Energy Agency*. 1977-1978. Paris: Organization for Economic Cooperation and Development. 67 pp. OECD Publications Center, 1750 Pennsylvania Ave. NW, Suite 1207, Washington, DC 20006.
The objective of the International Energy Agency is to assure the development and application of new energy technologies which can help reduce dependence on oil. Research projects are described in areas of energy conservation, coal technology, nuclear safety, geothermal, solar, biomass, ocean, wind, fusion, and hydrogen.

International Energy Agency. Workshop on Energy Data of Developing Countries. Paris: Organization for Economic Co-Operation and Development, 1979. OECD Publications and Information Center, Suite 1207, 1750 Pennsylvania Ave. NW, Washington, DC 20006. Vol. I. *Summary of Discussions and Technical Papers*. 128 pp. $10.00. Vol. II. *Basic Energy Statistics and Energy Balances of Developing Countries*. (in English and French.) 544 pp. $15.00.
Experts from developing countries present reports, and assemble statistics on energy production, trade, transformation, and consumption for 16 countries.

Kelley, Donald R. *The Energy Crisis and the Environment: An International Perspective*. New York, N.Y.: Praeger, 1977. 264 pp. $22.95.
The political dimension of energy and environmental policies is explored in diverse nations such as the U.S., the USSR, Europe, Japan, Brazil, and Iran. A variety of social and governmental systems, and a wide range of energy-related and environmental problems are represented.

Lucas, N.J.D. *Energy and The European Communities.* London: Europa, 1977. 175 pp.
  The author traces the history of energy in Europe since the Second World War, and the search by member states of the community for a common energy policy. The principal motives appear to be political rather than economic or technical.

Mangone, Gerald J., ed. *Energy Policies of the World.* New York, N.Y.: Elsevier. Vol. I, 1976, 387 pp., $19.50. *Canada, China, the Arab States, Venezuela, and Iran.* Vol. II, 1977, 320 pp., $18.50. *Indonesia, North Sea Countries, and the Soviet Union.*
  The authors seek to illuminate the background, conditions, and influences upon the energy policies of key foreign countries, and to examine available options for national development, international trade, and world peace.

Organization for Economic Cooperation and Development. *Energy Research and Development.* Paris: OECD, 1974. 243 pp.
  Energy problems, current research, and options for future development are analyzed from a worldwide perspective.

Pachauri, R.K. *Energy and Economic Development in India.* New York, N.Y.: Praeger, 1977. 208 pp. $19.50.
  The relationship of energy to economic, industrial, and agricultural development in India and other developing countries is the focus of this study. It assesses technologies, resources, and policies which could contribute to the most efficient use of energy in the next 20 years.

Russell, Jeremy. *Energy as a Factor in Soviet Foreign Policy.* Lexington, Mass.: Lexington Books, 1976. 264 pp. $21.95.
  Russell describes the production and use of major Soviet fuels, and analyzes the USSR's energy policy with regard to other countries.

Smil, Vaclav. *China's Energy: Achievements, Problems, Prospects.* New York, N.Y.: Praeger, 1976. 272 pp. $21.50.
  China has a high potential for the development of fossil fuels, hydro-energy, and unconventional sources of energy, but the patterns of usage and technology are only moderately advanced.

Stunkel, Kenneth R., ed. *National Energy Profiles.* New York, N.Y.: Praeger, 1979. 335 pp. $19.95.
  Patterns of energy use and energy strategies of ten nations are examined, in terms of variations in culture, economic development, ideology, political systems, and social tradition.

Scenarios for the Future: Limits to Growth and the Conserver Society

Callenbach, Ernest. *Ecotopia.* Berkeley, Calif.: Banyan Tree. 1975. 167 pp. $2.95 (EARS)
  This underground classic projects a future of stable-state, humanitarian society based upon renewable resources and coevolution with the biosphere. See also *Seriatim, an Ecotopian Journal,* in the periodicals section of this bibliography.

Canada, Department of Supplies and Services. *Canada As A Conserver Society: Resource Uncertainties and the Need for New Technologies.* The Committee on the

Implications of Conserver Society of the Science Council of Canada. Ottawa, Canada, 1978. 108 pp. $5.50. (UNIPUB)

Respect for the biosphere and concern for the future are the basis for recommendations for conservation, including public transit, building codes, discouraging wasteful practices, and studying the dis-economies of scale. Of interest to citizens of any industrialized country.

Daly, Herman E. *Steady State Economics: The Economics of Biophysical Equilibrium and Moral Growth*. San Francisco, Calif.: Freeman., 1977. 185 pp. $6.00.

Daly presents constructive arguments for the establishment of a steady state economy, and suggests measures for achieving it. Fission power is a good example of how growth, whether actual or projected, forces us to accept dangerous technologies that would never be acceptable or be needed with smaller populations living at less lavish standards of per capita consumption.

Goodman, Percival. *The Double E*. New York, N.Y.: Doubleday, 1977. $3.50.

The two "E"s are ecology and economy. This vision of an alternative future is based upon the mutual relations between organism and environment. Small, compact cities would operate on renewable energy systems with little pollution, and decentralization would be found to be more efficient than large scale technology.

Johnson, Warren. *Muddling Toward Frugality: A Blueprint for Survival in the 1980's*. Boulder, Colo.: Shambala, 1979. 252 pp. $2.95. (EARS).

A hopeful—even humorous—book, which explains how, in the face of dwindling resources, we will be exchanging the grand achievements of large scale technology for modest accomplishments on a more human scale. After accepting the reality of scarcity, we can adapt to a more fulfilling and sustainable way of life based on renewable resources.

Meadows, Dennis L., ed. *Alternatives to Growth—I: A Search for Sustainable Futures*. Cambridge, Mass.: Ballinger, 1977. 448 pp. $8.95.

Collected essays study the problems and opportunities inherent in a "steady state" society, a society no longer dependent on perpetual growth in population, energy use, and raw materials consumption.

Meadows, Dennis L.; Meadows, Donella H.; Randers, Jorgen; and Behrens, William W. III. *The Limits to Growth*. New York, N.Y.: Universe Books, 1972. 205 pp. $2.75. (FOE)

Based on a Massachusetts Institute of Technology study of the limits to exponential growth and the achievement of global equilibrium, this work depicts the role of energy with its depletion of non-renewable resources and resultant pollution.

Nash, Hugh, ed. *Progress As If Survival Mattered: A Handbook for a Conserver Society*. San Francisco, Calif.: Friends of the Earth, 1977. 320 pp. $6.95. (FOE) (EARS)

FOE's draft proposal for sane and practical planning for a future of freedom and permanence. Staff experts and well-known consultants explore 20 vital areas, including population, energy, health, transportation, the sea, defense and foreign policy, law, science & technology, jobs & the environment, education, agriculture, and wilderness.

Ophuls, William. *Ecology and the Politics of Scarcity*. San Francisco, Calif.: Freeman, 1977. 303 pp. $6.95.

An illuminating analysis of the interconnections of all things. Modern industrial civilization, with its exponential growth, misuse of energy and resources, and disruption of natural systems, is now confronted by implacable ecological imperatives. The only way out is to make the transition from exploitation to stewardship and low-energy, steady-state society as rapidly as possible. Critical bibliographic notes survey the literature.

Pirages, Dennis Clark, ed. *The Sustainable Society: Implications for Limited Growth.* New York, N.Y.: Praeger, 1977. 362 pp. $23.50.
Noted social scientists explore the issues surrounding the limits to growth controversy, focusing on the need for basing economic growth on renewable resources, and analyzing the impact of resource scarcity on social and political systems, and on international relations.

Robertson, James. *The Sane Alternative: A Choice of Futures.* River Basin Publishing Company, P.O. Box 30573, St. Paul, MN 55175. 1979. 152 pp. $4.95.
Robertson analyzes our present society and its problems of bureaucracy, energy and raw materials shortages, ecological disruption, and loss of feedback from citizens at the grass-roots level. A scenario is proposed for the transition to a sane, humane, and ecological (SHE) future.

Solomon, Lawrence. *The Conserver Solution: A Blueprint for the Conserver Society.* Pollution Probe Foundation, Canada. Garden City, New York: Doubleday, 1979. 206 pp. $6.95.
Conservation need not be overwhelmingly difficult, and it can mean more, not less. A conserver society would be more efficient, self-sustainable, and wholly regenerative.

Steinhart, John, et al. *Pathway to Energy Sufficiency: The 2050 Study.* San Francisco, Calif.: Friends of the Earth, 1979. 96 pp. $4.95. (FOE) (EARS)
What will the conserver society be like? Here is a hard-headed, hopeful look at institutions and technologies that can help us to solve the energy problem at a fraction of current costs.

Valaskakis, Kimon; Sindell, Peter; Smith, J. Graham; and Fitzpatrick-Martin, Iris. *The Conserver Society.* New York, N.Y.: Harper and Row, 1979. 286 pp. $4.95.
A "think-tank" drawn from Canadian government agencies and universities attempts to portray the kinds of society that would be indefinitely sustainable. Changes are proposed that would lead to less waste and greater efficiency, but the authors do not face up to the problems of resource depletion, limits to growth, and continued dependence on the "hard" energy path.

Voegell and Tarrant. *Survival 2001: Scenario from the Future.* New York, N.Y.: Van Nostrand Reinhold Company. 1975. 115 pp. $6.95. (EARS)
Workable ideas, with detailed engineering drawings, that could help solve our pressing environmental problems.

ENERGY CONSERVATION

References

Cowperthwaite, Tom, and Murphy, Ken, eds. *Guide to Federal Energy Conservation Programs*. Environmental Study Conference. Congressional Record, Vol. 125, No. 15, February 9, 1979. Available free from your Senator or Representative.

Describes federal programs, and where to obtain information regarding loans, tax credits, grants, audio-visual materials, exhibits, publications, and much more.

Gil, Efraim, ed. *Energy Efficient Planning: An Annotated Bibliography*. American Society of Planning Officials, 1313 East Sixtieth St., Chicago, IL 60637. $6.00.

The listings stress energy conservation, and include sections on land-use planning, transportation, and energy-efficient house design.

U.S. Department of Energy. *The Resource File: Practical Publications for Energy Management*. Washington, D.C., 1978. S/N 061-000-00040-2. 475 pp. $9.00. (USGPO)

An in-depth bibliography of action-oriented energy conservation publications.

Overviews and Issues

Abelson, Philip H., ed. *Energy: Use, Conservation, and Supply*. Washington, D.C.: American Association for the Advancement of Science, 1974. 154 pp.

A compendium of articles on the efficiency of energy use in the United States, conservation, food and all energy sources including developing technologies. Concludes that nuclear power is necessary despite its problems.

Abelson, Philip H., and Hammond, Allen L., eds. *Energy II: Use, Conservation, and Supply*. Washington, D.C.: American Association for the Advancement of Science, 1978. 201 pp. $6.00.

Further readings on the efficiency of energy use in the United States.

Armstrong, Joe E., and Harman, Willis. *Plausibility of a Restricted Energy Use Scenario*. Menlo Park, Calif.: Stanford Research Institute, 1975. 206 pp.

Surveys energy use, the necessity of conservation, and problems of transition to new lifestyles. Recommends steps for comprehensive planning now.

Canada, Department of Energy, Mines, and Resources. *Energy Conservation in Canada: Programs and Perspectives*. Report EP 77-7. Ottawa, Ontario, Canada:

Department of Energy, Mines and Resources, 1977. 56 pp.

This report is concerned with strategies to increase the efficiency of energy use in order to reduce the rate of growth of energy consumption in an environmentally and socially acceptable way. Analyzes opportunities for conservation in buildings, transportation, industry, energy supply, agriculture, and in the public sector.

Citizens' Advisory Committee on Environmental Quality. *Citizen Action Guide to Energy Conservation.* Citizens' Advisory Committee on Environmental quality, 1700 Pennsylvania Ave. NW, Washington, DC 20006. 1973. 62 pp. $1.75. (USGPO)

The possibilities for energy conservation in the home, workplace, industry, and transportation are explained in simple terms, with ideas for organizing community action to promote the practice of conservation.

Cunningham, William H., and Lopreato, Sally Cook. *Energy Use and Conservation Incentives: A Study of the Southwestern United States.* New York, N.Y.: Praeger, 1977. 216 pp. $18.50.

This study examines attitudes, behaviors, and energy consumption patterns, discusses policy implications of the data, and outlines new programs for energy conservation.

Darmstadter, Joel. *Conserving Energy.* Published for Resources for the Future. Baltimore, Md.: Johns Hopkins University Press, 1975. 105 pp. $2.95.

Explores patterns of consumption, energy saving practices, and policies to implement energy conservation in the New York area.

Dumas, Lloyd J. *The Conservation Response: Strategies for the Design and Operation of Energy-Using Systems.* Lexington, Mass.: Lexington Books, 1976. 320 pp. $19.00.

This excellent college text challenges the prevailing response to the energy problem: the attempt to expand the supply of energy resources to meet an unrestricted demand, regardless of consequences. The alternative is the conservation response, which can solve both energy and pollution problems. Strategies are presented for the conservation of energy in the areas of building design, heating & cooling, lighting, transportation, industry, food, and agriculture.

Environmental Law Institute State and Local Energy Conservation Project. Cambridge, Mass.: Ballinger.

This series provides information on legal and administrative strategies for conserving America's energy supplies, and the technical and economic soundness of these policies.

Volume 1. Tether, Ivan J. *Government Procurement and Operation.* 1977. 208 pp. $15.50.

Volume 2. Russell, Joe W., and Garrison, E. Grant. *Tax Strategies: Alternative to Regulation.* 1979. 152 pp. $15.00.

Volume 3. Wells, Frederick J. *Utility Pricing and Planning: An Economic Analysis.* 1979. 144 pp. $15.00.

Volume 4. Dean, Norman L. *Energy Efficiency in Industry: A Guide to Legal Barriers and Opportunities.* 1979. 192 pp. $16.50.

Volume 5. Thompson, Grant P. *Building to Save Energy: Legal and Regulatory Approaches.* 1979. 176 pp. $16.50.

Volume 6. Zaelke, Durwood J. *Saving Energy in Urban Transportation.* 1979. 256 pp. $17.50.

Volume 7. Harwood, Corbin Crews. *Using Land to Save Energy.* 1977. 336 pp.

$19.50.

Volume 8. Friedrich, Robert A. *Energy Conservation for American Agriculture.* 1979. 192 pp. $16.50.

Fritsch, Albert J. *The Contrasumers: A Citizens' Guide to Resource Conservation.* New York, N.Y.: Praeger, 1974. 182 pp. $3.50.

A very readable analysis of energy conservation, power resources, environmental protection, U.S. consumer culture and the crises it leads to. Provides guidelines for citizen action. (Education)

Griffin, James M. *Energy Conservation in the OECD, 1980-2000.* Cambridge, Mass.: Ballinger, 1978. 320 pp. $20.00.

The strengths and limitations of energy conservation in the countries of the Organization for Economic Cooperation and Development are evaluated, along with the determinants of consumption, possibilities of energy substitution, and the remaining gaps to be filled with increased energy production.

Hayes, Denis. *Energy: The Case for Conservation.* Washington, D.C.: Worldwatch Institute, 1976. 77 pp. $2.00. (EARS) (FOE)

Details the use of energy in the United States, and how half of this energy could be saved through conservation.

Organization for Economic Cooperation and Development. *Energy Conservation in the International Energy Agency.* OECD Publications Center, 1700 Pennsylvania Ave. NW, Washington, DC 20006. 55 pp. $6.00.

The results of the 1976 review of the conservation efforts of 17 member nations show the United States to be below average in achievement.

Sawhill, John C., ed. *Energy: Conservation and Public Policy.* The American Assembly, Columbia Univ. Englewood Cliffs, N.J.: Prentice-Hall, 1979. 259 pp. $5.95

Energy experts from various sectors present a forum of opinion on energy economics; conservation in transportation, buildings, industry, agriculture, and electrical generation; waste recovery; solar prospects; and government programs. Energy conservation is the Cinderella of our current energy options.

Schipper, Lee. *Energy Conservation: Its Nature, Hidden Benefits, and Hidden Barriers.* Berkeley, Calif.: Energy and Resources Group, University of California, 1975. UCID-3725. 92 pp. $5.00. (NTIS)

Shows that for each dollar invested in the highly mechanized energy sector, only a relatively few jobs and only a relatively small increment in Gross National Product result.

Schipper, Lee, and Lichtenberg, A.J. *Efficient Energy Use and Well-Being: The Swedish Example.* LBL 4430. Lawrence Berkeley Laboratory, and Energy Resources Group, University of California, Berkeley, CA 94720. 1976. 53 pp.

A detailed comparison is made between the energy consumption of the U.S. and that of Sweden. Sweden uses 55% of the U.S. per capita energy at essentially the same per capita income. The study indicates that more efficient energy use could in fact improve the U.S. economy.

Stanford Research Institute. *Comparison of Energy Consumption between West Germany and the United States.* NTIS #PB245-652-AS. $5.25. (NTIS)

West Germans use only 2/3 as much energy as Americans. It should be possible for the U.S. to substantially reduce the ratio of energy use to national income, without cutting living standards or economic growth.

Taylor, Vince. *Energy: The Easy Path*. Cambridge, Massachusetts: Union of Concerned Scientists, 1979. 175 pp. $4.50. (UCS)

Why nuclear power cannot make a substantial contribution to the energy supply problem over the next several decades is demonstrated by this study. The most immediate solution lies in the remarkable potential for reducing energy inputs without affecting the quality or quantity of energy services.

Taylor, Vince. *The Easy Path Energy Plan*. Cambridge, Mass.: Union of Concerned Scientists. 1979. 46 pp. $2.00. (UCS)

In a companion volume to *Energy: The Easy Path*, a program is proposed for meeting the energy supply problem through the implementation of currently available energy conservation technologies.

U.S. Congress. *Alternative Energy Conservation Strategies: An Economic Appraisal*. Washington, D.C., 1978. S/N 052-070-04545-1. 182 pp. $2.75. (USGPO)

The concept of total productivity is used to evaluate three conservation strategies.

U.S. Department of Energy. Conservation and Solar Applications. *International Energy Conservation: Comparative Law and Policy*. Proceedings from the 1978 International Conference on Energy Conservation. CONF 780274. Washington, D.C., 1979. 362 pp. $13.00. (NTIS)

Conservation may be the most readily available and least costly alternative energy resource, but laws, policies, incentirves, and information are needed for it to succeed. The conference provided concepts to be tailored to the various national customs, social needs, and political and economic realities.

Williams, Robert H., ed. *The Energy Conservation Papers*. A report to the Energy Policy Project of the Ford Foundation. Cambridge, Mass.: Ballinger, 1974. 400 pp. $22.50.

An analysis of energy, employment, consumer options, potential energy conservation through recycling and recovery from organic wastes, pollution control, and waste management.

Saving Energy in the Home

Albright, Roger. *547 Easy Ways to Save Energy In Your Home*. Charlotte, Vt.: Garden Way, 1978. 124 pp. $4.95.

Describes many things you can do yourself at little or no cost to keep comfortable with a minimum of heat. Considers insulation, heating, appliances, the automobile, and other areas.

Baker, Bill. *How To Beat the Energy Crisis and Still Live in Style*. New York, N.Y.: Putnam, 1979. 210 pp. $6.95.

This is a workable blueprint for living more cheaply, safely, and comfortably by stopping heat loss and waste in your home. It includes simple tips on insulation as well as aids to selecting a solar system.

Consumer Guide, eds. *Energy Savers Catalog*. New York, N.Y.: Putnam, 1977. 160 pp. $6.95.

Step by step instructions for homeowner insulation, care of heating and cooling systems, appliance maintenance, conservation of electricity and water, emergencies, auto gas consumption. Products recommended by name brands. Clear diagrams, and well organized for easy reference.

Derven, Ronald, and Nichols, Carol. *How to Cut Your Energy Bills.* Farmington, Mich.: Structures Publishing Company, 1976. 131 pp. $4.95.

Detailed photographs and diagrams show how to plug the energy leaks at home, control ventilation and lighting, heat and cool economically, and make the most efficient use of home appliances. Many specific and useful suggestions are included.

Eccli, Eugene, and Eccli, Sandra F. *Save Energy: Save Money.* Washington, D.C.: Community Services Administration, Office of Economic Oppotrunity, 1974. 40 pp. Available from the National Center for Community Action, 1711 Connecticut Ave., N.W., Washington, DC 20009.

Offers many practical suggestions for improving the energy efficiency of your home and appliances.

The Family Handyman. *The Family Handyman Practical Book of Saving Home Energy.* Blue Ridge Summit, Pa.: TAB Books, 1978. 240 pp. $5.95.

Here's how to become an energy expert in your own home, and save money without sacrificing comfort. Excellent illustrated step-by-step instructions.

Federal Energy Administration. *Home Energy Saver's Workbook.* #041-018-0016-8. Washington, D.C.: FEA. 29 pp. $.50. (USGPO)

A concise guide for determining measures that will make your home more energy efficient. Includes maps, tables, calculations, installation techniques, and other useful tips.

Friend, Gil. *Kilowatt Counter.* See ENERGY EDUCATION: RESOURCES

Fritsch, Albert. *Lifestyle Index 1977.* See ENERGY EDUCATION: RESOURCES

Hart, G. Kimball, and the editors of U.S. News and World Report Books. *How to Cut Your Energy Costs: A Guide to Major Savings at Home and on the Road.* Washington, D.C.: U.S. News and World Report Books, 1978. 272 pp. $7.95.

You can carry out your own cost saving analysis of energy improvements for your home, including appliances, clothing, food, and automobile, and make informed decisions about the many offerings on the market.

Hickok, Floyd. *Your Energy Efficient Home: Improvements to Save Utility Dollars.* Englewood Cliffs, N.J.: Prentice-Hall, 1979. 145 pp. $5.95.

You can be your own engineer and prevent heat loss from basement to attic, and cut fuel bills. You will also learn how the sun can become your home's heat source.

Jacobs, Madeleine, and Petersen, Stephen R. *Making the Most of Your Energy Dollars in Home Heating and Cooling.* National Bureau of Standards, Washington, DC 20234, 1975. 17 pp. $.70. (From Consumer Information, Pueblo, CO 81009)

A homeowner's guide to figuring an energy conservation budget, with cost and savings to be expected from home improvements such as insulation.

Kleeberg, Irene C. *The Home Energy Saver: All the Facts You Need to Save Energy Dollars.* New York, N.Y.: Butterick, 1977. 208 pp. $3.95.

A collection of energy-saving facts about home heating and cooling, insulation, lighting, automobiles, and much more.

Lawrence, Allen. *Slash Your Energy Bills.* Ambiente Environmental Concerns, P.O. Box 13622, San Antonio, TX 78213. 1977. 33 pp. 11" x 11". $1.95 postpaid.

This guide concisely covers the major conservation areas of interest to the consumer, including the design and location of the house, energy waste problems in the house, and electrical appliances.

Murphy, John A. *The Homeowner's Energy Guide: How to Beat the Heating Game.* New York, N.Y.: Crowell, 1976. 217 pp. $6.95.

This analysis of all home components shows how to calculate fuel costs and potential savings. A checklist is included.

Price, Billy, and Price, James. *Homeowner's Guide to Saving Energy.* Blue Ridge Summit, Pa.: Tab Books, 1976. 288 pp. $5.95. (EARS).

This is a well-illustrated how-to-do-it book, showing the homeowner how to cut electricity and fuel consumption.

Rothchild, John, and Tenney, Frank. *The Home Energy Guide: How to Cut Your Utility Bills.* New York, N.Y.: Ballantine, 1978. 247 pp. $1.95.

This book seeks to present a middle course between the trivial and the complicated solutions for the non-technical reader. It contains suggestions for an energy budget, reading labels and meters, appliance selection and care, life-cycle costing, insulation, solar possibilities, utilities and public power, and preparing for energy survival in emergencies. (Education)

Socolow, Robert H. *Saving Energy in the Home: Princeton's Experiments at Twin Rivers.* Cambridge, Mass.: Ballinger, 1978. 320 pp. $16.50.

The Twin Rivers Program in Energy Conservation in Housing studied the amount of energy used in a set of nominally identical townhouses, and how this could be modified through energy conservation techniques.

U.S. Department of Energy. *Tips for Energy Savers.* Washington, D.C., 1979. 29 pp. Free from Consumer Information Center, Pueblo, CO 81009.

A guide to saving energy and money on home heating, cooling, lighting, and appliances. (Education)

U.S. Department of Housing and Urban Development. *The Energy-Wise Home Buyer: A Guide to Selecting an Energy Efficient Home.* Washington, D.C., 1979. S/N 023-000-00518-2. 60 pp. $2.00. (USGPO)

Many useful tips are contained in this guide, such as features to look for in new and used homes, how to estimate energy costs, saving energy in the home, and a checklist for house inspection.

U.S. Department of Housing and Urban Development. *In the Bank . . . Or Up the Chimney? A Dollars and Cents Guide to Energy-Saving Home Improvements.* Washington, D.C.: Abt Associates, 1975. 72 pp. $2.00. (USGPO) (EARS) This material appears in other publications as *How to Insulate Your Home and Save Fuel,* Dover; *How to Keep Your House Warm in Winter, Cool in Summer,* Cornerstone; and *Energy-Saving Home Improvements,* Drake. Prices vary.

A clearly written and illustrated manual to help the homeowner plan do-it-yourself projects or seek professional services.

Conservation in Architecture and Buildings; The Energy-Efficient House; Insulation

Adams, Anthony. *Your Energy Efficient House.* Charlotte, Vt.: Garden Way Publishing, 1975. 118 pp. $4.95. (EARS)

Emphasizes non-mechanical concepts that should be considered in designing a new house or renovating an existing house, and outlines basic ways to use Nature's heating and cooling forces.

American Institute of Architects. *Saving Energy in the Built Environment: The AIA Policy.* American Institute of Architects, 1735 New York Ave. NW, Washington, DC 20006. Free booklet.
A discussion of some of the wider implications of saving energy in buildings. Additioal information on energy conservation is available.

Bender, Tom and DeMoll, Lane. *Building Value: Energy Design Guidelines for State Buildings.* Office of the State Architect, P.O. Box 1079, Sacramento, CA 95805. 1976. $3.25.
Design resources for buildings and landscaping, and evaluation including lifecycle costs.

Caudill, William Wayne: Lawyer, Frank D.; and Bullock, Thomas A. *A Bucket of Oil; The Humanistic Approach to Building Design for Energy Conservation.* Boston, Mass.: Cahners Books, 1974. 87 pp.
Suggests measures which can incorporate more human and ecological designs into our buildings, with savings of energy.

Cole, John N., and Wing, Charles. *From the Ground Up.* Boston, Mass.: Little, Brown, 1976. 252 pp. $7.95. (EARS)
This compendium of insights, information, and illustrations for building an energy-conserving shelter can save money, enhance comfort, and lead to a life of greater harmony with the natural world.

Construction Specification Institute. *Energy Conservation in Buildings: Techniques for Economic Design.* Washington, D.C.: American Institute of Architects, 1974, 180 pp. $20.00.
The economics and the technical aspects of reducing energy use in buildings are outlined in this guide.

Consumer Energy Council of America. *Building Energy Performance Standards.* Consumer Energy Council of America, 1990 M St. NW, Washington, DC 20036. 75 pp. Free.
A primer on the Department of Energy's New Conservation Initiative.

Dillon, J.B. *Thermal Insulation: Recent Developments.* Park Ridge, N.J.: Noyes Data Corporation, 1978. 339 pp. $39.00.
This study surveys the wide variety of materials, both natural and manufactured, which provide insulation because of their low thermal conductivity, for uses ranging from buildings to furnaces to LNG storage.

Dubin, Fred S., and Long, Chalmers G. *Energy Conservation Standards for Building Design, Construction, and Operation.* New York, N.Y.: McGraw-Hill, 1978. 413 pp. $22.50.
Architects and engineers will find the latest practical methods in this guide for managing energy in new buildings, and for modifying existing buildings. Tables and charts facilitate the measurement of energy flows and the determination of cost/benefit ratios.

Eccli, Eugene, ed. *Low Cost, Energy-Efficient Shelter.* Emmaus, Pa.: Rodale Press, 1976. 408 pp. $7.95. (EARS)
Information on how to make homes more energy-efficient, including use of passive solar heating systems. An extensive and practical reference on conservation measures in construction.

Goodland, Robert, ed. *Buildings and the Environment.* Millbrook, N.Y.: The Cary Arboretum, 1976. 263 pp. $10.00.

Contains articles on the ecology of housing, low-energy housing, gentle architecture, energy conservation, and construction codes and options.

Hand, A.J. *Home Energy How To.* New York, N.Y.: Harper & Row, a Popular Science Book, 1977. 258 pp. $9.95.
Explicit directions for upgrading your home insulation, saving on present heating and cooling systems, and producing your own home energy from the sun, wind, water, and biofuels.

Higson, James D. *Building and Remodeling for Energy Savings.* Solana Beach, Calif.: Craftsman, 1977. 319 pp. $15.00.
Energy efficiency can be improved by design features, new materials, and new equipment. Useful information on all systems including landscaping.

Hill, Burt, et al. *Planning and Building the Minimum Energy Dwelling.* Solana Beach, Calif.: Craftsman, 1979. 287 pp. $10.00.
The MED—Minimum Energy Dwelling—was built as a demonstration project by the federal government and private industry, with the goals of reducing energy consumption by at least 50% and of encouraging the building industry to adopt these energy saving features. Includes directions for adapting this design to other climates, conserving water, and disposing of waste. Gives examples of community planning in Davis, California, and in the ancient pueblos of the Southwest.

Hoffman, Douglas R. *The Energy-Efficient Church.* Total Environmental Action. New York, N.Y.: Pilgrim, 1979. 86 pp. $4.95. (TEA)
A non-technical guide to conserving energy and cutting fuel bills in a church, including reducing demand, insulation, controlling infiltration, and considering life-cycle costing of conservation and solar ventures.

Holloway, Dennis. *Ouroboros East: Towards an Energy Conserving Urban Dwelling.* Minneapolis, Minn.: School of Architecture, University of Minnesota. 224 pp. $5.95.
Describes a project to retrofit an existing home for maximum energy efficiency and alternate energy sources. This detailed analysis has wide application.

Institute for Local Self-Reliance. *Weatherization Materials Handbook.* Institute for Local Self-Reliance, 1717-18th St. NW, Washington, DC 20009. 1979. 128 pp. $6.00.
Keyed to the needs of the federal weatherization program, this handbook looks at the quality and effectiveness of different types of insulation, weatherstripping, and storm windows and doors. A manufacturers' directory is included.

Kern, Ken. *The Owner Built Home.* New York, N.Y.: Chas. Scribner and Sons, 1975. 374 pp. $6.95. (EARS) (TEA).
Practical tips on building an energy-efficient home, utilizing the surroundings of the house to the best advantage.

Knowles, Ralph. *Energy and Form: An Ecological Approach to Urban Growth.* Cambridge, Mass.: MIT Press, 1975. 176 pp. $28.00.
Discusses energy conservation through building design and how buildings, settlements, and regions could be planned to take advantage of natural cycles, such as the seasons, to conserve energy.

National League of Cities, U.S. Conference of Mayors. *Energy Conservation in*

Buildings: New Roles for Cities and Citizen Groups. NLC/USCM Publications Center, 1620 Eye St. NW, Washington, DC 20006. $3.00.
A useful guide for community planners. Other publications available.

Olgyay, Victor. *Design with Climate: Bioclimatic Approach to Architectural Regionalism.* Princeton, N.J.: Princeton University Press, 1963. 190 pp. $28.50.
Discusses the need for regionalized architectural solutions that are based on scientific analysis and are responsive to climatic conditions.

Project 2020. *How to Build a Superinsulated House: Cold Weather Edition.* College, Alaska: Project 2020, 1978. 38 pp. $3.00. (EARS)
Special techniques are illustrated for reducing heat loss and insulating houses in very cold climates.

Robinson, Steven, with Dubin, Fred S. *The Energy-Efficient Home. A Manual for Saving Fuel and Using Solar, Wood, and Wind Power.* New York, N.Y.: New American Library, 1978. 158 pp. $4.95.
A do-it-yourself guide to available systems and equipment for building a new energy-efficient home, or retrofitting an old home. Cost-effectiveness, tax breaks, and other useful information.

Schoen, Richard; Hirschberg, Alan S.; and Weingart, Jerome M. *New Energy Technologies for Buildings.* A report to the Energy Policy Project of the Ford Foundation. Cambridge, Mass.: Ballinger Publishing Co., 1975. 240 pp. $22.50.
Conservation and new technologies could reduce energy demand. Tells of barriers that must be surmounted, and makes recommendations for policy changes.

Shelter Publications. *Shelter II.* Bolinas, Calif.: Shelter, 1978. 224 pp. $9.50. (EARS)
A review of world-wide housing techniques, and a manual of design and construction for the first time house builder. Includes urban housing projects.

Steadman, Philip. *Energy, Environment, and Building.* Cambridge, England: Cambridge University Press, 1975. 287 pp. $5.95.
An excellent text, covering energy conservation and solar energy systems for buildings. Explains ways in which buildings can be designed to have a less destructive impact on the natural environment.

Stein, Richard. *Architecture and Energy.* Garden City, N.Y.: Anchor, 1977. 321 pp. $12.95.
Not only an indictment of our present practices—it outlines the choices we must make if we are to rediscover a rational path for architecture. Examines different types of buildings; energy, building and ecology; and principles of energy-saving architecture.

Sterling, Ray, director. *Earth-Sheltered Housing Design.* Underground Space Center, University of Minnesota. New York, N.Y.: Van Nostrand Reinhold, 1979. 318 pp. $9.95.
Architects and homeowners are offered guidelines for the construction of innovative and comfortable underground housing, using low-cost natural resources and energy-saving systems. Varied examples show adaptation to the natural surroundings, and advice is given on problems, products, and building codes.

Sunset Magazine, eds. *Do-It-Yourself Insulation and Weatherstripping for Year-Round Energy*

Saving. Menlo Park, Calif.: Lane, 1978. 80 pp. $2.95.

Clear text and illustrations explain how to find heat leaks and install insulation and weatherstripping.

Tatum, Rita, *The Alternative House: A Complete Guide to Building and Buying*. Danbury, N.H.: Reed Books, 1978. 160 pp. $6.95. (EARS)

Unusual and affordable housing solutions include solar homes, log cabins, mobile homes, creative subdivisions, and urban renewal housing.

Ulrey, Harry F. *Building Construction and Design*. Indianapolis, Inc.: Howard Sams and Company, Inc., 1970. 390 pp. $6.75. (EARS)

Intended to aid the designer, builder and homeowner to avoid or correct many common building faults that are directly affected by natural forces such as heat, light, noise, wind, water, and fire.

Underground Space Center, University of Minnesota. *Earth Sheltered Housing: Guidelines, Examples, References*. New York, N.Y.: Van Nostrand-Reinhold, 1978. 310 pp. $9.95. (EARS) (TEA)

A handsome volume which deals with the design, construction, problems, and policies related to earth sheltered houses and includes many illustrative examples.

U.S. Department of Commerce. *Life-Cycle Costing: A Guide for Selecting Energy Conservation Projects for Public Buildings*. Washington, D.C., 1978. S/N 003-003-01980-1. 70 pp. $2.75. (USGPO)

A step-by-step guide for conducting life-cycle cost evaluations of alternate energy/conservation retrofit projects, and selecting the most cost-effective designs for new buildings.

U.S. Department of Commerce, Office of Energy Policy and Programs. *Total Energy Management: A Practical Handbook on Energy Conservation and Management*. 1976. 54 pp.

Specific steps are described for reducing energy consumption in existing buildings.

U.S. Department of Energy. *An Assessment of Thermal Insulation Materials and Systems for Building Applications*. Washington, D.C., 1978. S/N 061-000-00094-1. 282 pp. $4.75. (USGPO)

The insulation industry is described, with assessments of insulation materials, testing, standards, and building codes.

Vale, Brenda, and Vale, Robert. *The Autonomous House: Design and Planning for Self-Sufficiency*. New York, N.Y.: Universe, 1975. 224 pp. $4.95. (EARS)

The authors tell how to build a home that can operate independently of gas, water, electric, and sewage utility services.

Wade, Alex. *A Design and Construction Handbook for Energy Saving Houses*. Emmaus, Pa.: Rodale, 1979. 416 pp. $15.95.

Specific information is provided to enable the owner-builder to design, finance, and build a custom-made, energy-efficient, reasonably priced house. Includes plans, and lists of architects, contractors, and suppliers.

Wade, Alex, and Ewenstein, Neal. *Thirty Energy-Efficient Houses You Can Build*. Emmaus, Pa.: Rodale, 1977. 316 pp. $8.95. (EARS) (TEA)

The authors describe practical construction techniques and materials that will save fossil fuels and money in either new or remodeled homes. Photographs, floor plans, and specifications are given for a variety of innovative houses which are elegantly simple as well as economical.

Waschek, Carmen, and Waschek, Brownlee. *Your Guide to Good Shelter: How to Plan, Build, or Convert for Energy Conservation.* Reston, Va.: Reston, 1978. 237 pp. $12.75.

A well-designed home should be structurally sound, functional, aesthetic, livable, and affordable. A realistic approach is offered for building a new home or retrofitting an existing home.

Wells, Malcolm. *Underground Designs.* Brewster, Mass.: Wells, 1977. 88 pp. $6.00. (EARS)

A collection of designs for underground buildings, with information on land, laws, structure, insulation, drainage, and landscaping.

Wing, Charles. *From the Walls In.* Boston, Mass.: Little Brown, 1979. 226 pp. $9.95. (TEA)

Information, advice, and illustrations to help retrofit an older home to enhance comfort and conserve energy.

Community Planning for Conservation and Energy Self-Reliance

City of Davis. *Davis Energy Conservation Report: Practical Use of the Sun.* City of Davis, Community Development Department, 226 F St., Davis, CA 95616. 1977. 128 pp. $5.00.

The comprehensive energy conservation program for the city is described, including building codes, planning, solar houses, and public education. Other publications are available from the Community Development Department. More material on Davis may be found in this section under Living Systems: *Planning for Energy Conservation,* and Public Resource Center: *The Davis Experiment;* also, Bainbridge et al: *Village Homes,* under *SOLAR HOMES AND ARCHITECTURE.*

Citizens' Energy Project. *Community Self-Reliance.* Washington, D.C.: Citizens' Energy Project, 1979. 175 pp. $5.00. (CEP)

More than a dozen technologies are presented to help local communities become self-reliant through the development of indigenous renewable energy resources and through energy conservation.

Coates, Gary, ed. *Eco Communities.* Harrisville, N.H.: Brick House, 1980.

This series of articles describes communities actively engaged in ordering their lifestyles according to sound ecological principles.

Diamond, Stuart, and Lorris, Paul S. *It's In Your Power: The Concerned Energy Consumer's Survival Kit.* New York, N.Y.: Rawson, 1978. 272 pp. $8.95.

Here are thousands of ideas to cut energy use and bills: how to buy or build wood stoves, solar heaters, and windmills; how to get federal funding for mass transit and cut waste in public buildings. A useful guide for taking control of your home and your community.

Federal Energy Administration/Department of Housing and Urban Development. *Urban Energy Management Study Final Report,* July 1976. (Available from DOE.) Vol. I, *Executive Summary.* 11 pp.; Vol. II, *Project Overview and Energy Consumption Survey,* 34 pp.; Vol. III, *Energy Supply and Demand,* 88 pp.; Vol. IV, *Energy Management Plan.* 29 pp. These four volumes are followed by the *Final*

Report Summary: Implementation. September, 1977, 62 pp.

This is a report of energy patterns, conservation practices, and a preliminary Urban Energy Management Plan for the City of Anaheim, California, and member cities of the California Innovation Group. The latest volume summarizes the implementation measures taken by these cities, and includes policies, codes, and data on lighting and vehicles.

Federal Energy Administration, Local Energy Management Program. *A Guide to Reducing . . . Energy Use Budget Costs.* Prepared under the joint efforts of the National Association of Counties, National League of Cities, and the U.S. Conference of Mayors. 1976. 93 pp. (From DOE, or NLC/USCM Publication Center, 1620 Eye St. NW, Washington, DC 20006.)

The study focuses on administrative commitment, employee programs, vehicle fleets, new and existing buildings, and how to initiate an energy conservation program.

Gilles, Janet. *A Community Project in Alternate Energy: Epoch B.* Epoch B., Evanston Environmental Association, 2024 McCormick Blvd., Evanston, IL 60201. 1978. 112 pp. $3.50.

An informal discussion evolved into a community-scale program of energy conservation. Technical appendices and resources included.

Greenberg, Phillip A. *Energy Policies and Programs of California Cities and Counties: A Survey.* Marin Citizens for Energy Planning, 24 H St., San Rafael, CA 94901. 1977. 92 pp. $6.50. ($3.50 for non-profit groups).

A reference tool for local governments, citizen groups, and anyone interested in energy at the community level. Programs and publications are described, and individuals, organizations, and agencies are listed in this well organized and useful guide.

Gunn, Anita. *A Survey of Model Programs: State and Local Solar/Conservation Projects.* Center for Renewable Resources, 1001 Connecticut Ave. NW, 5th floor, Washington, DC 20036. 1978. 14 pp. $1.25.

You and your community can glean many ideas from this survey of programs throughout the United States. Names and addresses of contact persons are included.

Hess, Karl. *Community Technology.* New York, N.Y.: Harper and Row., 1979. 107 pp. $2.95.

Hess's thesis is that any community can develop a technology perfectly appropriate to its needs and to its resources. He finds that we can learn much from the experience of a neighborhood in Washington, D.C. which for five years strove to become self-sufficient.

Hill, Burt. *Planning and Building the Minimum Energy Dwelling.* See *ENERGY CONSERVATION: CONSERVATION IN ARCHITECTURE & BUILDING.* Includes examples of community planning.

Institute for Local Self-Reliance. *Planning for Energy Self-Reliance: A Case Study of Baltimore.* Washington, D.C.: Institute for Local Self-Reliance, 1979. 111 pp. $12.00.

Various factors in a solar energy future are outlined, including government incentives, utility programs, financing, economic development potential, and the role of citizen involvement.

Institute for Local Self-Reliance. *Planning for Energy Self-Reliance: A Case Study of the District of Columbia.* Washington, D.C.: Institute for Local Self-Reliance, 1979.

286 pp. $12.00.

Energy conservation can lead to economic development, as shown in this framework for planning a municipal energy program.

Living Systems. *Planning for Energy Conservation.* Living Systems, Rte. 1, Box 170, Winters, CA 95694. 1976.

Many of the innovative plans of this group have been put into effect in the City of Davis, California, and in a state office building.

Morris, David, and Hess, Karl. *Neighborhood Power, the New Localism.* Boston, Mass.: Beacon Press, 1975. 180 pp. $4.95 (EARS)

This book shows how a potentially self-sufficient community can develop service networks, co-ops, collectice enterprises, and finally, neighborhood government.

Meyers, Phyllis, and Binder, Gordon. *Neighborhood Conservation: Lessons from Three Cities.* Washington, D.C.: The Conservation Foundation, 1977. 113 pp. $4.00.

Six case studies of neighborhood revitalization review the issues, needs, and trends in neighborhood conservation.

Okagaki, Alan, with Benson, Jim. *County Energy Plan Guidebook: Creating a Renewable Future.* Institute for Ecological Policies, 9208 Chjristopher St., Fairfax, VA 22031. 1979. 200 pp. $7.50/$15.

Renewable energy plans on a local and county level can be created with the aid of this comprehensive, non-technical tool. The long term goal is to combine the plans of the 3000 counties in the U.S. into a National Citizens' Energy Plan, and move toward a stable society based on environmentally sound, democratically controlled, renewable energy sources.

Oregon Office of Energy Research Planning. *Transition: A Book on Future Energy— Nuclear or Solar?* Portland, Ore.: Prometheus Unbound, 1975. 465 pp. $7.95. (EARS)

A classic study of the application of the principles of net energy analysis to a geographical area, the State of Oregon. Includes tables, charts, and energy flow diagrams.

Public Resource Center. *The Davis Experiment: One City's Plan to Save Energy.* The Elements, 1747 Connecticut Ave. NW, Washington, DC 20009. 72 pp. $2.00.

The Davis energy conservation experiement is described in this collection of codes, ordinances, drawings, photographs, and plans. Although designed to meet Davis' unique needs, many of these ideas will be applicable elsehwere.

Public Technology Inc. *Energy Conservation: A Management Report for State and Local Governments (7 pp) and Energy Conservation: A Technical Guide for State and Local Governments* (110 pp.). Funded by the National Science Foundation. Public Technology, Inc., 1140 Connecticut Ave. NW, Washington, DC 20036. 1975. $10.00.

The principles of energy conservation are outlined, with specific steps to be taken, and case studies.

Rickles, Robert N. *Energy in the City Environment.* Park Ridge, N.J.: Noyes Data Corporation, 1972. 173 pp. $12.50.

This report, based upon a symposium held in New York City, suggests measures for energy conservation in the transportation, residential, commercial, industrial, and electric sectors. Its findings are applicable to other urban areas as well.

Ridgeway, James, with Projansky, Carolyn S. *Energy-Efficient Community Planning: A Guide to Saving Energy and Producing Power at the Loca Level.* Emmaus, Pa.: J.G. Press, 1979. 218 pp. $9.95. (EARS)

Ridgeway describes a number of American communities that are using conservation policies and alternate energy systems to save and produce power. They are leading the way to a society based upon renewable resources. Examples of ordinances, plans, and projects encourage emulation.

ROMCOE. *Montclair Future Power: A Program to Enable a Community to Create Its Own Energy Future.* ROMCOE, 1115 Grant St., Denver, CO 80203. 1978. 58 pp. $3.75.

A middle-class urban neighborhood undertakes a community program through an energy fair, energy workshops, and a school greenhouse.

ROMCOE. *San Luis Future Power.* ROMCOE, 1115 Grant St., Denver, CO 80203. 1978. 40 pp. $3.75.

A rural community energy action program resulted in workshops and classroom sessions on energy conservation and low-technology solar power, and an increase in solar units in the area.

Stokes, Bruce. *Local Responses to Global Problems: A Key to Meeting Human Needs.* Washington, D.C.: Worldwatch Institute, 1978. 64 pp. $2.00. (FOE)

Self-help efforts of individuals and communities are becoming more successful in dealing with food, housing, health, and energy problems.

U.S. Department of Housing and Urban Development. *Energy Conservation Choices for the City of Portland.* Washington, D.C., 1977. S/N 023-000-00465-8 through S/N 023-000-00475-5. 1374 total pp. $35.25 total price. (USGPO)

Eleven volumes constitute the final report of a project to develop a comprehensive energy conservation plan, and recommend changes in codes, ordinances, and budgeting procedures.

Conservation in Industry and Food Processing

Brooks, Cindy. *The Case for Industrial Cogeneration.* New Jersey Public Interest Research Group, 32 West Lafayette, Trenton, NJ 08608. 1978. $5.00 for the entire report; $1.00 for a 10-page summary.

A study of conservation alternatives to increased energy consumption.

Casper, M.E., ed. *Energy-Saving Techniques for the Food Industry.* Park Ridge, N.J., Noyes Data Corporation, 1977. 657 pp. $39.00.

The aim of this book is to promote increased energy efficiency in the food industry. Detailed findings for various sectors are presented together with proposed goals.

Dubin, F.S., Mindell, H.L., and Bloome, S. *How to Save Energy and Cut Costs in Existing Industrial and Commercial Buildings. An Energy Conservation Manual.* Park Ridge, New York, N.Y.: Noyes Data Corporation, 1976. 725 pp. $24.00.

Written for maintenance men, operators, occupants, engineers, and architects, this book offers guidelines for an organized approach toward conserving energy. It finds that the investment is usually recovered through lower operating costs.

Green, Maurice B. *Eating Oil: Energy Use in Food Production.* Boulder, Colo.:

Westview Press, 1978. 205 pp. $12.50.

More and more energy must be used in food production as populations increase, and the law of diminishing returns applies. The author examines the efficiency of energy use in food production, and considers the problem of feeding the populations in those developing countries in which fossil fuel is not readily available.

Gyftopoulos, E.P.; Lazaridis, Lazaros J.; and Winder, Thomas F. *Potential Fuel Effectiveness in Industry.* Cambridge, Mass.: Ballinger, 1974. 112 pp. $7.95.

Thermodynamic availability analysis, general methods for fuel saving, and fuel saving in selected industries are covered in this technical report.

Leach, Gerald. *Energy and Food Production.* Survey, England: IPC House. 144 pp. $11.00.

Detailed information on the energy requirements of different methods of producing food, and opportunities for energy conservation.

Myers, John G. Project Director. *Energy Consumption in Manufacturing.* A Report to the Energy Policy Project of the Ford Foundation. Cambridge, Mass.: Ballinger, 1974. 656 pp. $25.00.

The manufacturing sector of the economy uses about 40% of all energy consumed in the U.S. This reference tool examines the energy use of some 30 industries, with projections to 1980, and a bibliography for each section.

Myers, John G., and Nakamura, Leonard. *Saving Energy in Manufacturing.* Cambridge, Mass.: Ballinger, 1978. 160 pp. $16.50.

Case studies of eight major energy-consuming industries—such as paper, chemicals, petroleum, and durable goods—describe the complexities involved in their efforts to conserve energy.

Pierotti, Anne, and Fritsch, Albert. *Energy and Food.* Washington, D.C.: Center for Science in the Public Interest, 1977. 80 pp. $6.00. (CEP)

A comprehensive examination of the sources and inputs of energy used in the production, processing, delivery, and marketing of 150 selected foods. Indicates that good energy conservation is compatible with good nutrition and good consumer buying practices.

Rimberg, David. *Utilization of Waste Heat from Power Plants.* Park Ridge, N.J.: Noyes Data Corporation, 1974. 175 pp. $18.00.

An examination of methods for productively using energy presently wasted on the environment.

Shinsky, Francis G. *Energy Conservation Through Control.* New York, N.Y.: Academic Press, 1978. 321 pp. $18.50.

Thermodynamics can be applied to energy conservation through the control of industrial processes such as steam generation, refrigeration, drying, distillation, and the heating, cooling, and ventilation of buildings.

Smith, Thomas E. *Industrial Energy Management for Cost Reduction.* Ann Arbor, Mich.: Ann Arbor Science Publishers, 1979. 214 pp. $22.50.

Engineers and managers will find many specific techniques for energy management in this practical guide to improved efficiency of energy use and the employment of alternative energy sources.

U.S. Congress. *Opportunities for Energy Savings in Crop Production.* Washington, D.C., 1978. S/N 052-070-04407-1. 269 pp. $3.75. (USGPO)

An evaluation of methods by which energy use in the major crop production activities may be reduced, for example, in nitrogen fertilizer production, crop drying, and irrigation.

U.S. Department of Agriculture. *Energy Accounting in the Food Processing Industry.* Washington, D.C., 1979. S/N 001-000-03961-0. 56 pp. $2.50. (USGPO)

This useful aid in energy policy formulation provides data on the food processing energy use by fuel, industry, and State.

U.S. Department of Energy. *Voluntary Business Energy Conservation Program.* Washington, D.C., 1978. S/N 061-000-00052-6. 156 pp. $3.25. (USGPO)

Semi-annual reports on the progress in energy conservation made by participants in this voluntary program.

U.S. Department of Commerce, National Bureau of Standards. *Waste Heat Management Guidebook.* Washington, D.C. $2.75. (USGPO)

Designed to help the engineer or energy manager to capture and recycle heat that is normally lost to the environment during industrial and commercial processes, and to promote an awareness of the energy conservation potential in industry and commerce.

APPROPRIATE TECHNOLOGY

References and Catalogs

Baldwin, J., and Brand, Stewart. *Soft-Tech.* A Co-Evolution Book. San Francisco, Calif.: Penguin, 1978. 175 pp. $5.00. (EARS)

This catalog provides access to tools, devices, books, and resources, and also includes articles on solar, wind, steam, biomass, transportation, and innovative housing.

Brand, Stewart, ed. *Whole Earth Catalog.* Sausalito, Calif.: Point, 1975. (18th Printing) 449 pp. $6.00.

Access to tools and information for self-sufficient living and alternative sources of energy, in the categories of whole systems, land use, shelter, soft technology, craft, community, nomadics, communications, and learning.

Brand, Stewart, ed. *Whole Earth Epilog.* Sausalito, Calif.: Point, 1974. 318 pp. $4.00.

A continuation of the *Whole Earth Catalog,* including an index of both the *Catalog* and the *Epilog.* Access to tools and information for self'sufficient living and alternative sources of energy.

Citizens' Energy Project. *Appropriate Technology Guide.* Citizens' Energy Project, 1110 Sixth St. NW, #300, Washington, DC 20001. 1979. 100+ pp. $4/$6. (CEP)

This study provides an overview of the model community-level appropriate technology programs under way around the country. These include alternative health care, housing, renewable energy, agriculture, transportation, communications, waste recycling, and other programs, as well as suggestions for launching similar programs in one's own community.

Consumer Guide, eds. *Whole House Catalog.* New York, N.Y.: Simon & Schuster, 1976. 320 pp. $7.95.

This large format guide to home maintenance, repair, and construction projects includes listings of brand name equipment and materials.

Horvitz, Cathy, Project Coordinator. *Tools for a Change. Proceedings of the Northeast Regional Appropriate Technology Forum.* National Science Foundation award C-ISP78-22988; GPO document #NSF/RA 790009. School of Business Administration, University of Massachusetts, Amherst, MA 01003. February, 1979. 226 pp.

The entire scope of appropriate technology was addressed by this forum, which made recommendations for action in the areas of agriculture and land use, business and economics, community involvement, education, energy, housing, government policy, transportation, and water and waste utilization.

Useful appendices list laws supporting appropriate technology, and forum participants. A most valuable tool!

Integrative Design Associates. *Appropriate Technology: A Directory of Activities and Projects.* Washington, D.C.: USGPO, 1977. 66 pp. $2.20. (USGPO)
   This survey by the national Science Foundation is an annotated directory of individuals and organizations, both private and governmental, and their projects. Additional sources of information are listed.

Rain Magazine, eds. *Rainbook: Resources for Appropriate Technology.* New York, N.Y.: Schocken, 1977. 251 pp. $7.95. (EARS)
   This illustrated catalog contains a wealth of information on everything from community economics to solar greenhouses. Brief articles assess what's happening in each field. Well organized and indexed data provide access to hundreds of organizations, individuals, publications, films, and other resources. A gold mine!

Tools for Self-Sufficient Living; Food, Agriculture, and Home Waste Management

Bendavid-Val, Avrom. *Starting Your Own Energy Business.* Washington, D.C.: Institute for Local Self-Reliance, 1978. 45 pp. $4.00. (EARS)
   People interested in new approaches to local economic development will profit from this analysis of four possible ventures: energy audits, storm doors and windows, cellulose insulation, and solar hot water heating.

Bender, Tom. *Sharing Smaller Pies.* Portland, Oreg.: *Rain Magazine*, 1975. 38 pp. $2.00. (EARS)
   An analysis of the energy and materials crisis. Discusses the economic, philosophic, and social/scientific basis for appropriate technology, renewable energy, and resource conservation. Lists the changes necessary in our society.

Clarke, Robin. *Building for Self-Sufficiency.* New York, N.Y.: Universe, 1977. 296 pp. $5.95 (EARS)
   The tools, materials, and systems for self-sufficient living are described in this product of the author's experience. A 43-acre farm was converted into a commune with a lifestyle that is independent with regard to food, water, energy, and materials.

Coe, Gigi. *Present Value: Constructing a Sustainable Future.* Office of Appropriate Technology, State of California. San Francisco, Calif.: Friends of the Earth, 1979. 96 pp. $5.95. (FOE)
   Here you can see how the "soft energy path" is actually at work in energy-efficient homes, commercial structures, and community developments that are economically feasible as well as functionally reliable. Energy production, resource conservation, and waste disposal are integrated in local systems to produce a sustainable lifestyle adaptable to a variety of climates.

Congdon, R.J., ed. *Introduction to Appropriate Technology: Toward a Simpler Life Style.* Emmaus, Pa.: Rodale Press, 1977. 224 pp. $6.95. (EARS)
   Features specific ways in which both developed and developing countries can introduce people-oriented technologies in all aspects of society. Outlines some radical economic changes which must be made in the industrial world.

DeMoll, Lane, and Coe, Gigi, eds. *Stepping Stones: Appropriate Technology and Beyond.* New York, N.Y.: Schocken, 1978. 204 pp. $7.95.

This companion volume to *Rainbook* offers the philosophical stepping stones that have helped shape the techniques, values, tools, and politics of appropriate technology, as well as responses to the question about what lies beyond A.T. It includes articles by E.F. Schumacher, Wilson Clark, Tom Bender, Howard Odum, Amory Lovins, and many others.

Dickson, David. *The Politics of Alternative Technology.* New York, N.Y.: Universe, 1974. 224 pp. $3.95. (EARS)

A coherent world view of the ideas behind alternative technology, and a damning indictment of modern technology on the grounds of wastefulness, pollution, and the alienation of man from nature.

Dunn, P.D. *Appropriate Technology: Technology With a Human Face.* New York, N.Y.: Schocken, 1979. 220 pp. $5.95.

This book presents the theory and practice of appropriate technology, including its application to developing countries, considering food and agriculture, water, health, buildings, industry, education, transport, and research.

Esbenshade, Henry. *Farming: Sources for a Social and Ecologically Accountable Agriculture.* Davis, Calif.: Alternative Agricultural Resources Project, 1976. 68 pp. $4.25. (EARS)

A sourcebook for resources on alternatives to the dominant energy-and-capital intensive approaches to food production and distribution.

Farallones Institute. *The Integral Urban House: Self-Reliant Living in the City.* Introduction by Sim Van der Ryn. San Francisco, Calif.: Sierra Club, 1979. 494 pp. $12.95.

The Integral Urban House is an idea, a model life-support system based on actual experience, that can provide a measure of self-reliance as it fulfills basic needs. This manual explains natural energy flows, conservation of energy, and waste management, as well as raising food crops. Required reading for anyone concerned with building a sustainable urban culture.

Fritsch, Albert. *99 Ways to a Simple Lifestyle.* New York, N.Y.: Doubleday, 1976. 324 pp. $3.50. (CEP) (EARS)

Ninety-nine essays propose simple alternatives to today's over-consumptive lifestyle through the conservation of human and natural resources. (Education)

Harper, Peter; Boyle, Godfrey; and the editors of *Undercurrents,* eds. *Radical Technology.* New York, N.Y.: Pantheon, 1976. 304 pp. $5.95. (EARS)

About technologies that could help create a more fulfilling society, with the growth of small scale techniques under workers' and consumers' control in the areas of food, energy, shelter, materials, and communication.

Howard Community College and Foundation for Self Sufficiency. *Essays on Food and Energy.* Howard Community College and Foundation for Self Sufficiency, 35 Maple, Catonsville, MD 21228. 1977. 184 pp. $5.00. (From Volunteers in Technical Assistance, 3706 Rhode Island Ave., Mt. Rainier, MD 20822.)

Twenty-five illustrated and referenced essays point the way to self sufficiency through conservation, solar energy, aquaculture, gardening, and alternative transportation.

Illich, Ivan. *Energy and Equity.* New York, N.Y.: Harper & Row, 1974. 84 pp. $.95.

Illich philosophizes on the current energy shortage, and finds that it is but one symptom of the major crisis that is afflicting our over-industrialized society. His solution is a return to a simpler and more satisfying form of living.

Illich, Ivan. *Tools for Conviviality.* New York, N.Y.: Harper and Row, 1973. 173 pp. $1.50. (EARS)
An appeal to construct a society based on tools to which we all have access, and which we will direct and use to meet our own felt needs.

Jackson, Wes. *The Last Free Meal: An American Agriculture for the Future.* (Title tentative.) San Francisco, Calif.: Friends of the Earth, 1980. 144 pp. $4.95. (FOE)
American agriculture, preoccupied with raising yields and profits, is strip-mining our best crop land as it consumes great quantities of oil. Jackson proposes a new system that will grow continuously like a natural ecosystem does.

Kern, Ken, and Kern, Barbara. *The Owner Built Homestead: A How To Do It Book.* New York, N.Y.: Scribner, revised 1977. 394 pp. $7.95. (EARS) (TEA)
The homestead is a maturing organism, not just a static plan. The homesteader must examine natural factors and ecological relationships to understand himself and his family on the site, and find solutions to his problems.

Lappé, Frances Moore, and Collins, Joseph, with Fowler, Cary. *Food First: Beyond The Myth of Scarcity.* Boston, Mass.: Houghton Mifflin, 1977. 466 pp. $10.95. (EARS)
Lappe tackles the question of why there is hunger in a world of plenty, and finds the causes in the giant corporate and bureaucratic obstacles to quality food production. Worldwide consumer and farmer awareness can lead to the rise of democratic communities necessary to a healthy and productive society.

Leckie, Jim, et al. *Other Homes and Garbage: Designs for Self-Sufficient Living.* San Francisco: The Sierra Club, 1975. 320 pp. $9.95. (EARS) (TEA)
A guide to environmental engineering, house design, generation of electricity, solar heating, waste handling, and water supply. Very practical, with diagrams, formulas, and references. Outstanding in this area.

McCullagh, James C., ed. *Pedal Power: In Work, Leisure, and Transportation.* Emmaus, Pa.: Rodale, 1977. 133 pp. $4.95. (EARS)
The vast potential for pedal-powered devices in the workshop, kitchen, farm, and homestead is demonstrated in this book, which also tells of human muscle power in history and in the Third World. Many tools and vehicles are described.

McHarg, Ian. *Design with Nature.* Garden City, N.Y.: Doubleday/Natural History Press, 1969. 198 pp. $6.95. (EARS)
An outspoken critic of the traditional notion that urban development must be imposed upon the landscape, regardless of the ecological consequences. New knowledge may be applied to actual environments in designing with nature.

Marks, Vic, ed. *Cloudburst—A Handbook of Rural Skills and Technology.* Book People, Berkeley, Calif.: Cloudburst Press, 1973. 128 pp. $5.95. (EARS)
An introduction to the arts, skills, and technologies of living and working on the land. Addresses the basic problems facing the people seeking to decentralize society and repopulate the countryside.

Marks, Vic, ed. *Cloudburst 2.* Book People, Berkeley, Calif.: Cloudburst Press, 1976. 128 pp. $5.95. (EARS)
More of the arts, skills, and technologies of living and working on the land.

Merrill, Richard, ed. *Radical Agriculture.* New York, N.Y.: Harper and Row, 1976. 459 pp. $6.95. (EARS)
Alternatives to our present energy-intensive form of agriculture are explored in this collection of articles.

Papenak, Victor. *Design for the Real World.* New York, N.Y.: Bantam, 1971. 378 pp. $2.95. (EARS)
There is a need for more practical and safe designs for many common products, especially those intended for use in the Third World.

Papanek, Victor, and Hennessey, James. *How Things Don't Work.* New York, N.Y.: Pantheon, 1977. 152 pp. $4.95. (EARS)
Many modern applicances, tools, and devices don't work efficiently, durably, or safely, and must be replaced by more useful and ecologically sound products.

Simple Living Collective of the American Friends Service Committee. *Taking Charge: Personal and Political Change Through Simple Living.* New York, N.Y.: Bantam, 1977. 343 pp. $1.95. (EARS)
The Collective takes a new look at energy, food, economics, health, and personal and community growth, and makes practical suggestions for changes in our daily lives, our communities, and the world.

Stoner, Carol Hupping. *Goodbye to the Flush Toilet.* Emmaus, Pa.: Rodale, 1977. 285 pp. $6.95. (EARS) (TEA)
Workable alternatives to the flush toilet are described by Stoner, along with principles of composting, and ways of saving water and money in the home.

Todd, Nancy Jack, ed. *The Book of the New Alchemists.* New York, N.Y.: Dutton, 1977. 174 pp. $6.95. (EARS)
This large and handsome volume presents plans for self-sustaining agriculture, aquaculture, bioshelters, and simple living.

Traister, John. *Do-It-Yourself Guide to Modern Energy-Efficient Heating and Cooling Systems.* Blue Ridge Summit, Pa.: TAB Books, 1977. 280 pp. $5.95.
Detailed directions are given for the selection, maintainance, and repair of a wide range of modern heating and cooling systems.

Van der Ryn, Sim. *The Toilet Papers.* New York, N.Y.: Capra Press, 1978. 124 pp. $3.95. (EARS)
A history of the management of organic wastes is followed by practical plans for dry toilets, compost privies, and grey water systems.

Wallace, Daniel, ed. *Energy We Can Live With: Approaches to Energy That Are Easy on the Earth and Its People.* Emmaus, Pa.: Rodale, 1976. 168 pp. $3.95.
Forty essays on energy use and conservation, including solar heating, methane, composting toilets, and a variety of alternate energy ideas. An excellent reader for students. (Education)

Warshall, Peter W. *Septic Tank Practices.* Garden City, N.Y.: Doubleday, 1979. 76 pp. $3.95. (TEA)
A guide to the conservation and re-use of household wastewaters.

Yudelson, Jerry, and Nelson, Lynn. *Right Livelihood, Work, and Appropriate Technology.*

The Habitat Ctr, 162 Christen Dr., Pacheco, CA 94553. 1976. 128 pp. $7.50.
A report to the California Office of Appropriate Technology on the relationships between jobs, economic development, and appropriate technology. It holds that work should be socially useful and meaningful.

Appropriate Technology in the Third World

Brace Research Institute of McGill University, and the Canadian Hunger Foundation. *A Handbook on Appropriate Technology.* From CHF, 75 Sparks St., Ottawa, Ontario, Canada K1P 5A5. 1977. 240 pp. $8.50.
Case histories demonstrate how appropriate technology has solved specific problems in the developing world; exhaustive references are provided.

Brown, Norman L., ed. *Renewable Energy Resources and Rural Applications in the Developing World.* American Association for the Advancement of Science. Boulder, Colo.: Westview Press, 1978. 168 pp. $15.00.
Developing countries have been hard hit by price increases for the oil upon which they depend primarily for industrial growth. Non-commercial energy sources such as firewood, dung, and agricultural residues are in short supply, and forests are disappearing. The author looks to small scale, decentralized technologies for exploiting renewable energy sources to provide solutions to the problem of rural energy needs.

Cecelski, Elizabeth; Dunkerley, Joy; and Ramsay, William. *Household Energy and the Poor in the Third World.* Washington, D.C.: Resources for the Future, Inc., 1979. 152 pp. $6.75.
This is the report of a research project on energy needs and possibilities for the poor in developing countries, with emphasis on household use. It explores the possibilities of unconventional technologies, such as biogas, solar, wind, and mini-hydro. The study concludes that energy is used with great inefficiency in many parts of the developing world; that there are great opportunities for important savings; and that cultural and institutional factors must be considered in changing energy technologies.

Darrow, Kenneth, and Pam, Rick. *Appropriate Technology Sourcebook.* Stanford, Calif.: Volunteers in Asia Press, 1976. 304 pp. $4.50. (EARS)
Ideas and projects gathered from many lands show people in developing countries new ways to store food, build shelter, and utilize simple renewable energy sources.

Eckholm, Erik. *The Dispossessed of the Earth: Land Reform and Sustainable Development.* Washington, D.C.: Worldwatch, 1979. 48 pp. $2.00. (FOE) (EARS)
Conflicts rooted in inequality of land ownership are becoming more acute in country after country.

Jequier, Nicolas. *Appropriate Technology: Problems and Promises.* Paris: Development Centre of the Organisation for Economic Co-Operation and Development, 1976. 344 pp.
Principles, innovations, information networks, policies, and applications of appropriate technology in the developing world.

Makhijani, Arjun, with Poole, Alan. *Energy and Agriculture inb the Third World.* Cambridge, Mass.: Ballinger, 1975. 192 pp. $8.95.

More efficient use of biological energy resources is necessary to solve the energy problems of under-developed countries. These resources include wood, wastes, and human and animal labor.

National Academy of Sciences. *Energy for Rural Development: Renewable Resources and Alternative Technologies for Developing Countries.* Washington, D.C.: NAS, 1976. 306 pp. (From the Commission on International Relations, National Academy of Sciences, 2101 Constitution Ave., N.W., Washington, D.C. 20418.)

Each technology is described and its potential application outlined, with technical information and international references.

VITA. *Environmentally Sound Small Scale Agricultural Projects: Guidelines for Planning.* Volunteers in Technical Assistance, 3706 Rhode Island Ave., Mt. Rainier, MD 20822. 1979. 103 pp. $3.95 + $.60 postage.

Representatives from organizations concerned with Third World countries analyze the relationship of agriculture to the natural environment, and offer practical guidelines for the management of water supply, erosion, nutrients, and pests. A cost/benefit analysis for small scale projects is included.

Recycling and Resource Recovery

Environmental Action Foundation. *Resource Recovery: Truth and Consequences.* Environmental Action Foundation, 1346 Connecticut Ave. NW, Washington, DC 20036. 1977. 77 pp. $3.50.

A review of the resource recovery systems in operation, the economics and energy behind resource recovery, and a reference to government and environmental groups and individuals concerned with this issue.

Environmental Action Foundation. *Talking Trash: Proceedings of the Meeting of the National Coalition on Solid Waste.* Environmental Action Foundation, 1346 Connecticut Ave. NW, Washington, DC 20036. 1977. 112 pp. $3.50.

Input from citizens, the Environmental Protection Agency, and other experts on the Resource Conservation and Recovery Act; high-technology resource recovery and source separation systems; and cutting down on packaging.

Goldstein, Jerome. *Recycling: How to Reuse Wastes in the Home, Industry, and Society.* New York, N.Y.: Schocken, 1979. 238 pp. $6.95.

Do you want to kick the garbage habit? Here is how to begin recycling at home, cut back on waste at its source, convert garbage into energy and fertilizer, and put industrial wastes to work. New technologies and public policies are needed for the health of our economy and our ecology, and for the saner use of our resources.

Goldstein, Jerome. *Sensible Sludge: A New Look at a Wasted Natural Resource.* Emmaus, Pa.: Rodale, 1977. 192 pp. $5.95.

Much of the energy, petroleum, and money currently spent on synthetic fertilizers could be saved by the proper treatment and utilization of sludge for adding nutrients to farmlands, parks, and gardens, and for reclaiming stripmined regions.

Hayes, Denis. *Repairs, Reuse, Recycling: First Steps Toward a Sustainable Society.* Washington, D.C.: Worldwatch Institute, 1978. 38 pp. $2.00. (FOE) (EARS).

Hayes looks at current resource supplies, and how they are used and wasted, and at energy and environmental constraints. Policy changes, small changes in technology, and public education could bring tremendous changes in curbing wasteful practices.

Institute for Local Self-Reliance. *Waste Utilization: Citizen's Information Packet*, Volume I. Washington, D.C.: Institute for Local Self-Reliance, 1979. 56 pp. $4.00.
High-technology resource recovery plants pose both economic and environmental problems.

Institute for Local Self-Reliance. *Waste Utilization: Citizen's Information Packet*, Volume II. Washington, D.C.: Institute for Local Self-Reliance, 1979. 87 pp. $4.50.
Government policy and its effect on the recycling of municipal solid wastes are detailed in this packet, with testimony from recycling experts.

Seldman, Neil. *Garbage in America: Approaches to Recycling*. Institute for Local Self-Reliance, 1717 18th St. NW, Washington, DC 20009. 1976. 45 pp. $2.50. (EARS)
This survey of current approaches to resource recovery in the United States considers source reduction, waste management, and recycling systems.

Quimby, Thomas H.E. *Recycling: The Alternative to Disposal*. Resources for the Future. Baltimore, Md.: Johns Hopkins University Press, 1975. 133 pp. $9.50.
The generation and disposal of residuals is the focus of this study, which gives details of available methods, and the quantities of solid residuals, paper, and corrugated containers involved.

U.S. Congress. *Materials and Energy From Municipal Waste*. Washington, D.C., 1979. S/N 052-003-00692-8. 284 pp. $6.00. (USGPO)
Important questions about the feasibility of resource recovery, recycling, and reuse are addressed.

Wentworth, Marchant. *Resource Recovery: Truth or Consequences*. Washington, D.C.: Environmental Action Foundation, 1977. 78 pp. $3.50. (EARS)
Home source separation and local collection systems are compared with the huge solid waste recovery plants; the former method is the more economical way to go.

ALTERNATIVE SOURCES OF ENERGY

Overviews and Issues

Alternative Sources of Energy. *Access: Information and People.* ASE, Rt. 2, Box 90A, Milaca, MN 56353, 1974. $1.25 (ASE) (EARS)

Contains listings of the ASE mail lending library. Topics include solar and wind energy, fuels from organic matter, and other energy related materials.

Alternative Sources of Energy. *Agriculture and Energy.* Alternative Sources of Energy, Rt. 2, Milaca, MN 56353. May/June 1979. 56 pp. $2.00. (ASE) (EARS)

The focus is on the agricultural applications of renewable energy sources for small farms, stressing the importance of a decentralized, labor-oriented, self-sufficient agricultural economy.

Alternative Sources of Energy. *An Alternative Technology Equipment Directory.* ASE, Rt. 2, Box 90A, Milaca, MN 56353. $2.00. (ASE) (EARS)

Names and addresses, and prices for energy equipment. Sections include energy and resource conservation, solar energy, wind power, water power, organic fuels, waste disposal, architecture and water distillation.

Alves, Ronald, and Milligan, Charles. *Living With Energy: Alternative Sources in Your Home.* New York, N.Y.: Penguin, 1978. 128 pp. $5.95. (EARS)

Practical and economical ways to use alternative energy in any structure and any climate. 266 illustrations. Introduction by Ralph Nader.

Boyle, Godfrey. *Living on the Sun: Harnessing Renewable Energy for an Equitable Society.* London: Marion Boyers, 1975. 127 pp. $4.95.

Tells how to conserve energy, and harness the power in plants, wind, water, and solar energy in a decentralized society. The utilization of low cost, easily recycled, more efficient and accessible sources will provide a firmer foundation for fraternity among mankind.

Canada, Department of Supplies and Services. *Environmentally Appropriate Technology, Renewable Energy, and Other Developing Technologies for a Conserver Society in Canada.* Canada: Supplies and Services, 1977. 155 pp. $9.00. (UNIPUB)

A review of current environmentally safe technologies for the use of renewable energy sources such as solar, biomass, hydro, and wind. Considers social as well as technical feasibility.

Clark, Peter, and Landfield, Judy. **The Natural Energy Workbook.** Visual Purple Productions, Box 996, Berkeley, CA 94701, 1974. 128 pp. $3.95.

Homemade alternative energy plans for the person who likes to build. Stresses the application of locally regenerative sources (sun, wind, water, and photosynthetic fuels) to local needs.

Clegg, Peter. *New Low-Cost Sources of Energy for the Home*. Charlotte, Vt.: Garden Way Publishing Co., 1975. 252 pp. $7.95 (EARS) (TEA)
Basic principles of solar energy, wind power, water power, water/waste systems, and wood heating; diagrams and illustrated catalogs.

Davis, A.B., and Schubert, R.P. *Alternative Natural Energy Sources in Building Design*. Blacksburg, Va.: Passive Energy Systems, 1977. 252 pp. $7.95. (EARS)
Provides basic design criteria in alternate technology for both the professional and the amateur. Covers energy conservation and integrated systems.

Eccli, Sandy, ed. *Alternative Sources of Energy: Practical Technology and Philosophy for a Decentralized Society*. New York, N.Y.: A Continuum Book. Seabury Press, 1974. 277 pp. $7.95.
This large format volume describes alternative technologies, strategies for building a network of groups, and the philosophy and politics of energy.

Energy Probe. *The Renewable Energy Handbook*. Energy Probe, 43 Queens Park Cres. E., Toronto, Ontario, Canada, M5S 2C3. 1976.
Of interest to non-Canadians as well as Canadians, this manual examines the potential for renewable energy in Canada, and covers energy alternatives both technologically and economically.

Hagel, John III. *Alternative Energy Strategies: Constraints and Opportunities*. New York, N.Y.: Praeger. 1976. 204 pp. $19.50.
A consideration of alternative energy programs to meet the needs of the world's principal energy consuming nations, and policy options in terms of technological, economic, political, and environmental factors.

Halacy, D.S., Jr. *Earth, Water, Wind, & Sun*. New York, N.Y.: Harper & Row 1977. 186 pp. $8.95.
Provides useful information on the potentials of alternative energy sources, as well as data on costs, feasibility, and environmental impact.

Hartnett, James P. ed. *Alternative Energy Sources*. New York, N.Y.: Academic Press, 1976. 328 pp. $31.50.
The technologies of fluidized bed coal combustion, coal gasification, solar thermal systems, solar furnace, and geothermal energy are described in this collection of papers.

Merrill, Richard, and Gage, Thomas, eds. *Energy Primer: Solar, Water, Wind, and Biofuels*. New York, N.Y.: Dell, Revised edition, 1978. 256 pp. $7.95. (EARS)
All renewable forms of energy, energy conservation, and solar architecture are explained in this comprehensive and semi-technical book. Many devices are suitable for application in small scale systems.

Mother Earth News. *Handbook of Homemade Power: Some Concrete Answers to the Energy Crisis*. New York, N.Y.: Bantam, 1974. 374 pp. $2.50. (EARS)
Articles and interviews with people using a variety of alternative energy sources.

New England Congressional Caucus, Energy Task Force. *New England Rural Energy Sources*. New England Congressional Caucus, 53 D St. SE, Washington, DC 20003. $6.00. A summary is free.

Wood, small-scale hydro, solar, and wind can help solve the area's energy problems.

Pierson, Richard E. *Technician's and Experimenter's Guide to Using Sun, Wind, and Water Power.* West Nyack, N.Y.: Parker, 1978. 270 pp. $10.95.

Private power means thrift and independence, according to Pierson, who encourages the individual to build his own electrical generation system. He supplies data and plans for a variety of low cost energy installations.

Prenis, John, ed. *Energy Book #1: Natural Sources and Backyard Applications.* Philadelphia, Pa.: Running Press, 1975. 112 pp. $4.00. (EARS)

An overview of possible alternative sources of energy, both practical and experimental, with articles by well known authors.

Prenis, John, ed. *Energy Book #2: More Natural Sources and Backyard Applications.* Philadelphia, Pa.: Running Press, 1977. 125 pp. $5.00. (EARS)

Written by people with first-hand experience in the field, these articles describe the latest developments and future possibilities for using energy from the sun, wind, methane, plants, and trash.

Ridgeway, James, and Conner, Bettina. *New Energy: Understanding the Crisis, and a Guide to an Alternative Energy System.* Boston, Mass.: Beacon, 1975. 224 pp. $7.95.

After an examination of the history of the energy industry, energy resources, and energy policy, the authors make a proposal for an alternative energy system, democratically organized, with ecologically sound use of the nation's resources.

Skurka, Norma, and Naar, Jon. *Design For a Limited Planet: Living with Natural Energy.* New York, N.Y.: Ballantine Books, 1976. 215 pp. $6.95 (EARS)

Alternate energy houses are described in text, diagrams, and photographs, providing a close look at the many ways to live a cleaner, more natural life by harnessing the resources of sun, wind, and water.

Stanford University Institute for Energy Studies. *Alternative Energy Futures: An Assessment of U.S. Options to 2025.* Institute for Energy Studies, Stanford University, Stanford, Calif., 1979. Executive Summary, 41 pp., $3.00. Full Report, 632 pp., $30.00.

The purpose of this study was to identify the energy supply and demand systems to 2025 in scenarios with different criteria for energy-related decisions. Criteria weighed were national policies, shortages, costs, breakthroughs in research and development, and perceived impacts of energy systems on the environment.

Stoner, Carol. *Producing Your Own Paper: How to Make Nature's Energy Sources Work for You.* New York, N.Y.: Vintage Books, 1975. 322 pp. $3.95. (EARS)

An excellent "how-to" book with many diagrams and tables for the do-it-yourselfer.

Szczelkun, Stefan A. *Survival Scrapbook #3: Energy.* New York: Schocken Books, 1974. 114 pp. $3.95.

A practical guide to energy systems that can be built, used, and controlled by individuals and small communities: solar, wind, fire, water, and bio-gas.

United Nations Conference on New Sources of Energy: Solar Energy, Windpower, and Geothermal Energy. Solar 2. Rome, August 1961. Seattle, Wash.: Cloudburst, 1978. 315 pp. $8.50. (EARS)

A newly available classic for the self-reliant: solar pioneers from many countries describe projects for water heating, space heating, solar drying and cooking, and heat storage, including both usual and unusual applications of solar energy.

U.S. Department of Energy. *Distributed Energy Systems in California's Future.* Interim Report. Environmental Office of Technology Impacts. Prepared by the Lawrence Berkeley Laboratory, Lawrence Livermore Laboratory, University of California at Berkeley, and the University of California at Davis. Washington, D.C., 1978. HCP/P7405-01 and -02. Vol. I, 287 pp. Vol. II, 357 pp. Vol. I and Vol. II are combined in HCP/P7405-3, available as S/N 061-000-0068-2 from USGPO.

Contributors from a broad set of disciplines critically examine energy futures based on renewable energy sources, and using distributed, as opposed to centralized, technologies. A major stimulus to this project was Amory Lovins' *Soft Energy Paths.* The aspects studied included feasibility, economics, impacts, implications, and the policies and measures needed to implement such a future.

Wade, Gary; Hartmann, Michael, and Hartmann, Susan. *Homegrown Energy: Power for the Home and Homestead.* New York, N.Y.: Scribner, revised 1976. 144 pp. $3.95.

An indexed guide to companies that supply alternative energy products.

Wolfe, Ralph, and Clegg, Peter. *Home Energy for the Eighties, plus: Complete Catalog on Alternate Energy Systems.* Charlotte, Vt.: Garden Way, 1979. 264 pp. $10.95.

This mine of practical information for the home owner covers energy conservation; solar, wind, and water power, and wood heat. A unique feature is a catalog section at the end of each chapter, describing and comparing products and equipment.

BIOMASS

Fuels from Biomass; Biogas and Methane

Auerbach, Les. *A Homesite Power Unit: Methane Generator.* Madison, Conn.: Alternative Energy Systems, 1973. 50 pp. $5.00.
  Topics include planning, design, construction and operation of home power units.

Bell, Boulter, Dunlop and Keiller. *Methane, Fuel of the Future.* Prism Press, Stable Court, Chelmington, Dorchester, Dorset, DT20HB, 1973. 84 pp. $2.95.
  Explains methods of generation and uses of methane fuel.

Bio-Gas of Colorado. *Methane on the Move: Small Anerobic Digesters.* Arvada, Colo.: Bio-Gas of Colorado, Inc., 1977. 96 pp. $2.00.
  Experiments were conducted to determine yield coefficients of different manures, and the economic feasibility of small-scale digesters.

Coppinger, Elizabeth; Baylon, David; and Smith, Ken. *Design and First Year Operation of a 50,000 Gallon Anaerobic Digester at the State Honor Dairy Farm, Monroe, Washington.* Ecotope Group, 2332 E. Madison, Seattle, WA 98112. 1978. 87 pp. $5.75.
  This is the report of a farm demonstration project, describing the design, components, biological systems, net energy, and economics.

Fry, John. *Methane Digesters for Fuel Gas and Fertilizer.* Woods Hole, Mass.: New Alchemy institute, 1973. 47 pp. $4.00.
  Explains the background and presents plans for small scale methane generators using very low technology and readily available materials.

Fry, John. *Practical Building of Methane Power Plants for Rural Energy Independence.* Santa Barbara, Calif.: Standard Printing, 1974. 96 pp. $12.00. (EARS)
  Includes working diagrams, directions for operation, and the solutions to problems of methane power plants.

House, D. *The Compleat Biogas Handbook.* Aurora, Ore.: At Home Everywhere, 1978. 403 pp. $8.00. (EARS)
  Biogas is an alternative source of energy, easily and cheaply made from any organic material such as leaves, straw, grass, and manure.

International Development Research Centre. *Biogas Technology in the Third World: A Multidisciplinary Review.* 1978. 132 pp. $10.00. (UNIPUB)
  Biogas generation is a small-scale technology that offers the possibility for more decentralized approaches to energy supply. This review examines technical, economic, and social aspects of this energy option, with case studies from six Asian countries.

Meynell, Peter John. *Methane: Planning a Digester*. New York, N.Y.: Schocken, 1978. 150 pp. $4.95. (EARS)

The history and current uses of methane as an energy source are described, along with a survey of existing processes and research programs, and advice on the construction of a digester.

Mitsui, Akira, et al, eds. *Biological Solar Energy Conversion*. New York, N.Y.: Academic Press, 1977. 454 pp. $19.75.

An anthology of papers presented at a conference sponsored by the U.S.-Japan Cooperative Science Program, the U.S. National Science Foundation, and the Japanese Society for the Promotion of Science. The areas under study include the capture and utilization of solar energy, the synthesis of organic compounds from carbon dioxide, nitrogen fixation and the production of single cell protein, and practical applications. Harnessing plant potential to grow our energy is an idea whose time has come.

Price, Elizabeth C., and Cheremisinoff, Paul N. *Biogas Production and Utilization*. Ann Arbor, Mich.: Ann Arbor Science Publishers, 1980. $20.00.

Background, theory, and practice are presented in this technical work on the generation of biogas from organic wastes as an alternative energy source.

Robertson, Ernest E. *Bioconversion: Fuels from Biomass*. Philadelphia, Pa.: Franklin Institute, 1977. 72 pp. $8.95.

Many possibilities exist for converting urban solid wastes, and agricultural and forest residues into real energy. Planners, legislators, and individuals can begin to put this inexpensive and inexhaustible resource into use.

Singh, Ram Bux. *Bio-Gas Plant*. India: Gobar Gas Research Station. 1975. 94 pp. $10.00. (from Mother Earth News, P.O. Box 70, Hendersonville, NC 28739).

The design, operation, and economics of bio-gas plants are described, including different types which are suitable for various climates.

Skov, Niels A., and Papworth, Mark L. *The Pegasus Unit*. Olympia, Wash.: Pegasus, 1974. 132 pp. $9.95. (EARS)

Germany solved its petroleum shortage in the 1930's with the gasification of substitute fuels, including wood, peat, and coal.

U.S. Department of Energy. *Environmental Development Plan: Fuels from Biomass, 1977*. Washington, D.C., 1978. S/N 061-000-00086-1. 53 pp. $2.30. (USGPO)

An examination of the health, environmental, safety, social, and economic issues involved in the production and conversion of biomass.

U.S. Department of Energy. Solar Energy Research Institute. *A Survey of Biomass Gasification*. SERI/TR-33-239. Washington, D.C., 1979. (USGPO) (NTIS)

Vol. I. *Synopsis and Executive Summary*. 43 pp. $4.50. Vol. II. *Principles of Gasification*. 241 pp. $9.50. Vol. III. *Current Technology and Research*.

Numerous technologies are described, and recommendations are made for the rapid development of coal and biomass gasification to meet needs in the near future.

Washington Center for Metropolitan Studies. *Capturing the Sun Through Bioconversion*. Washington Center for Metropolitan Studies, 1717 Massachusetts Ave. NW, Washington, DC 20036. 1976. 861 pp. $18.00.

These proceedings of a conference sponsored by ERDA, FEA, EPA, NSF, AAAS and other organizations offer the most comprehensive source of information on bioconversion. Included are discussions of biomass sources such as urban, industrial, agricultural, and forestry wastes; ocean farming;

processes and products; economic, social, and environmental impacts; and international aspects.

Alcohol Fuels; Gasohol

Cheremisinoff, Nicholas P. *Gasohol for Energy Production.* Ann Arbor, Mich.: Ann Arbor Science Publishers, 1979. 142 pp. $14.95.
   Outlines the options and processes available for producing synthetic fuels from biomass, the development of a nation-wide alcohol-gasoline fuel system, and the benefits and problems of alcohol fuels.

Colucci, Joseph M., and Gallopoulos, Nicholas E., eds. *Future Automotive Fuels: Prospects, Performance, Perspectives.* New York, N.Y.: Plenum Press, 1977. 380 pp. $39.50.
   Automotive fuel accounts for almost half of the petroleum used in the United States. This study describes efforts of industry and government to find solutions to the problems of future fuel needs. It discusses supply and demand, maximizing energy use, fuel technologies, hydrocarbons from coal and oil shale, methanol, hydrogen, hydrazine, and the social and economic impacts of drastic increase in the synthetic fuels industry.

Frazier, Jack. *Auto Fuels of the 1980's.* Indian Mills, W.Va.: Solar Age Press, 1978. 71 pp. $3.95. (CEP)
   The adoption of alternative auto fuels in inevitable, despite the opposition of the multinational energy elite. Blends of methanol and gasoline will be used first. Methanol can be produced from garbage, agricultural waste, and certain crops. Brazil has a crash program for producing methanol from sugarcane and manioc. Methane gas from coal seams would also be an excellent fuel. These new fuels will be less polluting, more efficient, and give improved performance.

Hoye, David. *Solargas, and How to Easily Make Your Own Auto and Heating Fuel for Pennies a Gallon.* Los Angeles, Calif.: International Publishers, Second edition, 1979. 202 pp. $7.95.
   Although the title may imply otherwise, this manual focuses on the production of liquid fuels. In a non-technical manner, it explains how alcohol can be made from various organic materials and wastes; how to construct and operate anything from a backyard solar still to a small commercial enterprise; and how to use alcohol in cars, trucks, and furnaces.

Lincoln, John Ware. *Methanol and Other Ways Around the Gas Pump.* Charlotte, Vt.: Garden Way Publishing Co., 1976. 134 pp. $4.95. (EARS)
   The author describes the production and use of methanol and other fuels for motor vehicles, as well as car design and instructions for engine conversion. He also tells the story of the powerful anti-methanol lobby.

Mandeville, Michael Wells. *Solar Alcohol: The Fuel Revolution.* Ambix, P.O. Box 353, Port Ludlow, WA 98365. 1979. 127 pp. $8.95.
   Ethyl alcohol is the world's safest fuel—efficient and non-polluting, and is presently used in Brazil and elsewhere. Basics are explained, such as what alcohol is, where it can be obtained, the solar-biomass machine, and simple steps for production and use. Needs for research and policy change are outlined. Design and layout of each page convey ideas and relationships clearly, and make this an excellent resource for the secondary teacher. See also Ambix under ORGANIZATIONS. (Education)

Paul, J.K., ed. *Methanol Technology and Application in Motor Fuels*. Park Ridge, N.J.: Noyes Data Corporation, 1978. 470 pp. $54.00.

Methanol can be produced from a number of unusual and renewable sources, utilized as an automotive fuel, and converted into gasoline.

U.S. Department of Energy. *Biomass-Based Alcohol Fuels: The Near-Term Potential for Use in Gasoline*. Washington, DC, 1978. S/N 061-000-00151-03. 71 pp. $2.50. (USGPO)

The requirements and prospects for the development of a nationwide alcohol-gasoline fuel system by the year 1990 are surveyed in this report.

U.S. Department of Energy. *Status of Alcohol Fuels Utilization Technology for Highway Transportation*. Washington, DC, 1978. S/N 061-000-00129-8. 144 pp. $3.50. (USGPO)

Here are the results of engine, vehicle, and fuel testing, and a review of the status of alcohol utilization technologies.

Energy from Solid Waste

Anderson, Larry K., and Tillman, David A., eds. *Fuels from Waste*. New York, N.Y.: Academic Press, 1977. 230 pp. $31.00.

This volume is an overview of present technologies and programs to produce energy from organic waste, from sources such as municipal solid waste, feedlot waste, and agricultural and wood wastes.

Cheremisinoff, Paul N., and Morresi, Angelo C. *Energy From Solid Wastes*. New York, N.Y.: Marcel Dekker, 1976. 505 pp. $35.00.

Tremendous savings, both environmental and economic can be realized through converting solid wastes into heat and power. This book describes technologies presently in use in the United States and in Europe.

DeRenzo, D.J., ed. *European Technology for Obtaining Energy From Solid Waste*. Park Ridge, N.J.: Noyes Data Corporation, 1978. 281 pp. $39.00.

The recovery of energy from solid waste is now an established technique for conserving energy, especially in Western Europe. Systems are outlined, case studies detailed, and national overviews, problem analyses, maps, and combustion unit censuses presented.

DeRenzo, Dorothy. *Energy from Bioconversion of Waste Materials*. Park Ridge, N.J.: Noyes Data Corporation, 1977. 223 pp. $32.00.

This book describes practical arrangements and equipment, large and small, for the anaerobic decomposition of organic wastes to produce methane gas, thus providing partial solutions to the energy and solid waste problems.

Golueke, Clarence G. *Biological Reclamation of Solid Wastes*. Emmaus, Pa.: Rodale, 1977. 272 pp. $5.95.

Intended for professionals in waste management and for concerned laymen, this book describes the principles, technologies, and economic factors in treating organic wastes, including composting, sludge spreading, anaerobic digestion, yeast and ethanol production, and photosynthetic reclamation.

Institute for Local Self-Reliance. *Municipal Composting*. Washington, DC: Institute for Local Self-Reliance, 1980. approx. 40 pp. $4.00.

Composting methods, economic feasibility, and government policy are examined, with case studies to help community planners.

International Development Research Centre. *Compost, Fertilizer and Biogas Production from Human and Farm Wastes in the People's Republic of China.* 1978. 94 pp. $6.00. (UNIPUB)

 The design, construction and operation of various technologies for the treatment of wastes are described in this collection of papers.

Jackson, Frederick R. *Energy from Solid Waste.* Park Ridge, N.J.: Noyes Data Corporation, 1974. 163 pp. $24.00.

 Provides information on the burning of solid wastes to create steam directly, and on the pyrolysis of wastes, yielding pyrolysis gas or oil.

Jewell, William. *Bio-Conversion of Agricultural Waste for Energy Conservation and Pollution Control.* Oak Ridge, Tenn.: ERDA 1976. (TIC)

 A new design for a small lo-cost digester.

Jewell, William, J. *Energy, Agriculture, and Waste Management.* Ann Arbor, Mich.: Ann Arbor Science Publishers, 1977. 540 pp. $27.50.

 The Proceedings of the 1975 Cornell Waste Management Conference concentrate on the energy consumed in food production; the technology and energy costs of pollution control; and the potential for producing energy from agricultural wastes.

Mathematical Science Northwest, Inc. *Feasibility Study: Conversion of Solid Waste to Methanol or Ammonia.* Prepared for the City of Seattle by Mathematical Sciences Northwest, Inc., 4545 Fifteenth Ave. NE, Seattle, WA 98105. 1974. 185 pp.

 This study assesses various processes for the conversion of waste into methanol and ammonia, the use of methanol as a motor vehicle fuel, and the use of ammonia for fertilizer. Environmental, marketing, and financial considerations are also discussed. It concludes that large plants would be economically feasible.

National Academy of Sciences. *Methane Generation from Human, Animal, and Agricultural Wastes.* National Academy of Sciences, 2101 Constitution Ave. NW, Washington, DC 20418. 1977. 131 pp.

 Gas production systems, safety concerns, economic feasibility, technology, public health hazards, and research and development needs are described in this study.

Wood Energy;
Stoves & Fireplaces

Cheremisinoff, Nicholas P. *Wood for Energy Production.* Ann Arbor, Mich.: Ann Arbor Science Publishers, 1980. 200 pp. $20.00.

 A survey of the latest technologies and future trends in the use of wood as an energy source, including the use of wood wastes and the production of liquid fuels by indirect bioconversion techniques.

Curtis, Chris, and Post, Don. *Be Your Own Chimney Sweep.* Charlotte, Vt.: Garden Way, 1979. 112 pp. $4.95.

 Here you will find out how to clean your chimneys and stoves effectively, and how to prevent heat loss and fires.

Daniels, M.E. *Fireplaces and Wood Stoves.* New York, N.Y.: Bobbs-Merrill, 1977. 192 pp. $12.50.

This manual for homeowners and handymen explains how to build many types of fireplaces and how to install wood stoves. It also covers maintenance, safety, possible problems, and insulating materials. Excellent photos and diagrams.

Eckholm, Eric P. *The Other Energy Crisis: Firewood.* Washington, DC: Worldwatch Institute, 1975. 22 pp. $2.00. (FOE)
 The shortage of firewood affects a third of mankind, and deforestation is leading to soil erosion, flooding, and creeping deserts.

Food and Agriculture Organization of the United Nations. *Charcoal.* FAO, U.N., 1974. 97 pp. $4.25. (UNIPUB)
 There is presently a revival of interest in wood charcoal as a renewable fuel. Manufacturing techniques, world trade, and the industry's future are described here.

Gay, Larry. *The Complete Book of Heating with Wood.* Charlotte, Vt.: Garden Way Publishing Co., 1974. 128 pp. $3.95. (EARS) (TEA)
 Information on finding and preparing wood for burning, types of wood stoves, and heat exchangers.

Harrington, Geri. *The Wood Burning Stove Book: How to Beat the Energy Crisis.* New York, N.Y.: Collier, 1977. 175 pp. $6.95.
 A bit different in its approach, this guide begins with the history and ecology of woodburning, with its advantages and disadvantages, and then describes the various types of stoves and fireplaces, and the art of gathering wood.

Hiser, Michael, *Wood Energy.* Ann Arbor, Mich.: Ann Arbor Science Publishers, 1978. 152 pp. $15.00.
 There are many possibilities for using wood as an energy source; some of the projects in progress include the utilization of forest biomass, and electric power generation.

Ivins, David. *The Complete Book of Woodburning Stoves.* New York, N.Y.: Drake, 1978. 158 pp. $6.95.
 The woodburning stove is one of the oldest, simplest, and most economical systems of heating the home. This guide describes different types of stoves and how to select them, safety, and firewood.

Ross, Bob, and Ross, Carol. *Modern and Classic Woodburning Stoves: A Complete Guide.* Woodstock, N.Y.: Overlook, revised 1978. 158 pp. $4.95. (EARS).
 Heating with wood can be sound ecology and economy as well. This guide explains combustion, and stove selection and operation. The authors describe houses designed to be heated with wood, or wood integrated with other fuels or with a solar heating system.

Shelton, Jay. *Wood Heat Safety.* Charlotte, Vt.: Garden Way, 1979. 180 pp. $8.95.
 Taking the right precautions makes woodburning an economical, enjoyable, and safe energy alternative. Explains building and fire codes, and how to safely reduce clearances.

Shelton, Jay, and Shapiro, Andrew. *The Woodburners Encyclopedia.* Waitsfield, Vt.: Vermont Crossroads Press, 1977. 155 pp. $7.95. (EARS) (TEA)
 Answers questions about wood heating, including feasibility, cost, safety, installation, and operation. Includes list of manufacturers and specification charts.

Soderstrom, Neil, *Heating Your Home With Wood*. New York, N.Y.: Harper and Row, 1978. 199 pp. $3.95.

The author explains the theory of heat and its application to woodburning fireplaces, stoves, and furnaces, and the cutting and seasoning of wood.

Sullivan, George. *Wood-Burning Stoves*. New York, N.Y.: Cornerstone, 1978. 128 pp. $4.95.

A clear text and good illustrations explain how to choose, install, and maintain wood stoves, make your fireplace more efficient, and obtain firewood.

Twitchell, Mary. *Wood Energy: A Practical Guide to Heating with Wood*. Charlotte, Vt.: Garden Way, 1978. 172 pp. $7.95. (EARS)

Fireplaces, chimneys, stoves, and wood supplies are described in detail, trouble sources pinpointed, and remedies offered. Equipment is listed and compared, and directions given for selection, installation, and operation.

Vivian, John. *Wood Heat*. Revised edition. Emmaus, Pa.: 1978. 448 pp. $7.95. (EARS)

There are many ways in which we can make wood a safe, efficient source of heat in our homes—and even use the ashes.

Wik, Ole. *Wood Stoves: How to Make and Use Them*. Anchorage, Alaska: Alaska Northwest, 1977. 194 pp. $5.95. (EARS)

Advice is given on choosing the right stove for your needs, and getting the most out of it; many types are illustrated, including some which can be built at home.

FOSSIL FUELS

Overviews and International Issues

Blair, John J. *The Control of Oil.* New York, N.Y.: Pantheon, 1976. 441 pp. $15.00.
This well-documented book relates how the world markets were divided up by internatioal cartel agreements, and how the supply of oil is controlled. It emphasizes the need for developing new technologies, and for the regulation or breaking up of the monopoly power.

Charles River Associates, Inc. *OPEC: Policy Implications for the United States.* New York, N.Y.: Praeger, 1979. 350 pp. $18.50.
Explores the economic impact of OPEC, the oil shortage, and the increase in oil prices, and considers the response of the United States and possible alternative policies.

Cheng, Chu-yuan. *China's Petroleum Industry: Output Growth and Export Potential.* New York, N.Y.: Praeger, 1976. 268 pp. $24.95.
A discussion of the prospects and problems of China's fast-growing petroleum industry, including technology import, capital investment, and export policy.

Choucri, Nazli, with Ferraro, Vincent. *International Politics of Energy Interdependence: The Case of Petroleum.* Lexington, Mass.: Lexington Books, 1976. 272 pp. $21.95.
After a consideration of shifts in economic interdependence, the authors find that a global energy regime is necessary to accomodate the conflicting objectives of energy producers and consumers, and national preferences and priorities.

Dam, Kenneth W. *Oil Resources: Who Gets What How?* Chicago, Ill.: University of Chicago Press, 1976. 193 pp. $4.95.
The allocation and development of natural resources, particularly oil, are problems of growing international concern. After an examination of the policies of Great Britain, Norway, and the U.S., the author suggests that an auction system would be most beneficial.

Eckbo, Paul L. *The Future of World Oil.* Cambridge, Mass.: Ballinger, 1976. 160 pp. $20.00.
This volume is designed as a tool for decision-makers in industry and government in unraveling the complex structures of the world oil market and the uncertainties of its future development.

Edens, David G. *Oil and Development in the Middle East.* New York, N.Y.: Praeger, 1979. 220 pp. $16.95.
The author analyzes Middle Eastern economic underdevelopment in terms of resource imbalance brought about by the rise in the value of oil reserves

and the relative resource poverty in all other areas.

Engler, Robert. *The Brotherhood of Oil*. Chicago, Ill.: University of Chicago Press, 1977. 337 pp. $12.50.
    Details of the politics behind the operations of the oil industry, and a proposal to examine public control of domestic energy resources.

Ezzati, Al. *World Energy Markets and OPEC Stability*. Brookhaven National Laboratory. Lexington, Mass.: Lexington Books, 1978. 224 pp. $18.95.
    The author presents a model designed to closely approximate market behavior which can be used to determine equilibrium prices, supply, demand, imports, and exports for each of the major regions of the world.

Fritsch, Albert. *Major Oil*. Washington, DC: Center for Science in the Public Interest, 1974. 56 pp. $4.00. (CEP)
    A factbook containing historical highlights, world-wide and domestic production operations, and economic data on the eight largest U.S. companies.

Gelb, Bernard, and Pliskin, Jeffrey. *Energy Use in Mining: Patterns and Prospects*. Cambridge, Mass.: Ballinger, 1979. 192 pp. $18.50.
    Data on energy consumption and technological change in the extractive industries, and legal constraints in this field. Covers iron, copper, bauxite, coal, oil, and gas extraction.

Keto, David B. *Law and Offshore Oil Development: The North Sea Experience*. New York, N.Y.: Praeger, 1978. 150 pp. $16.95.
    Patterns of offshore oil development and laws governing licensing, safety, and environmental protection are described in this study. The author concludes that national or international bodies should promulgate detailed laws and regulations before any large-scale operations are undertaken.

Mancke, Richard B. *Mexican Oil and Natural Gas: Political, Strategic, and Economic Implications*. New York, N.Y.: Praeger, 1979. 200 pp. $18.95.
    The potential of Mexico's recent discovery of oil and gas resources is assessed, together with a consideration of how this will affect the Mexican economy, U.S. supplies, OPEC, and world trade.

Medvin, Norman. *The Energy Cartel: Who Runs the American Oil Industry?* New York, N.Y.: Vintage Books, 1974. 205 pp. $1.95.
    The author tells how the oil industry combines with banks and insurance companies to control the world's supply of energy, and therefore the world itself. He makes recommendations on regulation and pricing.

Moran, Theodore H. *Oil Prices and the Future of OPEC: The Political Economy of Tension and Stability in the Organization of Petroleum Exporting Countries*. Washington, DC: Resources for the Future, 1978. 108 pp. $5.75.
    Commitments to growth and social betterment leave little slack in OPEC national budgets, and thus preclude output reductions for any extended period.

National Research Council, National Academy of the Sciences, 2101 Constitution Ave. NW, Washington, DC 20418. *Mineral Resources and the Environment*. 1975. 348 pp. $8.25.
    These estimates of America's energy resources are lower than previous governmental reports.

Odell, Peter R. *Oil and World Power*. New York, N.Y.: Penguin, Revised Edition,

1979. 272 pp. $3.95.

The traumatic events in the oil world since 1973 are recounted, with their diverse geographic, political and economic factors, and implications for international relations.

Probstein, Ronald, and Gold, Harris. *Water in Synthetic Fuel Production: The Technology and Alternatives.* Cambridge, Mass.: Massachusetts Institute of Technology Press, 1978. 296 pp. $9.95.

The large-scale synthesis of fuels from coal and oil shale involves both promise and constraints, especially the requirement for large amounts of fresh water, and the production of polluted water. Most of these reserves are located in the arid West. Technologies for minimizing water consumption and pollution are being developed.

Safer, Arnold E. *International Oil Policy.* Foreword by Senator Edward M. Kennedy. Lexington, Mass.: Lexington Books, 1979. 192 pp. $13.95.

The basic concepts of U.S. energy policy are challenged, with a call for more active leadership in oil price determination, and diversification in the search for energy solutions.

Sampson, Anthony. *The Seven Sisters: The Great Oil Companies and the World They Shaped.* New York, N.Y.: Bantam, 1976. 395 pp. $2.25.

Tells the story of the cartelization of the earth's most precious commodity, and reveals the role oil plays in making and breaking governments and economics.

Solberg, Carl. *Oil Power: The Rise and Imminent Fall of an American Empire.* New York, N.Y.: New American Library, 1976. 326 pp. $2.25.

The history of "black gold" involves politicians and scandals, international entanglements, and subsidies and profits. However, the power of the American oil industry may be coming to an end as we move to new sources of energy.

U.S. Department of Energy. *Fossil Energy Research and Development Program.* Washington, DC, 1978. S/N 061-000-00040-2. 475 pp. $9.00. (USGPO)

A search for new and promising ways to provide for future energy needs.

U.S. Executive Office of the President, Council on Environmental Quality. *The World Oil Market in the Years Ahead.* Washington, DC, 1979. S/N 041-015-00114-1. 80 pp. $4.00. (USGPO)

An analysis of the outlook for the world oil market over the next few years, and long-term trends.

White, Irvin L., et al. *North Sea Oil and Gas: Implications for Future U.S. Development.* Norman, Okla.: University of Oklahoma Press, 1974. 176 pp. $2.95.

This study, sponsored by the Council on Environmental Quality, assesses North Sea oil and gas resources and technologies, compares them with U.S. operations, and finds lessons to be learned.

Williams, Edward J. *The Rebirth of the Mexican Petroleum Industry: Developmental Directions and Policy Implications.* Lexington, Mass.: Lexington Books, 1979.

A discussion of the socio-economic impact of Mexico's new oil wealth, the implications for domestic and foreign policy, and future policy alternatives.

Willrich, Mason, et al. *Administration of Energy Shortages: Natural Gas and Petroleum.* Cambridge, Mass.: Ballinger, 1975. 320 pp. $22.50.

A critique of government energy administration and regulation, with recommendations for future policy.

Windsor, Philip. *Oil: A Guide Through the Total Energy Jungle*. Boston, Mass.: Gambit, 1976. 182 pp. $8.95.

Examines the world's dependence on oil, the way the oil industry works, and the nature of the changes in the past few years. Holds that the solution must be political, on a multinational scale.

Petroleum, Oil Shale, and Natural Gas

Ahern, William R., Jr. *Oil and the Outer Coastal Shelf: The Georges Bank Case*. Cambridge, Mass.: Ballinger, 1973. 164 pp. $17.50.

Explores the economic, environmental, legal, and political aspects of offshore drilling.

Baker, J.M., ed. *Marine Ecology and Oil Pollution*. New York, N.Y.: Halsted Press, 1976. 566 pp. $60.00.

A useful book for those concerned with oil installations, and the intertidal and offshore monitoring and toxicity testing of oils and disperants.

Berry, Mary Clay. *The Alaska Pipeline*. Bloomington, Ind.: Indiana University Press, 1975. 320 pp. $10.95.

An evaluation of the impact on the Alaskan native of the pipeline, and the role played by the law and the American political process in resolving the problems.

Boesch, Donald F.; Hershner, Carl H.; and Milgram, Jerome H. *Oil Spills and the Marine Environment*. An Energy Policy Project of the Ford Foundation. Cambridge, Mass.: Ballinger, 1974. 144 pp. $8.95.

This is an analysis of marine oil pollution, including aspects of marine biology, oceanography, biochemistry, oil drilling and transport practices, and government regulation. The need for further research is pointed out, since the technology for the prevention, control, and clean-up of oil spills is now based on very limited information of the impacts upon marine ecology.

Carmichael, Frank R. *Offshore Drilling Technology*. Park Ridge, N.J.: Noyes Data Corporation, 1975. 392 pp. $36.00.

Describes techniques including drilling ships, platforms and subsea facilities.

Dye, Lee. *Blowout at Platform A: The Crisis That Awakened a Nation*. Garden City, N.Y.: Doubleday, 1971. 231 pp.

This account of the blowout at the Union Oil well at Santa Barbara, California on January 28, 1969 provides details of the disaster, describes the peril to the ocean and marine life, and discusses the relationship of the oil industry to other industries and to the Federal government.

Food and Agriculture Organization. *Impact of Oil on the Marine Environment*. FAO, U.N., 1977. 250 pp. $10.50. (UNIPUB)

The 2 to 20 million tons of oil that is discharged annually into the oceans has far-reaching effects upon deoxygenation, heating, gaseous exchange, microbial populations, and complex biosystems.

Kash, Don E., ed. *Energy Under The Oceans: A Technological Assessment of Outer Continental Shelf Gas and Oil Operations*. Norman, Okla.: University of Oklahoma Press, 1973. 378 pp. $20.00.

This study, under a grant from the National Science Foundation, considers anticipated consequences beyond economic cost-benefits and technology in its assessment of the full range of social and environmental impacts.

Kimball, Vaughn S. *Waste Oil Recovery and Disposal.* Park Ridge, N.J.: Noyes Data Corporation, 1975. 267 pp. $24.00.

The recovery and disposal of waste oil are of interest both from the standpoints of conservation of energy resources and the protection of the environment. Techniques include incineration and microbial decomposition.

Manning, Harvey. *Cry Crisis: Rehearsal in Alaska.* San Francisco, Calif.: Friends of the Earth, 1974. 313 pp. (FOE)

A study of the Alaskan oil resources, the environmental impact of the pipelines and the supertanker shuttle, and alternative proposals for a rational energy policy.

Mansvelt-Beck, Frederik W., And Wiig, Karl M. *The Economics of Offshore Oil and Gas Supplies.* Lexington, Mass.: Lexington Books, 1977. 176 pp. $16.00.

The authors analyze the economics of offshore drilling, the costs of production, production methods, and geologic formations.

McDonald, Angus. *Shale Oil.* Washington, DC: Center for Science in the Public Interest, 1974. 68 pp. $4.00.

A critical study which points out the problems of water supply, land reclamation, and destruction of wildlife, and questions whether the program would be a net energy gain or loss.

Mostert, Noel. *Supership.* New York, N.Y.: Warner Books, 1974. 382 pp. $1.95.

A combination of thorough research, love of the sea, and literary talent have produced this grim and compelling account of the dangers of supertankers, and the resulting pollution of the world's oceans—a continuing catastrophe that may be irreversible.

Perrini, Edward M. *Oil from Shale and Tar Sands.* Park Ridge, N.J.: Noyes Data Corporation, 1975. 307 pp. $36.00.

A survey of mining, refining, and separation processes for the recovery of petroleum from shale and tar sands, based upon U.S. patent literature.

Pimlott, Douglas; Brown, Dougald; and Sam, Kenneth. *Oil under the Ice: Offshore Drilling in the Canadian Arctic.* Ottawa, Ontario: Canadian Arctic Resources Committee, 1976. 178 pp.

Due to exceptionally hazardous drilling conditions, to proceed to drill without adequate knowledge of the environment, or effective clean-up capability, is to accept the risk of uncontrollable spills with severe environmental and social impacts.

Potter, Jeffrey. *Disaster by Oil: Oil Spills, Why They Happen, What They Do, How We Can End Them.* New York, N.Y.: macmillan, 1973. 301 pp. $7.95.

Here are case studies of supertankers aground and offshore drilling blow-outs, as well as descriptions of the damage to marine life, food chains, and the vital supply of food from the ocean. Corporations are interested mainly in profits, and government policies have been ineffective.

Sittig, Marshall. *Oil Spill Prevention and Removal Handbook.* Park Ridge, N.J.: Noyes Data Corporation, 1974. 466 pp. $36.00.

Discusses prevention and control of spills from various sources, removal, ultimate disposal, costs and economics, and effects on the environment.

Sittig, Marshall. *The Petroleum Industry. 1978: Energy Saving and Environmental Control.* Park Ridge, N.J.: Noyes Data Corporation, 1978. 374 pp. $39.00.

A number of approaches to saving energy and avoiding pollution, and the retrofitting necessary to meet changing requirements, are described in this volume.

Wardley-Smith, J., ed. *The Prevention of Oil Pollution.* New York, N.Y.: Wiley, 1979. 309 pp. $39.95.

Practical advice is given on preventing the occurrence of oil pollution through techniques applicable to exploration, production, transportation, refining, storage, and industrial and commercial usage of oil.

Winslow, Ron. *Hard Aground: The Story of the Argo Merchant Oil Spill.* New York, N.Y.: Norton, 1978. 286 pp. $10.95.

Reporter Winslow reconstructs this disaster at sea from interviews and testimony.

Yen, T.F. *Science and Technology of Oil Shale.* Ann Arbor, Mich.: Ann Arbor Science Publishers, 1976. 226 pp. $9.95.

An examination of oil shale resources in the United States, the technology presently in use, recent research, and environmental concerns.

Liquefied Natural Gas

Davis, Lee Niedringhaus. *Frozen Fire: Where Will It Happen Next?* San Francisco, Calif.: Friends of the Earth, 1979. 298 pp. $6.95. (FOE) (EARS)

This is a citizen's guide to one of the most promising—and frightening—of the new fuels. The technology for liquefied natural gas demands perfection, since a leak could result in a firestorm as escaping gas ignites. The costs and the risks of the LNG program will be borne by the public, while the profits go to this rising international industry. Most LNG comes from OPEC countries, thus continuing our energy dependence.

U.S. Congress. *Liquefied Natural Gas: Safety, Siting, and Policy Concerns.* Washington, DC, 1978. S/N 052-070-04566-3. 147 pp. $2.50. (USGPO)

Proceedings of the Congressional Research Service Seminar provide orientation on public policy issues associated with LNG.

U.S. Congress, Office of Technology Assessment. *Transportation of Liquefied Natural Gas.* #052-003-00436-4. Washington, DC, 1977. 101 pp. $2.50. (USGPO)

A factual description of LNG systems and facilities and the federal regulatory process, and a critical review of technical and political problems Public awareness and concerns are reviewed, and recommendations proposed.

U.S. Department of Energy. *Synthesized Gaseous Hydrocarbon Fuels.* Washington, DC, 1978. S/N 061-000-00105-1. 291 pp. $5.25. (USGPO)

Coal, hydrocarbon liquids, oil shales, tar sands, and bioconvertible materials are considered as potential sources for gaseous fuels.

U.S. General Accounting Office. *Liquefied Energy Gases Safety.* Washington, DC, 1978. (USGPO)

This three-volume report analyzes the safety issues involved, identifies problem areas, and recommends corrective action to reduce risks.

Vol. 1. *Executive Summary and Report Chapters.* S/N 020-000-00167-4. 641 pp.

$7.00.

Vol. 2. *Appendices.* S/N 020-000-00165-8. 485 pp. $6.50.

Vol. 3. *Federal Agency Comments.* S/N 020-000-00166-6. 173 pp. $3.75.

Van der Linde, Peter, with Hintze, Naomi A. *Time Bomb.* Garden City, NY: Doubleday, 1978. 183 pp. $6.95.

The whole issue of liquefied natural gas and the threat it presents to us and to our environment is investigated in this book. The explosive force of LNG is second only to a nuclear holocaust, yet facilities are sited in heavily populated areas, and are not provided with adequate safeguards.

Coal

Atomic Energy Commission, Office of Information Services, Technical Information Center. *Coal Processing: Gasification, Liquefaction, Desulfurization. A Bibliography, 1930-1974.* TID 3349, 1974. 757 pp. $13.60. (NTIS)

Contains the bulk of U.S. and foreign scientific and technical information, arranged in broad subject categories and indexed.

Berkowitz, N. *An Introduction to Coal Technology.* New York, N.Y.: Academic Press, 1979. 345 pp. $32.50.

This text discusses the origins and properties of coal; handling and processing, including gasification and liquefaction; and environmental aspects such as pollution and pollution abatement.

Braunstein, H.M.; Copenhaver, E.D.; and Pfuderer, H.A. *Environmental, Health, and Control Aspects of Coal Conversion: An Information Overview.* Oak Ridge, Tenn.: Oak Ridge National Laboratory, 1977. Vol. 1. #0-238-328; Vol. 2. #0-238-329. (USGPO)

Volume 1 summarizes technical information on the origin and properties of coal, conversion processes, process effluents, and coal products.

Volume 2 presents technical information on environmental interactions, microbial interactions, plant interactions, trace elements, and effects on humans and animals.

Coal Age Magazine. Coal Age Operating Handbook of Coal Surface Mining and Reclamation. New York, N.Y.: McGraw-Hill, 1978. 448 pp. $19.50.

This handbook has been compiled from recent issues of *Coal Age Magazine,* and includes discussions of surface mining methods, reclamation, transportation of coal, and federal regulations.

Darcey, D., McMahon, G., Burns, E., et al. *Strip Mine Blasting: A Study of Vibrational Pollution.* Washington, DC: Center for Science in the Public Interest, 1977. 124 pp. $7.50. (CEP)

This study documents the massive toll in human environmental damages resulting from strip mine blasting practices, and suggests measures to alleviate these problems.

Doyle, William S. *Deep Coal Mining: Waste Disposal Technology.* Park Ridge, N.J.: Noyes Data Corporation, 1976. 392 pp. $36.00.

Discusses methods to prevent and control pollution associated with deep mining of coal.

Doyle, William S. *Strip Mining of Coal: Environmental Solutions.* Park Ridge, N.J.: Noyes Data Corporation, 1976. 353 pp. $32.00.

Describes surface mining of coal, land use and methods, land reclamation technology, and sediment and erosion control.

Fort Union Coal Field Symposium, Sponsored by Montana Academy of Sciences, Eastern Montana College. Five Volumes. $8.75 from Eastern Montana College Bookstore, Billings, MT 59101.
    A technical compilation on the development and use of coal resources, including social impact considerations.

Gordon, Richard L. *Coal in the U.S. Energy Market.* Lexington, Mass.: Lexington Books, 1978. 240 pp. $17.95.
    An economic analysis of the U.S. coal industry, consumption patterns, the economics of fuel choice, and regulations affecting production and use.

Gordon, Richard L. *U.S. Coal and the Electric Power Industry.* Published for Resources for the Future. Washington, DC: Johns Hopkins University Press, 1975. 213 pp.
    A study of the problems involved in the utilization of coal as compared with other fossil fuels and nuclear energy. Analyzes costs, environmental effects, and new technologies, and presents scenarios for future fuel choices.

Hartnett, James P., ed. *Alternative Energy Sources* includes fluidized bed coal combustion and coal gasification. See *ALTERNATIVE SOURCES OF ENERGY.*

Hoffman, E.J. *Coal Conversion.* Laramie, Wyo.: The Energy Company, 1978. 450 pp. $55.00.
    The researcher and engineer will find this to be a valuable reference for coal conversion research, technology, chemical fundamentals, methodology, and calculations.

Howard-Smith, I., and Werner, G.J. *Coal Conversion Technology.* Park Ridge, N.J.: Noyes Data Corporation, 1976. 133 pp. $24.00.
    Describes over 100 processes for the transmutation of coal into more useful and acceptable synthetic fuels.

Komanoff, Charles. *A Comparison of Nuclear and Coal Costs.* and other works. See *NUCLEAR ENERGY: ECONOMICS.*

Lamb, George H. *Underground Coal Gasification.* Park Ridge, N.J.: Noyes Data Corporation, 1977. 255 pp. $36.00.
    In situ gasification of coal appears to have great promise in alleviating some of the problems associated with the production, transportation, and burning of coal. Experimental equipment and set-ups are reviewed.

Meyers, Robert A. *Coal Desulfurization.* New York, N.Y.: Marcel Dekker, 1977. 254 pp. $29.75.
    The current state of coal reserves, reasons for sulfur removal, desulfurization techniques, and cost effectiveness of different processes are considered in this reference tool for the researcher.

Miller, Saunders. *The Economics of Nuclear and Coal Power.* See *NUCLEAR ENERGY: ECONOMICS.*

Morgan, Mark. *The Enforcement of Stripmining Laws.* Washington, DC: Center for Science in the Public Interest, 1975. 120 pp. $4.00. (CEP)
    A study of the inadequate enforcement of laws in Kentucky, West Virginia, and Pennsylvania. Recommendations are proposed.

Morgan, Mark, and Moss, Edwin. *Citizen's Blasting Handbook.* Washington, DC: Citizens' Energy Project, 1978. 70 pp. $2.00. (CEP)

Laws and strategies are studied for dealing with the many problems created by the impact of coal mine blasting upon the health and property of nearby residents.

Murray, Francis X., ed. *Where We Agree: Report of the National Coal Policy Project.* Center for Strategic and International Studies, Georgetown University. Boulder, Colo.: Westview Press, 1978. Vol. 1, 337 pp. Vol. 2, 477 pp.
Leaders from industry and environmental groups seek consensus on national policy issues related to the use of coal in an environmentally and economically acceptable manner.

National Academy of Sciences/National Academy of Engineering. *Rehabilitation Potential of Western Coal Lands.* A Report to the Energy Policy Project of the Ford Foundation. Cambridge, Mass.: Ballinger, 1974. 228 pp. $8.95.
Here is an evaluation of the trade-offs between energy production, consumption of resources, and environmental quality. This study analyzes the expected environmental impact of surface mining, onsite energy conversion technologies, economic development, and the limiting factor of water supply.

Richardson, Francis W. *Oil from Coal.* Park Ridge, N.J.: Noyes Data Corporation, 1975. 387 pp. $36.00.
Describes the operational details of many coal liquefaction processes.

Rosenbaum, Walter A. *Coal and Crisis: The Political Dilemmas of Energy Management.* New York, N.Y.: Praeger, 1978. 124 pp. $15.95.
To develop coal as a major energy source, changes in the federal regulatory structure will be necessary, and environmental standards may have to be modified.

Stern, Gerald M. *The Buffalo Creek Disaster.* New York, N.Y.: Vintage, 1976. 307 pp. $2.45.
Stern tells the story of one of the worst man-made disasters in our history: how a coal waste refuse pile which dammed a stream in West Virginia collapsed and devastated sixteen small communities—and the pattern of corporate neglect which made it possible.

Torrey, S., ed. *Trace Contaminants from Coal.* Park Ridge, N.J.: Noyes Data Corporation, 1978. 294 pp. $39.00.
Trace elements released by the burning of coal have a potential for ecological contamination. This report outlines how they are disseminated through air, water, and ecosystems; public health and ecological effects, and emission control.

Tyner, Wallace E., and Kalter, Robert J., with Wold, John P. *Western Coal: Promise or Problem.* Lexington, Mass.: Lexington Books, 1978. 208 pp. $18.00.
All major issues involved in developing federally owned western coal are covered in this study of leasing policy, stripmining costs, resource availability, and locations of future coal developments.

U.S. Congress, Office of Technology Assessment. *The Direct Use of Coal: Prospects and Problems of Production and Combustion.* Washington, DC, 1979. S/N 052-003-00664-2. 411 pp. $7.00. (USGPO)
The benefits and risks of a massive shift to coal are assessed: the social, economic, physical, and biological implications, and the impacts upon public health and the environment.

U.S. Department of the Interior. *Draft Environmental Statement: Federal Coal Management Program.* Washington, DC, 1978. S/N 024-011-00099-2. 753 pp. $8.50. (USGPO)

Various alternatives for a federal coal management program and their possible impacts are assessed.

Witt, Matt. *In Our Blood.* Washington, DC: Highlander Research and Education Center, 1979. 90 pp. $6.95.

Witt takes the reader into the coal mines and into the minds of those who work there, relating the everyday hazards, the struggles for better working conditions, and the history of the United Mine Workers Association.

Yaverbaum, Lee. *Fluidized Bed Combustion of Coal and Waste Materials.* Park Ridge, N.J.: Noyes Data Corporation, 1977. 267 pp. $39.00.

Feasible processes are detailed for fluidized bed combustion, a method for removing sulfur and obtaining energy from high-sulfur coal and obnoxious wastes, and also for utilizing many low-grade fuels directly.

You Can't Put It Back: A West Virginia Guide to Strip Mine Opposition. The Land Use and Environmental Rights Committee of the Mountain Community Union & Save Our Mountains, Inc., Box 573, Hamlin, WV 25523. 1976. 79 pp. $2.50.

This handbook explains the economics of the coal industry, the need for tax reform, and how to organize the opposition. It is applicable to problems in other areas as well as in West Virginia.

GEOTHERMAL ENERGY

Technology and Applications

Armstead, H. Christopher, ed. *Geothermal Energy: A Review of Research and Development.* Paris: UNESCO, 1977. 186 pp. $21.50. (UNIPUB)
Presents basic theories, practical developments, and applications in the fields of geothermal exploration, utilization, and economics.

Berman, Edward R. *Geothermal Energy.* Park Ridge, N.J.: Noyes Data Corporation, 1975. 336 pp. $24.00.
Describes the nature and extent of geothermal resources and the currently available technology for exploiting geothermal energy.

Bierman, Sheldon L.; Stover, David F.; Nelson, Paul A.; and Lamont, William, Jr. *Geothermal Energy in the Western United States: Innovation Versus Monopoly.* New York, N.Y.: Praeger, 1978. 490 pp. $25.00.
A study of the relationship between petroleum companies and the utilities, and how the development of geothermal energy might be affected by marketing considerations and geothermal holdings of the large petroleum companies.

Collie, M.J., ed. *Geothermal Energy: Recent Developments.* Park Ridge, N.J.: Noyes Data Corporation, 1978. 445 pp. $40.00.
This review covers recent developments in technology, and the management of problems such as inefficiency in conversion to electricity, corrosion, and pollution. Geothermal energy is not expected to play a large overall role in the United States, but it can have regional significance in the Western States, and in developing countries having volcanic regions.

Edmunds, Stahrl, and Rose, Adam. *Geothermal Energy and Regional Development: The Case of Imperial County, California.* New York, N.Y.: Praeger, 1979. 280 pp. $19.95.
This study presents a model for regional energy analysis, focusing on the technical, economic, and social aspects of geothermal energy development. It finds geothermal economically feasible and competitive with fuel oil in the production of electricity.

The Futures Group. *A Technology Assessment of Geothermal Energy Resource Development.* NSF—RA—X—75-011. Washington, DC: U.S. Government Printing Office. 500 pp. $6.00. (USGPO)
Suggests the potential futures for geothermal energy in the U.S., and makes evaluations and recommendations.

Geothermal Project, Office of Biological Services, U.S. Fish and Wildlike Service,

Department of the Interior. *Geothermal Handbook.* NP-21172. ERDA/TIC. 1976. 194 pp.
A discussion of the development of geothermal resources and their environmental impact.

Geothermal World. *Geothermal World Directory.* Geothermal World, 18014 Sherman Way, Suite 169, Reseda, CA 91335. 400 pp.
A comprehensive reference guide to national and international geothermal research, exploration, and development.

Hartnett, James P., ed. *Alternative Energy Sources* includes geothermal energy. See *ALTERNATIVE SOURCES OF ENERGY.*

Jet Propulsion Laboratory, California Institute of Technology. *Conference on Research for the Development of Geothermal Resources.* NSF—RA—N—159. Sponsored by the National Science Foundation. Pasadena, Calif., 1974. 349 pp.
Overview of research programs, exploration and assessment of specific sites, environmental and legal aspects, and advanced technologies.

Kruger, Paul, and Otte, Carel, eds. *Geothermal Energy: Resources, Production, Stimulation.* Stanford, Calif.: Stanford University Press, 1973. 360 pp. $17.50.
Contains the full proceedings of a symposium held by the American Nuclear Society in June 1972. The papers provide a comprehensive review of information on geothermal heat as an energy source.

Lindsey, Michael, and Supton, Paul. *Geothermal Energy: Legal Problems of Resource Development.* Stanford University Environmental Law Society, Stanford Law School, Stanford, Calif., 1974. 150 pp. $3.95.
A description and evaluation of geothermal resources on public lands, with a summary of the legal problems inhibiting their development.

Milora, Stanley L., and Tester, Jefferson W. *Geothermal Energy as a Source of Electric Power: Thermodynamic and Economic Design Criteria.* Cambridge, Mass.: MIT Press, 1976. 186 pp. $16.25.
Engineers and researchers wil find technical and economic data for calculations involved in geothermal power conversion in this text. After assessment of the resource base, the authors conclude that geothermal power generation costs can compete with those of fossil fuels and nuclear power, and that the resources are large enough to have an impact on our economy.

Tatsch, J.H. *Geothermal Deposits: Origin, Evolution, and Present Characteristics.* Sudbury, Mass.: Tatsch Associates, 1976. 270 pp. $84.00.
A global mechanism is provided for explaining the characteristics of geothermal deposits, and for predicting the locations and characteristics of other heterogeneities that may be associated with hidden reserves.

United Nations. *Proceedings of the Second U.N. Symposium on the Development and Use of Geothermal Resources.* San Francisco, Calif., 1976. 3 vols. Approx. 2500 pp.
Experts from around the world presented papers on resource development, geothermal systems, exploration, environmental factors, technology, applications, economics, and legal aspects.

U.S. Congress. *Energy From Geothermal Sources.* Washington, DC, 1978. S/N 052-070-04717-8. 165 pp. $2.75. (USGPO)
Most aspects of geothermal energy are considered: history, geology, technology, global distribution, economics, environmental impact, and legal

status.

U.S. Department of the Interior. *Impact Prediction Manual for Geothermal Development.* Washington, DC, 1978. S.N 024-010-00494-1. 156 pp. $4.00. (USGPO)
    Information on the environmental impacts of air, water, and noise pollution from geothermal projects upon fish and wildlife and their habitats.

U.S. Energy Research and Development Administration. *Definition Report: Geothermal Energy Research, Development, and Demonstration Program.* Springfield, Va.: ERDA, 1975. $5.45. (NTIS)
    Provides a general review of geothermal technologies, and describes the federal effort in relation to geothermal energy.

U.S. Energy Research and Development Administration. *Geothermal Resources: A Bibliography.* TID 3354-R1. Springfield, Va.: ERDA, July 1976. 335 pp., plus approximately 300 pp. indices. $16.25. (NTIS)
    An annotated and indexed listing of the geothermal literature.

Wahl, Edward. *Geothermal Energy Utilization.* New York, N.Y.: Wiley, 1977. 302 pp. $22.00.
    The novice, student, and professional will find much information in this volume on the design and technology of systems for the production of electricity from geothermal energy, distributing thermal energy, and recovering minerals.

HYDROGEN AND FUEL CELLS

Technology and Applications

Bockris, J. O'M. *Energy: The Solar Hydrogen Alternative.* New York, N.Y.: Halsted Press, 1976. 365 pp. $27.50.

Explains how liquid hydrogen could solve the energy storage problem and be converted into electricity by the use of fuel cells. Discusses safety, transportation, and alternative economies.

Dickson, Edward M.; Ryan, John W.; and Smulyan, Marilyn H. *The Hydrogen Economy: A Realistic Appraisal of Prospects and Impacts.* New York, N.Y.: Praeger, 1977. 332 pp. $22.95.

The economic feasibility, costs, and impacts of the use of hydrogen fuel are discussed, and compared with other alternatives. Extensive research and development in the very near future is urged by the authors.

Federal Council on Science and Technology, Synthetic Fuels Panel. *Hydrogen and Other Synthetic Fuels.* Washington, DC: Government Printing Office, 1972. 131 pp.

The panel concludes that synthetic fuels from non-fossil sources appear to be the most likely alternative for supplying longterm needs for gaseous and liquid fuels.

Mathis, David A. *Hydrogen Technology for Energy.* Park Ridge, N.J.: Noyes Data Corporation, 1976. 285 pp. $32.00.

Explores the advantages and disadvantages of the use of hydrogen as a universal fuel, and the methods for storing, handling and transferring hydrogen.

McDougall, A.O. *Fuel Cells (Energy Alternative Series).* New York, N.Y.: Halsted Press, 1976. 200 pp. $11.95.

Explains how a fuel cell operates in direct electrochemical energy conversion, and describes working fuel battery systems, and the economics of fuel cell operation.

Noyes, Robert, ed. *Fuel Cells for Public Utility and Industrial Power.* Park Ridge, N.J.: Noyes Data Corporation, 1977. 325 pp. $42.00.

Fuel cells are generators of electricity containing no moving parts except small extraneous pumps. This work describes the advantages, types, applications, and marketing considerations of fuel cells.

Stanford Research Institute. *The Hydrogen Economy.* Menlo Park, Calif.: Stanford Research Institute, 1976. 389 pp.

Forecasts that hydrogen will be an important factor in the long-term energy economy. Assesses the problems, costs, and possible applications.

U.S. Energy Research and Development Administration. *Hydrogen Fuels: A Bibliography.* TID 3358. ERDA Office of Public Affairs/Technical Information Center, Feb. 1976. 203 pp. $12.50. (NTIS)

Citations of domestic and foreign publications, arranged in subject categories and cross-indexed.

NUCLEAR ENERGY

References, Overviews, and Issues

Ahmed, S. Basheer. *Nuclear Fuel and Energy Policy.* Lexington Books, 1979. 192 pp. $17.00.

An analysis of the economics of the nuclear fuel cycle, including the uranium industry, mining, milling, and enrichment, and fuel fabrication, with price forecasts.

American Nuclear Society. *Questions and Answers: Nuclear Power and the Environment.* American Nuclear Society, 555 N. Kensington Ave., La Grange Park, IL 60525. 1979. 128 pp. $4.00.

The views of the industry on energy independence, economics, reliability, radiation, waste disposal, safety, benefit/risk, insurance, breeder reactors, fusion, and alternative technology are presented here.

Bello, Walden; Hayes, Peter; and Zarsky, Lyuba. *'500-Mile Island'—The Philippine Nuclear Reactor Deal.* In *Pacific Research,* Vol. X No. 1, June 1979. Pacific Studies Center, 867 W. Dana, #204, Mountain View, CA 94041. 45 pp. $1.50.

A series of articles examining the nuclear industry's encroachment on the lives of the Filipinos, Australian aborigines, Micronesians, and Native Americans, and the commercial and political interests behind this technology.

Berger, John J. *Nuclear Power: The Unviable Option.* Palo Alto, Calif.: Remparts Press, 1976. 384 pp. $4.50. (EARS) Also, Revised Edition, New York, N.Y.: Dell, 1977. 381 pp. $2.50.

An analysis of nuclear power and its backers, it economics and its risks. Nuclear technology, clean energy alternatives, and the rising tide of citizen action are also described. Comprehensive, carefully researched, and eminently readable.

Bupp, Irvin C., and Derian, Jean-Claude. *Light Water: How the Nuclear Dream Dissolved.* New York, N.Y.: Basic Books, 1978. 241 pp. $10.00.

Only ten years ago the light water nuclear technology had achieved a monopoly in the United States and Europe, but it is now at the point of collapsing. Although the authors are nuclear advocates, they are highly critical of the self-delusion and oversell engaged in by the industry and government in the promotion of nuclear power, and deplore the secrecy surrounding nuclear safety issues.

Croall, Stephen. *The Anti-Nuclear Handbook.* See *ENERGY EDUCATION: BOOKS FOR YOUNG PEOPLE.*

Duffy, Gloria, and Adams, Gordon. *Power Politics: The Nuclear Industry and Nuclear Exports.* New York, N.Y.: Council on Economic Priorities, 1978. 131 pp. $5.00. (EARS)

The global nuclear energy market is the subject of this study, which provides data on reactor exports, the activities of the major U.S. nuclear companies here and abroad, and on U.S. government policies.

Eichholz, Geoffrey G. *Environmental Aspects of Nuclear Power.* Ann Arbor, Mich.: Ann Arbor Science Publishers, 1977. 683 pp. $37.50.

A text intended for nuclear engineers, the nuclear industry, environmental scientists, and energy policy makers. It includes data on radiation emitted by nuclear facilities, by the transportation of nuclear materials, and by radioactive wastes. The effects of thermal and air pollution, changes in local meteorology, and the discharge of other toxic effluents are also discussed.

Elliott, Dave. *The Politics of Nuclear Power.* London: Pluto Press, 1978. 142 pp. $4.95.

Questions are raised concerning the effects of the new industry on employment, trade unions, health and safety, and who pays and who benefits. Alternative energy sources and political strategies of the anti-nuclear movement are also discussed.

Environmental Action Foundation. *Countdown to a Nuclear Moratorium.* Washington, D.C.: Environmental Action Foundation, 724 Dupont Circle Building N.W., 20036, 1976. 197 pp. $3.00. (EARS)

A collection of articles on the issues of safety, economics, civil liberties, and energy demand, by Gofman, Tamplin, Gravel, Comey, Clark, Hayes, and others.

Foreman, Harry, ed. *Nuclear Power and the Public.* Minneapolis, Minn.: University of Minnesota Press, 1970. 273 pp. $9.00.

A symposium on health hazards to the public from nuclear power, ecological considerations in siting, radioactivity's physiological effects, thermal pollution, regulation of radiation, and policies affecting society's energy needs.

Francis, John, and Abrecht, Paul, eds. *Facing Up to Nuclear Power.* World Council of Churches. Philadelphia, Pa.: Westminster Press, 1976. 244 pp. $3.95.

Nuclear proponents and nuclear critics argue about the potential benefits and the unavoidable risks of large scale use of nuclear power, exploring economic, ecological, and ethical issues, developing countries, world peace, and alternative energy options.

Garvey, Gerald. *Nuclear Power and Social Planning: The City of the Second Sun.* Lexington, Mass.: Lexington Books, 1977. 192 pp. $16.00.

The integration of American nuclear policy and social planning is proposed, with considerations of nuclear technology, economics and risks; fusion, power parks, and inter-regional nuclear bargains.

Gofman, John W. *"IRREVY": An Irreverent, Illustrated View of Nuclear Power. A Collection of Talks from Blunderland to Seabrook IV.* Committee for Nuclear Responsibility, Main P.O. Box 11207, San Francisco, CA 94101. 1979. 246 pp. $3.95.

With piercing wit and anger Dr. Gofman points out the folly and the injustice of the nuclear technology which amounts to the license to commit random murder against the population. Anti-nuclear activists will find many useful quotations and cartoons on the effects of radiation and radioactive waste, nuclear weapons, law versus justice, civil disovedience, and an explanation of why nuclear power holds such charm for the energy planners.

Gofman, John W., and Tamplin, Arthur R. *Poisoned Power: The Case Against Nuclear Power Plants Before and After Three Mile Island.* Emmaus, Pa.: Rodale, 1971, revised 1979. 353 pp. $9.95.

Since Three Mile Island, the public has become more aware of the dangers of radiation, and of the monumental non-preparation of the utilities and the Nuclear Regulatory Commission. This book points out the health hazards to this and future generations, and the lies and cover-ups by government and industry. It also offers an alternative program, and a guide to citizen action.

Gyorgy, Anna, and Friends. *No Nukes: Everyone's Guide to Nuclear Power.* South End Press, Box 68, Astor Station, Boston, MA 02123. 1978. 288 pp. $8.00. (EARS) (Re-Source)

No activist should be without this useful reference. If you want to know about the history of atomic power, the nuclear fuel cycle, health dangers, economics, politics, or radioactive waste, it is all there and can be located quickly. There are also reports and maps from all over the world and the United States showing the location of nuclear reactors, and giving details of the citizens' movement to stop nuclear power. A section on alternative energy options is included.

Hayes, Denis. *Nuclear Power: The Fifth Horseman.* Washington, DC: Worldwatch Institute, 1976. 68 pp. $2.00. (FOE) (EARS)

Outlines the nuclear fuel cycle and its problems; nuclear weapons proliferation, terrorism, and the implications for society.

Inglis, David R. *Nuclear Energy: Its Physics and Its Social Challenge.* Reading, Mass.: Addison-Wesley, 1973. 395 pp. $5.95.

Designed for use as a college text, it gives insights into both the scientific and humanistic aspects of the problems of nuclear energy and nuclear weapons as a background for political judgments. Objective and very readable.

International Atomic Energy Agency. *Catalogue.* Vienna: IAEA Publications, 1978/79. 247 pp. U.S. address: UNIPUB, 345 Park Ave. South, New York, NY 10010.

Lists all publications of the agency, such as directories, bibliographies, technical reports, proceedings and periodicals in the field of nuclear science. Gives complete details, including summaries of contents. Publications are in English, French, Russian, and Spanish.

International Atomic Energy Agency. *Directory of Nuclear Reactors.* Vienna: IAEA Publications, annual volumes from 1959 to date. (UNIPUB)

Gives complete information on nuclear reactors throughout the world.

International Atomic Energy Agency. *Nuclear Power and Its Fuel Cycle.* Proceedings of an international conference at Salzburg, May 2-13, 1977.

Eight large volumes contain research papers on general energy prospects, integrated planning of the fuel cycle, reprocessing, standards for radioactivity management, nuclear safety, nuclear power in developing countries, nuclear power and public opinion, and an index.

Jungk, Robert. *Brighter Than a Thousand Suns.* New York, N.Y.: Penguin, 1970.
Excellent historical account of the early years of nuclear development.

Jungk, Robert. *The New Tyranny: How Nuclear Power Enslaves Us.* New York, N.Y.:
Warner, 1979. 268 pp. $2.50.
In this frightening indictment of the international nuclear establishment,
Jungk reveals the full extent of the dangers posed by nuclear power and
nuclear weapons. The risks entailed in the use of nuclear energy demand ever-
increasing security, surveillance, intimidation, and abridgment of human
rights and democratic freedom. An infallible *Homo atomicus* must be created to
maintain nuclear facilities. Our hope lies in the growing movement toward
the Soft Energy Path. Appendices include notes on the Three Mile Island
accident, and resource lists.

Kadiroglu, Osman K.; Perlmutter, Arnold; and Scott, Linda. *Nuclear Energy and
Alternatives.* Proceedings of the International Scientific Forum on an
Acceptable Nuclear Energy Future of the World. Cambridge, Mass.: Ballinger,
1978. 768 pp. $42.95.
Planning for future global energy requirements, and world developments
to meet this demand, requires the consideration of the economic and political
implications, environmental impact, proliferation and safeguards, and waste
disposal problems.

Karam, R.A., and Morgan, Karl Z., eds. *Environmental Impact of Nuclear Power Plants.*
Proceedings of a conference held Nov. 1974 at Georgia Institute of
Technology. Elmsford, N.Y.: Pergamon Press, 1976. 546 pp.
A meeting of experts from government, industry, and universities to study
the environmental impact of various power sources, especially nuclear, and
the cost-benefit ratios of each. One participant found the time scale and the
acreage which will be required to store radioactive wastes both staggering and
unacceptable. John Gofman offered critical comments on the nuclear
industry.

Knelman, Fred H. *Nuclear Energy. The Unforgiving Technology.* Edmonton, Canada:
Hurtig, 1976. 264 pp. $4.95.
Dr. Knelman believes that the people must have the power and knowledge
to determine the sources of energy, rather than be forced to accept the
decisions of "experts" of the global nuclear establishment. The author
identifies the safety and economic pitfalls of nuclear energy, and charts the
history of Canadian groups oposed to nuclear weapons and nuclear energy.
Conservation is offered as an alternative.

Lanoue, Ron. *Nuclear Plants: The More They Build, The More You Pay.* Center for
Study of Responsive Law, P.O. Box 19367, Washington, DC 20036. 1977. 92
pp. $5/$10.
Explains why nuclear power is as bad for our pocketbook as it is for our
health and safety. Data on energy efficiency, alternative energy technologies,
costs, problems, government subsidies, jobs, and citizen action strategies.
Invaluable to the activist.

Lomenick, T.F., and Nuclear Safety Information Center. *Earthquakes and Nuclear
Power Plant Design.* Oak Ridge, Tenn.: Oak Ridge National Laboratory, 1970.
215 pp.
Technical paper on earthquake and tsunami effects, and designs required to
accomodate these motions. Specific site studies included.

Lovins, Amory. *Is Nuclear Power Necessary?* London: FOE Ltd., 1979. 50 pp. $4.00. (FOE)

Lovins examines the potential ability of nuclear power, in an international context, to reduce dependence on imported oil. He finds nuclear power inadequate and uneconomical, since it supplies only a special and very expensive form of energy—electricity—whilst most needs are for lower quality and cheaper forms of energy. Alternative investments in efficiency improvements, transitional fossil fuel technologies, and renewable energy sources can provide relief more quickly and easily, and at a much lower cost.

McPhee, John. *The Curve of Binding Energy.* New York, N.Y.: Ballantine Books, 1973. 170 pp. $1.50.

Discusses nuclear security, material unaccounted for by the AEC, the prospect of private nuclear proliferation, and the inevitability of a serious accident.

Metzger, H. Peter. *The Atomic Establishment.* New York, N.Y.: Simon & Schuster, 1972. 318 pp. $8.95.

Examines the politics of nuclear power, and points out the shortcomings of the Atomic Energy Commission and government regulation of the hazards of the atomic industry and the nuclear weapons program.

Myers, Desaix III. *The Nuclear Power Debate: Moral, Economic, Technical, and Political Issues.* New York, N.Y.: Praeger, 1977. 166 pp. $16.95.

The author seeks to provide a basic understanding of primary issues, rather than pass judgment on the costs and benefits. Questions are raised concerning public policy and corporate social responsibility, the long range consequences of nuclear power development, safety, economics, and technology.

Nader, Ralph, and Abbotts, John. *The Menace of Atomic Energy.* New York, N.Y.: Norton, Revised Edition, 1979. 431 pp. $4.95.

Recent developments are included in this definitive handbook on the environmental, social, and economic aspects of nuclear power. It relates how the industry began, how it works, and how the government regulates and promotes it. This is a book of solutions, with suggestions and resources for citizens who wish to become involved in the controversy.

Nealey, Stanley. *Nuclear Power and the Public.* Battelle Human Affairs Research Center. Lexington, Mass.: Lexington Books, 1979.

Attitudes on nuclear power and general energy issues are analyzed in this survey of many aspects such as pollution, waste disposal, safety, health, proliferation, and terrorism.

Nero, Anthony V., Jr. *A Guidebook to Nuclear Reactors.* Berkeley, Calif.: University of California Press, 1979. 289 pp. $9.95.

Writing for the layman, Nero provides information on the basic reactor design features of various types of reactors and fuel cycles now available, and the advantages and liabilities associated with their use. He assumes that reliance on nuclear power will continue to increase in the near future, since the nations of the world seem unwilling to set limits on the growth of energy use. Good illustrations, glossary, and index add to the usefulness of this encyclopedia.

Noyes, Robert, ed. *Offshore and Underground Power Plants.* Park Ridge, N.J.: Noyes Data Corporation, 1977. 308 pp. $42.00.

Various proposals have been made for the siting of nuclear and fossil fuel plants offshore and underground. Among the factors to be considered are the availability of cooling water, proximity to load centers, land use, and the effects of possible accidents upon nearby populations and the environment.

Nuclear Energy Policy Study Group. *Nuclear Power Issues and Choices.* Sponsored by the Ford Foundation and administered by the MITRE Corporation. Cambridge, Mass.: Ballinger, 1977. 418 pp. $8.95.
The economics of coal and nuclear power are examined, and both are found to be suitable short-term choices. However, nuclear power is not considered critical to future economic development. The advantages of conservation are also noted. The hazards of nuclear proliferation and the plutonium economy are pointed out, but nuclear waste and safety problems are minimized. This report is unlikely to please either pro- or anti-nuclear forces.

Patterson, Walter C. *The Fissile Society.* London: Earth Resources Research, 1977. 117 pp. $3.50.
Patterson recapitulates the history of the development of the nuclear industry and its blood ancestor, nuclear weaponry. He then describes the potential dangers of an exponential electricity growth curve and the increasing dependency of society upon electricity.

Patterson, Walter C. *Nuclear Power.* Middlesex, England: Penguin Books, 1976. 304 pp. $3.50. (EARS)
Surveys the development of worldwide nuclear power and its hazards. Delineates the technical, economic, social, and political issues with wit and clarity.

Pederson, Erik S. *Nuclear Power.* Ann Arbor, Mich.: Ann Arbor Science Publishers, 1978. Vol. 1, *Nuclear Power Plant Design.* 558 pp. Vol. 2, *Nuclear Power Project Management.* 397 pp. $37.50 per volume, or $60.00 for the set.
Designed as a reference or a text for nuclear designers, engineers, and plant managers, and libraries, these volumes cover all aspects of this field.

Penner, S.S. *Energy: Volume III. Nuclear Energy and Energy Policies.* Reading, Mass.: Addison-Wesley, 1976. 713 pp. $19.50.
This series of lecture notes for advanced physical science majors deals with all nuclear technologies, including fusion. In formulating energy policies, many factors must be considered, such as population growth, food production, worldwide energy use, energy-induced climatological changes, energy conservation, and the comparative hazards of different energy sources.

Pringle, Lawrence. *Nuclear Power from Physics to Politics.* See *ENERGY EDUCATION: BOOKS FOR YOUNG PEOPLE.*

Stockholm Conference. *ECO II: Atomic Reactor Safety Hearings. August-September 1972.* San Francisco, Calif.: Friends of the Earth. 120 pp. $5.00. (FOE)
Eleven reports from the AEC's hearings on the emergency core-cooling system. Contains Amory Lovins' devastating analysis of the breeder reactor.

Stockholm Conference. *ECO III: Nuclear Industry Meetings. November 1973.* San Francisco, Calif.: Friends of the Earth. $5.00. (FOE)
Seven issues, unbound, cover meetings of the Atomic Industrial Forum and the American Nuclear Society. Contains embarrassing questions and relevant news the reactor-sellers want to gloss over.

Stockholm Conference. *ECO VI: Nuclear Industry Meetings. Novermber 1975.* San Francisco, Calif.: Friends of the Earth. $5.00. (FOE)

Five issues, unbound. An account of how the professional societies of the nuclear industry met to cover up the atom's dangers.

Stockholm International Peace Institute. *The Nuclear Age.* Cambridge, Mass.: Massachusetts Institute of Technology Press, 1975. 275 pp. $6.95.

A non-technical study of nuclear power, reactor operation, safeguards, waste, weapons and the non-proliferation treaty. Contains a useful glossary.

Union of Concerned Scientists. *The Nuclear Fuel Cycle: A Survey of the Public Health, Environmental, and National Security Effects of Nuclear Power.* Boston, Mass.: Massachusetts Institute of Technology Press, 1975. 275 pp. $5.25. (FOE) (EARS) (UCS)

Explores the major technical problems and the potential dangers of each step in the nuclear fuel cycle, from uranium mining to the hoped-for disposal of radioactive waste.

Vermont Public Interest Research Group. *The Final Shutdown: A Vermont PIRG White Paper on Decommissioning.* Vermont PIRG, 26 State St., Montpelier, VT 05602. 1979. $2.00.

The problems of nuclear power plant decommissioning are addressed in this study, which points out the failure of federal regulation and the need to develop plans and assure adequate funds.

Warnock, Donna. *Nuclear Power and Civil Liberties: Can We Have Both?* Washington, DC: Citizens' Energy Project, 1978. 120 pp. $5.00/$7.00. (CEP)

Violation of civil liberties and an eventual police state are inherent in the nuclear society because of the necessity of maintaining stringent safeguards against potential terrorists. There are already documented cases of the harassment and surveillance of nuclear opponents and persons involved in nuclear work.

The Controversy Over Nuclear Power

Abalone Alliance and the University of California Nuclear Weapons Laboratory Conversion Project. *First There Was the Bomb, Then . . . Came Atoms For Peace.* Abalone Alliance, 944 Market St., Rm. 307, San Francisco, CA 94102. 1979. 104 pp. $1.50.

An illustrated handbook of recent articles on nuclear power and nuclear weapons issues, and the political and technological links between them. Also considers the impact on health and public welfare, and energy alternatives. Lists California safe-energy organizations.

Citizens' Energy Project. *Nuclear Quotes Book.* Citizens' Energy Project, 1110 Sixth St. NW, #300, Washington, DC 20001. 1978. 26 pp. $2.25. (CEP)

This is a well illustrated collection of quotes on nuclear power and safe alternatives, from experts and public figures, ranging from the ridiculous to the sublime. It is a good resource for newsletter writers, who are invited to plagiarize.

Ebbin, Steven, and Dasper, Raphael. *Citizen Groups and the Nuclear Power Controversy: Uses of Scientific and Technological Information.* Cambridge, Mass.: MIT Press, 1974. 292 pp. $6.95.

Traces citizen involvement in nuclear power issues, and cites specific cases.

Makes recommendations to provide greater public understanding of scientific and technological issues, ensure judicious consideration of matters of public concern, and allow for more adequate public participation in the decision-making process.

Faulkner, Peter. *The Silent Bomb: A Guide to the Nuclear Power Controversy.* New York, N.Y.: Vintage/Friends of the Earth International, 1977. 382 pp. $3.95. (EARS)
This is an arsenal of articles and testimony by nuclear critics, with new explanatory material by Faulkner, that reveals the inner workings of the nuclear industry, and the financial and governmental interests behind it. It includes the testimony of the three General Electric engineers who resigned.

McTaggart, David, with Hunter, Robert. *Greenpeace III: Journey Into the Bomb.* New York, N.Y.: Morrow, 1979. 372 pp. $10.95.
The engrossing saga of the Greenpeace ketch which sailed into the fallout zone of the French H-bomb tests in the South Pacific points up the efficacy of dramatic protests. There is also a necessity for an accompanying groundswell of public opinion against nation states that ruthlessly pursue their own perceived "self-interests".

Laitner, Skip. *Citizens' Guide to Nuclear Power.* Washington, DC: Center for Study of Responsive Law, 1975. 94 pp. $5.00.
Includes a brief overview of nuclear power; specific suggestions for challenging power plant economics and emergency planning; evacuation plans and the law; citizen action strategies; legislative remedies; and references.

Lewis, Laura, and Morell, David. *Nuclear Power and Its Opponenets: A New Jersey Case Study.* Center for Environmental Studies, Princeton University May 1977. 138 pp.
A study of citizen groups in the nuclear power debate—their motives, dynamics, membership, strategies, and effectiveness in contributing to public participation in energy decisions.

Lewis, Richard S. *The Nuclear Power Rebellion: Citizens vs. the Atomic Industrial Establishment.* New York, N.Y.: Viking Press, 1972. $8.95.
A critical, non-technical review of the AEC's programs, including radioactive waste management. Lewis also examines the politics of nuclear power and citizen protest.

National No Nukes Strategy Conference. National No Nukes Report, 628 Rubel Ave., Louisville, KY 40204. August 1978. 47 pp. $2.00.
This excellent handbook on anti-nuclear organizing contains regional summaries and nationwide lists of contacts and organizations.

Nelkin, Dorothy. *Nuclear Power and Its Critics: The Cayuga Lake Controversy.* Ithaca, N.Y.: Cornell University Press, 1971. 128 pp.
A case study of the citizens' struggle to prevent nuclear power development at Cayuga Lake. Illustrates the need to consider environmental concerns in the design and siting of nuclear power plants, and the need for coordinated regulatory activities on state, local, and federal levels.

Novick, Sheldon. *The Electric War—The Fight Over Nuclear Power.* San Francisco, Calif.: Sierra Club Books, 1976. 376 pp. $12.50. (EARS)
People in the forefront of the controversy speak for themselves: scientists, officials, politicians, miners, plant employees, and concerned citizens opposed to nuclear power. Reveals what the nuclear industry is, how it came into

being, and the extent of its effects.

Olson, McKinley C. *Unacceptable Risk: What You Should Know About Nuclear Power After Three Mile Island*. New York, N.Y.: Bantam, 1979. 310 pp. $2.95. (EARS)
Olson chronicles the history of the citizens' anti-nuclear movement, and tells how to become involved. He describes nuclear technology, the dangers of radiation, and the involvement of the federal government with the nuclear industry. Three Mile Island was a warning that nuclear power is an unacceptable—and unnecessary—risk.

Wasserman, Harvey. *The Energy War: Reports from the Front*. Westport, Conn.: Lawrence Hill, 1979. 253 pp. $5.95. (ReSource)
A series of articles and eye-witness news stories relates the hazards of nuclear power, and the on-going campaigns against reactor projects in New England, Texas, California, Southeast Asia, Japan, and elsewhere. Alternatives to nuclear power and the movement toward a solar society are also discussed.

Economics

Gaines, Linda; Berry, Stephen R., and Long, Thomas Veach II. *TOSCA: The Total Cost of Coal and Nuclear Power*. Cambridge, Mass.: Ballinger, 1978. 136 pp. $17.50.
A demand model is developed to determine what mix of coal-fired and nuclear-powered plants will achieve the minimum total social cost.

Komanoff, Charles. *A Comparison of Nuclear and Coal Costs*. Komanoff Energy Associates, 475 Park Ave. South, 32nd floor, New York, N.Y. 10016. 1978. 178 pp. $10.00.
A comprehensive analysis of nuclear and coal generating costs, including capital costs, the nuclear fuel cycle, coal mining, plant reliability, financing costs, and the reasons why costs are increasing.

Komanoff, Charles. *Nuclear Plant Performance Update 2*. Komanoff Energy Associates, 475 Park Ave. South, 32nd floor, New York, N.Y. 10016. 1978. 114 pp. $3.00.
This statistical review of U.S. reactor capacity factors includes data through 1977. Another review will be forthcoming in 1980.

Komanoff, Charles. *Nuclear Power Costs: Past, Present, Future*. Komanoff Energy Associates, 475 Park Ave. South, 32nd floor, New York, NY 10016. 1979. 13 pp. $1.50.
Testimony was presented before the U.S. House Interior Committee on July 12, 1979, comparing the capital costs of nuclear power to those of coal, oil, and gas. Also included were estimates of the effect of the Three Mile Island accident on nuclear costs, and how energy efficiency improvements contribute to energy supply.

Komanoff, Charles. *Power Plant Escalation: Nuclear and Coal Capital Costs and Economics*. (title tentative). Komanoff Energy Associates, 475 Park Ave. South, 32nd floor, New York, NY 10016. 1979. Approx. 200 pp. $12.00.
A major study of construction costs of recent nuclear and coal plants, and a projection of future costs.

Komanoff, Charles. *Power Plant Performance: Nuclear and Coal Capacity Factors and Economics*. Council on Economic Priorities, 84 Fifth Ave., New York, NY 10011.

1976. 214 pp. $10.00. A 6-page summary is $1.00 from CEP or EARS.

A challenge to the Long Island Lighting Company's assertion that installing two nuclear units would save $2 billion in life-cycle costs as compared to coal fired plants.

Miller, Saunders, and Severance, Craig. *The Economics of Nuclear and Coal Power.* New York, N.Y.: Praeger, 1976. 172 pp. $17.50.

A book review in Barron's business publication said, "If the top executives of every electric utility in the nation . . . read (this book) . . . most nuclear plant construction plans would be scrapped." Miller's research concludes that the uranium shortage will become severe, that coal-fired plant performance records are superior to those of nuclear plants, and that to rely upon nuclear fission as a primary source of energy would constitute economic lunacy.

Morgan, Richard. *Nuclear Power: The Bargain We Can't Afford.* Washington, DC: Environmental Action Foundation, 1977. 96 pp. $3.50. (EARS)

Do you wonder why the utilities and the government find nuclear power profitable? Do you know the extent of the hidden costs that must be borne by the taxpayers now and far into the future? This book is laced with quotable facts, and includes tips on how to challenge nuclear expansion in your area.

Ramsay, William. *Unpaid Costs of Electrical Energy: Health and Environmental Impacts from Coal and Nuclear Power.* Washington, DC: Resources for the Future, 1978. 202 pp. $4.95.

The health, safety, and environmental costs of coal and nuclear power are compared, from mine through the generating system.

U.S. Congress. *Federal Government Incentives to Coal and Nuclear Energy.* Washington, DC, 1979. S/N 052-070-05445-4. 65 pp. $3.00. (USGPO)

Details of the various federally provided incentives to the coal and nuclear industries.

U.S. Congress, House Committee on Government Operations. *Nuclear Power Costs.* Washington, DC, 1978. House Report #95-1090. #PB-28647. $8.00. (NTIS)

In this controversial report on the economic costs of nuclear power, nuclear critics cite the hidden and the still uncalculated costs of the entire nuclear fuel cycle.

Wisconsin Environmental Decade. *The Nuclear Economics Question.* Wisconsin Environmental Decade, 114 E. Mifflin St., Madison, WI 53703. 1978. 92 pp. $2.00.

Nuclear power would be 83% more expensive for Wisconsin than coal-fired plants, according to this response to the utility's plans for expansion.

Future Technology: Breeder Reactors and Fusion

Chow, Brian G. *The Liquid Metal Fast Breeder Reactor: An Economic Analysis.* Washington, DC: American Enterprise Institute for Public Policy Research, 1150 17th St., NW, Washington, DC 20036. 1975. 76 pp. $3.00.

Examines the Nuclear Regulatory Commission's cost-benefit analysis of the breeder program, and calls for the redistribution of research funds to more promising energy sources.

Cochran, Thomas B. *The Liquid Metal Fast Breeder Reactor: An Environmental and Economic Critique.* Baltimore, Md.: The Johns Hopkins University Press, 1974. 271 pp. $6.95.

Analyzes the economic costs, environmental impact, and safety aspects of the LMFBR and concludes that it should receive a lower priority of Federal funding.

Fuller, John G. *We Almost Lost Detroit.* New York, N.Y.: Readers' Digest Press, 1975. 272 pp. $1.95. (EARS)

The documented account of the near-disaster at the Liquid Metal Fast Breeder Reactor near Detroit; other accidents are also described.

Häfele, W.; Holdren, J.P.; Kessler, G.; and Kulcinski, G.L. *Fusion and Fast Breeder Reactors.* Laxenburg. Austria: International Institute for Applied Systems Analysis. Revised 1977. 506 pp.

The liquid metal fast breeder reactor (LMFBR) and the deuterium-tritium fusion reactor (TOKAMAK) are compared. Both reactors can potentially produce practically unlimited—but possible expensive—amounts of energy.

Hagler, M.O., and Kristiansen, M. *An Introduction to Controlled Thermonuclear Fusion.* Lexington, Mass.: Lexington Books, 1977. 208 pp. $18.00.

The theory of fusion and the present status of thermonuclear research are reviewed in this technical treatise.

Kammash, Terry. *Fusion Reactor Physics: Principles of Technology.* Ann Arbor, Mich.: Ann Arbor Science Publishers, 1977. 495 pp. $36.00.

Suitable for the general scientific reader, this college text provides comprehensive coverage of basic processes in fusion reactors, present status of development, and future prospects.

Montefiore, Hugh, and Gosling, David, eds. *Nuclear Crisis: A Question of Breeding.* Dorchester, England: Prism, 1977, 165 pp. $2.50.

Expert British witnesses testify on needs and goals of society, economic and social risks of fast breeder reactors, technical feasibility, and alternatives.

U.S. Department of Energy. *Final Report of the Ad Hoc Experts Group on Fusion.* Washington, DC, 1978. S/N 061-000-00102-6. 24 pp. $1.30. (USGPO)

The current state of fusion energy research is reviewed, with recommendations for the direction of future research.

World Survey of Major Facilities in Controlled Fusion Research. 1976 Edition: *Nuclear Fusion* Special Supplement 1976. International Atomic Energy Agency, 1976. 866 pp. $48.00. (UNIPUB)

Contains detailed information by device type, including laser, and research activities of the scientific staffs of many nations.

Proliferation, Nuclear Weapons, and War

Aldridge, Robert C. *The Counterforce Syndrome: A Guide to U.S. Nuclear Weapons and Strategic Doctrine.* Institute for Policy Studies, 1901 Q Street NW, Washington, DC 20009. 1978, 1979. 86 pp. $3.95.

Do you know what the Pentagon has in store for you? Aldridge, an aeronautical engineer who resigned from Lockheed in 1973, tells how "counterforce"—massive disabling first-strike capability—has replaced the doctrine of "deterrence". He describes weapons systems, including the Trident and the MX, and discusses some of the obstacles to disarmament, such as the drive for profits by weapons manufacture, and the fear of job loss.

Barton, John H., and Weiler, Lawrence D., eds. *International Arms Control: Issues and Agreements*. Palo Alto, Calif.: Stanford University Press, 1976. 444 pp. $12.95.
This text traces the history of disarmament efforts, and discusses national security policy, the ethics of war, and the effectiveness of strategic doctrines.

Chayes, Abram, and Lewis, W. Bennett, eds. *International Arrangements for Nuclear Fuel Reprocessing*. Cambridge, Mass.: Ballinger, 1977. 252 pp. $16.50.
A Pugwash symposium focuses on the technical, political, and economic issues in multinational control of the nuclear fuel reactor cycle.

Cubie, James. *Myths and Realities: Nuclear Power, Nuclear Bombs*. Center for Study of Responsive Law, Box 19367, Washington, DC 20036. 60 pp. $4.00.
The evidence presented here disposes of the myth that exported nuclear technology will be used for peaceful purposes only, and shows the reality of international nuclear proliferation, and what options remain.

Epstein, William. *The Last Chance: Nuclear Proliferation and Arms Control*. New York, N.Y.: Free Press, 1976. 342 pp. $14.95. (EARS)
Provides a basic history of the proliferation of nuclear arms, and attempts at its control. Epstein analyzes the dilemma posed to world security and makes recommendations, for what may be the last chance for human survival.

Glasstone, Samuel, and Dolan, Philip J. *The Effects of Nuclear Weapons*. U.S. Department of Defense and Department of Energy. Washington, DC: USGPO, 1977. 653 pp. $7.00. #008-046-00093-0 (USGPO).
A comprehensive analysis of the characteristics of nuclear explosions and their effects upon exposed persons, structures, and terrain, biological and genetic effects, and radiation pathology.

Gompert, David C; Mandelbaum, Michael; Garwin, Richard L.; and Barton, John H. *Nuclear Weapons and World Politics: Alternatives for the Future*. The 1980's Project/Council on Foreign Relations. New York, N.Y.: McGraw Hill, 1977. 369 pp. $6.95.
Four nuclear regimes are proposed for the control of weapons and the problems they pose for international peace and progress, with a consideration of the potential for destruction and the dilemmas of political choice. Views range from "nuclear weapons foster stability" to "nuclear weapons are an intolerable menace."

Greenwood, Ted, Feiveson, Harold A., and Taylor, Theodore B. *Nuclear Proliferation: Motivations, Capabilities, and Strategies for Control*. The 1980s Project Studies/Council on Foreign Relations. New York, N.Y.: McGraw Hill, 1977. 210 pp. $4.95
An investigation into the political and security objectives of nations, the expansion and management of the international nuclear industry, and possible strategies for the international control of nuclear power. Scenarios for three alternative fission futures are presented. Although the authors do not consider non-nuclear alternatives, they present important information and viewpoints.

Griffiths, Franklyn, and Polanyi, John C. *The Dangers of Nuclear War*. University of Toronto Press, 33 East Tupper St., Buffalo, NY 14203. 1979. 197 pp. $5.95.
The 30th Pugwash Symposium, held in Toronto in May 1978, was attended

by scholars from eleven countries, who pondered the issues of nuclear proliferation, weapons, and the arms race; the developments which threaten nuclear war; and whether war will be averted through wisdom or through luck. The idea of 'winning' a nuclear war must be abandoned, considering the totally disastrous consequences for civilization. Fatalism must be replaced by new patterns of international conduct. This sober analysis merits the careful attention of both statesmen and the general public.

Johnson, Brian. *Whose Power to Choose?* International Institute for Environment and Development. Leigh-on-Sea, Essex, England: Temtex, 1977. 79 pp. $2.75.
  What are the politics of proliferating plutonium? How does the International Atomic Energy Agency both promote and control atomic energy? The author proposes strategies and reforms to avoid dependence on plutonium, offer developing countries a greater range of choice in planning for their energy needs, and solve problems of safeguards and nuclear waste disposal.

Kapur, Ashok. *International Nuclear Proliferation: Global Diplomacy and National Perceptions.* New York, N.Y.: Praeger, 1979. 250 pp. $20.00.
  The technical and political limitations of international nuclear safeguards as perceived by the non-nuclear nations.

Lens, Sidney. *The Day Before Doomsday: An Anatomy of the Nuclear Arms Race.* Garden City, New York: Doubleday, 1977. 274 pp. $8.95.
  A devastating indictment of the U.S. nuclear arms policy, and a feasible plan to defuse this growing menace to civilization.

Libby, Leona M. *The Uranium People.* New York, N.Y.: Scribner's, 1979. 335 pp. $15.95.
  The story of the Manhattan Project and the fourteen scientists who built and tested the first A-bombs and H-bombs is told—without apologies—by the lone woman of the group. Recommended by Dr. Edward Teller.

Phillips, John A., and Michaelis, David. *Mushroom: The Story of the A-Bomb Kid.* New York, N.Y.: Pocket Books, 1978. 265 pp. $2.50.
  Here is how a Princeton physics student took some textbooks and information supplied by government and industry, and designed an atomic bomb powerful enough to wipe out one fourth of Manhattan—and how the government reacted. It is an entertaining book, but carries serious messages of the need for stricter nuclear safeguards, and the threat of nuclear proliferation.

Rochlin, Gene I. *Plutonium, Power, and Politics: International Arrangements for the Disposition of Spent Nuclear Fuel.* Berkeley, Calif.: University of California Press, 1979. 397 pp. $22.95.
  The worldwide diffusion of commercial nuclear technology contributes to the spread of nuclear weapons and threatens world peace. This study explores the international options for the regulation of the back end of the nuclear fuel cycle, and the economic, political, technological, and environmental factors involved.

U.S. Congress. House Committee on International Relations, and Senate Committee on Government Affairs. *Nuclear Proliferation Factbook.* Washington, DC, 1977. (USGPO)
  A sourcebook on the many aspects of the development of nuclear power and nuclear weapons.

U.S. Congress. Office of Technology Assessment. *The Effects of Nuclear War.* Washington, DC, 1979. S/N 052-003-00668-5. 151 pp. $4.75. (USGPO)

What would be the impact of a nuclear war upon the civilian population, the economics, and the societies of the U.S. and the USSR?

U.S. Congress. Office of Technology Assessment. *Nuclear Proliferation and Safeguards.* New York, N.Y.: Praeger, 1977. 288 pp. $22.95.

The major issues of nuclear proliferation and methods of control are analyzed, and suggestions made for increased safeguards.

U.S. Congress. *Reader on Nuclear Nonproliferation.* Washington, DC, 1978. S/N 052-070-04804-2. 504 pp. $5.25. (USGPO)

Forty-one articles illustrate the range of recent thinking on the prospect of the further spread of nuclear weapons.

Wohlstetter, Albert; Gilinsky, Victor; Gillette, Robert; and Wohlstetter, Roberta. *Nuclear Policies: Fuel Without the Bomb.* Cambridge, Mass.: Ballinger, 1978. 128 pp. $16.50.

Essays from the California Seminar on Arms Control and Foreign Policy address the technical, political, and economic aspects of nuclear proliferation as nations search for new energy sources and nuclear technology spreads around the world.

Radiation

Brodine, Virginia. *Radioactive Contamination.* Scientists' Institute for Public Information. New York, N.Y.: Harcourt, Brace, and Jovanovich, 1975. 190 pp. $6.95. (EARS)

Excellent presentation of the sources of radioactivity and the effects of radioactive emissions upon human life and the environment.

Caldicott, Helen, M.D. *Nuclear Madness.* Brookline, Mass.: Autumn Press, 1978. 120 pp. $3.95. (EARS)

Despite the melodramatic title, this eloquent yet reasonable book is packed with solid information. Dr. Caldicott, a pediatrician and nuclear critic, contends that nuclear technology threatens life on our planet with extinction. This is confirmed by her well-documented account of radiation, the nuclear fuel cycle, nuclear weapons, and the policies and deceptions employed by government and industry. She concludes with a call for citizen action to halt this suicidal course.

Cushing, C.E. Jr. *Radioecology and Energy Resources.* Proceedings of the Fourth National Symposium on Radioecology. New York, N.Y.: Halsted Press, 1976. 401 pp. $25.00.

An examination of the radioecological problems associated with the development of energy sources, and the effects of radionucleotides and ionization radiation in aquatic and terrestrial ecosystems.

Eichholz, Geoffrey G., and Poston, John W. *Principles of Nuclear Radiation Detection.* Ann Arbor, Mich.: Ann Arbor Science Publishers, 1979. 379 pp. $29.95. Laboratory Manual, 200 pp. $14.95.

The principles and operation of radiation detectors used in nuclear technology, medical practices, and radiation protection are explained in this text for nuclear engineers, health physicists, and radiologists.

Environmental Policy Institute. *Plutonium in the Workplace: An Assessment of Health and*

Safety Procedures for Workers at the Kerr-McGee Plutonium Fuel Fabrication Facility.
Environmental Policy Institute, 317 Pennsylvania Ave. SE, Washington, DC
20003. 1979. 100 pp. $3.00.
A report on the inadequacies in quality control and security, material
unaccounted for, and the shocking conditions under which workers operated.

Environmental Policy Institute. *Radiation Standards and Public Health.* Proceedings of
a Second Congressional Seminar on Low-Level Ionizing Radiation, Feb. 10,
1978. Environmental Policy Institute, 317 Pennsylvania Ave. SE, Washington, DC 20003. 274 pp. $4.00.
A panel including the Congressional Environmental Study Conference, the
Environmental Policy Institute, the Atomic Industrial Forum, scientists, and
public health officials addressed questions concerning the potential health
effects of low-level ionizing radiation and the adequacy of current protective
standards. Includes testimony of Drs. Bross, Mancuso, Sternglass, Tamplin,
and others.

Healy, J.W., ed. *Plutonium: Health Implications for Man.* Health Physics Society.
Oxford, England: Pergamon Press, 1976. 191 pp.
This collection of scientific papers presented at the Second Los Alamos Life
Sciences Symposium covers methods of minimizing exposure to plutonium,
waste management, toxicity, and environmental pathways for the
redistribution of plutonium. It concludes that risk evaluation is a societal, not
a scientific problem.

Holzman, David. *Nuclear Power: The Invisible Killer.* Citizens' Energy Project, 1110
Sixth St. NW, Suite 300, Washington, DC 20001. 1978. 17 pp. $1.60. (CEP).
A well-documented discussion of the effects of low-level radiation and the
studies which have been made in this area, and the efforts of the U.S.
government to cover up nuclear health problems.

Honicker vs. Hendrie: A Lawsuit to End Atomic Power. Book Publishing Company, 156
Drakes Lane, Summertown, TN 38483. 1978. 152 pp. $5.00. (EARS).
The petition of Jeannine Honicker to the Nuclear Regulatory Commission
contains the most complete, readily available account of the health effects of
nuclear power and radiation. The results of numerous studies are cited, as
well as jurisprudential principles. (See also: *Shutdown* for the testimony of Drs.
Gofman and Sternglass in this suit.)

Huver, Charles W.; Dixon, Gertrude A; Jacobsen, Naomi; and Dixon, George.
Methodologies for the Study of Low-Level Radiation in the Midwest. Dr. John W. Gofman,
Chief Consultant. Millville, Minn.: Anvil Press, 1979. 200 pp. $5.00 + $.50
postage. A pamphlet summary of portions of *Methodologies,* for classroom and
general use is entitled *Nuclear Waste: The Time Bomb in Our Bones.* 18 pp. $1.25.
Both are available from LAND Educational Associates Foundation, Inc., 3368
Oak Ave., Stevens Point, WI 54481.
Low-level radiation is everyone's business. Information has been withheld
from the public on this crucial issue, and it is time for the truth. This carefully
researched six-year study details the sources of radiation; the pathways to
humans; the geographical areas, foods, and people that are at the greatest risk;
and the hidden danger of the slowly accumulating nuclear wastes in human
cells.

Laws, Priscilla W. *Medical and Dental X-Rays: A Consumer's Guide to Avoiding
Unnecessary Radiation Exposure.* Public Citizen Health Research Group, 2000 P
St., NW, Washington, DC 20036. 1974. 71 pp. $3.25.

Many qualified professionals believe that a significant portion of the present exposure to diagnostic x-rays is unnecessary. This guide explains the effects and risks of x-rays and how to minimize your exposure.

Lyon, W.S. *Progress and Problems in Radioelement Analysis.* Ann Arbor, Mich.: Ann Arbor Science Publishers, 1980. 500 pp. $29.95.
Written for the environmental scientist and the nuclear engineer, this text provides procedures and techniques for the study of radioelements, and methods for monitoring radioactivity in the environment.

MassPIRG. *Nuclear Power Plants: Unsafe for Workers.* Massachusetts Public Interest Research Group, 233 N. Pleasant St., Amherst, MA 01002. 1979. approx 90 pp. $2.00
Medical researchers have demonstrated strong links between workers' exposure to low-level radiation and high rates of leukemia and other cancers. Nevertheless, workers continue to be exposed to dangerous levels of radiation. Recommendations include lower exposure limits, strict enforcement of regulations, plant design changes, and coverage of workers by OSHA.

Meyer, Leo A. *Nuclear Power in Industry: A Guide for Tradesmen and Technicians.* Second Edition. Chicago, Ill.: American Technical Society, 1974. 137 pp. $5.25.
This manual on atomic power and radioactivity includes basic information on measuring radioactivity, its effects, and protection from radiation.

NIRS. *Resource Guide on Low-Level Radiation.* Nuclear Information and Resource Service, 1536 16th St. NW, Washington, DC 20036. 1979. 4 pp. $.50.
A list of resource people and organizations concerned with this issue.

International Atomic Energy Agency. *Seminar on Radiological Safety Evaluation Doses and Application of Radiological Safety Standards to Man and the Environment.* Portoroz, Slovenia, 1974. Vienna: International Atomic Energy Agency, 1974.
A highly technical study of population dose evaluation and standards for man and his environment, organized by the International Atomic Energy Agency and the World Health Organization, with the support of the United Nations Environment Programme. Includes basic concepts, methodology, potential harm, and ecological effects.

Shutdown! Nuclear Power on Trial. Summertown, Tenn.: Book Publishing Company, 1979. 191 pp. $4.95.
The petition of *Honicker vs Hendrie* calls upon the Nuclear Regulatory Commission to suspend licenses of the nuclear industry pending a complete investigation of the biological effects of low-level ionizing radiation. The expert testimony of Dr. John W. Gofman and Dr. Ernest Sternglass is presented in this report, along with an account of the Three Mile Island and other nuclear accidents. (See also *Honicker vs. Hendrie* for further data on radiation.)

Sternglass, Dr. Ernest. *Low-Level Radiation.* San Francisco, Calif.: Friends of the Earth, 1973. 240 pp. $5.95. (out of print)
Finds troubling correlations between the fallout from nuclear tests and reactors, with increased incidence of leukemia and foetal damage, and tells of the barriers thrown up to prevent letting the public know about it. Holds that the dangers of radiation have been underestimated.

United Nations. *Sources and Effects of Ionizing Radiation.* United Nations, 1977. 725 pp.

$28.00. (UNIPUB)

Natural and man-made sources of radiation are covered, including nuclear fallout, nuclear power, industrial and medical uses of radiation, and radioactive consumer products. Risks of exposure are estimated.

U.S. Department of the Interior. *The Radiation Hazard in Mining.* Washington, DC, 1977. S/N 023-019-00025-0. 24 pp. $1.50. (USGPO).

The occurrence of lung cancer caused by radioactive dust in underground mines, and the sources of radon daughters are investigated in this report.

Whitman, Lawrence. Fire Safety in the Atomic Age. See *NUCLEAR ENERGY: SAFETY.*

Wolfe, Sidney M., M.D. *Atomic Worker's Guide to the Most Unsafe Atomic Power Plants in 1977.* Health Research Group, 2000 P St. NW, Washington, DC 20036. 1979. 19 pp. $3.45.

A ranking of 40 plants by the amount of worker radiation exposure, and suggestions for change.

Woolard, Robert F., MD, and Young, Eric R., MD. *Health Dangers of the Nuclear Fuel Chain and Low-Level Ionizing Radiation. A Bibliography/Literature Review.* Prepared by the Environmental Health Committee of the British Columbia Medical Association, and the Physicians for Social Responsibility. Available from the Physicians for Social Responsibility, P.O. Box 295, Cambridge, MA 02238, and PSR, 944 Market St., Rm 808, San Francisco, CA 94102. 1979. 64 pp. $3.50.

Many studies relating to the health dangers of radiation and the nuclear fuel cycle are included in this annotated bibliography, which often quotes extensively from the works cited. The introduction sets forth the position of the Physicians for Social Responsibility on these issues.

Radioactive Waste Management

Deese, David A. *Nuclear Power and Radioactive Waste: A Sub-Seabed Disposal Option?* Lexington, Mass.: Lexington Books, 1978. 224 pp. $18.00.

Outlines the radioactive waste problem and disposal possibilities, together with their political and legal complications, and national and international aspects.

Gilmore, W.R. *Radioactive Waste Disposal, Low and High Level.* Park Ridge, N.J.: Noyes Data Corporation, 1977. 356 pp. $39.00.

Present radioactive waste management practices at government and commercial facilities are outlined in detail. Processes under development, and proposals for long-term solutions are also presented. This work is based mainly on federally financed studies.

International Atomic Energy Agency. *Management of Radioactive Wastes from the Nuclear Fuel Cycle.* Vienna: IAEA, 1976. Vol. 1, 395 pp. $25; Vol. 2, 424 pp., $26.

Technical research papers presented at a symposium organized by the IAEA and the OECD cover all aspects of radioactive waste management. Of major importance was the technology for incorporating high-level liquid wastes from reprocessing operations into solid forms, such as calcines, glasses, or ceramics.

Lipschutz, Ronnie D. *Radioactive Waste: Politics, Technology, and Risk.* Cambridge, Mass.: Ballinger, 1980. 246 pp. $7.00. (UCS)

The Union of Concerned Scientists investigates the problems of radioactive waste: where it comes from, why it is dangerous, how the government has managed waste in the past, and what the government proposes to do with radioactive waste in the future. Appendix on foreign waste management programs.

MHB Technical Associates. *Spent Fuel Disposal Costs.* Natural Resources Defense Council, 122 E. 42nd St., New York, NY 10017. 1978. 230 pp. $5/$15.

The costs of the U.S. Department of Energy's Spent Fuel Policy are evaluated in terms of the type of plan chosen, use of intermdeiate waste storage sites, delays, problems, and geological uncertainties. The costs may be $40 billion by the year 2000, adding 10% to 20% to utility bills. Plant decommissioning and ecological costs would add to this total.

U.S. Department of Energy. *Report of Task Force for Review of Nuclear Waste Management.* Washington, DC, 1978. DOE/ER-004/D, U.S. Directorate of Energy Research, Washington, DC 20585. 166 pp.

The report recommends federal management of all nuclear wastes, and considers available technologies, costs, decommissioning of obsolete nuclear power plants, and public relations issues.

U.S. Department of Energy. Energy Technology, Office of Nuclear Waste Management. *Environmental Aspects of Commercial Radioactive Waste Management.* DOE/ET-0029. 1979. 3 vols. approx. 1200 pp. (NTIS)

An assessment of the environmental effects of various systems of radioactive waste management which considers atmospheric effects, resource commitments, dose calculations, and health, ecological, and socioeconomic effects.

U.S. Department of Energy. Energy Technology, Office of Nuclear Waste Management. *Technology for Commercial Radioactive Waste Management.* DOE/ET-0028. 1979. 5 vols. approx. 2400 pp. (NTIS)

A review of the technology for waste treatment, interim storage, transportation, final isolation, decommissioning, thorium fuel cycle, and management systems.

WashPIRG. *Nuclear Waste: A National Waste Repository at Hanford.* Washington Public Interest Research Group, FK-10, University of Washington, Seattle, WA 98195. Revised 1979. 49 pp. $3/$5. Free summary with S.A.S.E.

Hanford, Washington may become a permanent burial site for the nation's nuclear waste. However, many problems remain to be solved, such as methods for disposal, geologic uncertainties, transportation of wastes and probable accidents, decommissioning of nuclear power plants, and political considerations.

Willrich, Mason, and Lester, Richard K. *Radioactive Waste: Management and Regulation.* New York, N.Y.: The Free Press, 1977. 138 pp. $13.95.

An analysis of existing laws and policies in the U.S. regarding radioactive waste management finds that the responsibility is divided between government and industry, that there are now no institutions adequate for the safe management of radioactive waste in the future, and that there is no comprehensive program for regulation. The long-lived toxicity of radioactive waste will present a major challenge for governments throughout the nuclear age and beyond.

Regulation, Legislation, and the Law

Carolina Environmental Study Group. *The Price-Anderson Act Decision.* Carolina Environmental Study Group, 824 Henley Place, Charlotte, NC 28207. March, 1977. 16 pp. $1.00.

Here is the text of U.S. District Judge James B. McMillan's decision declaring unconstitutional the Price-Anderson Act, which sets limits on liability for damages resulting from nuclear power plant accidents. However, the U.S. Supreme Court reversed the decision in June, 1978, stating that the Price-Anderson Act "bears a relationship to Congress's concern for stimulating the involvement of private enterprise in the production of electric energy through the use of atomic power" . . . which is . . . "ample justification for placing nuclear accident victims in a special category."

Greenberg, Phillip A., Task Force Chairperson. *Radioactive Materials in California: A Survey of Regulatory Issues in Industrial, Research, Power Generation, and Other Uses; Environmental Monitoring; Facility Decontamination and Decommissioning; Transportation.* Huey D. Johnson, Secretary for Resources. The California Resources Agency, 1416 Ninth St., Sacramento, CA 95814. April 1979. Executive Summary, 127 pp. + appendices; Complete Report, 469 pp. + appendices.

This comprehensive survey also addresses seismic safety, emergency planning, training of personnel, and State waste repository sites. Recommendations are made for improving the regulation of these hazardous substances. This report should be of value to other states considering these problems.

Klema, Ernest D., and West, Robert. *Public Regulation of Site Selection for Nuclear Power Plants. Present Procedures and Reform Proposals. An Annotated Bibliography.* Washington, DC: Resources for the Future, 1977. 129 pp. $5.75.

Present procedures and problems in the siting regulations for nuclear power plants are outlined, and alternative procedures are investigated, with the aim of reducing the long lead time for approval, yet fulfilling regulatory objectives of public health and safety, protecting environmental values, and providing for participation of affected interest groups. One hundred and fifty abstracts from the siting literature are included.

Lewis and Clark Law School, Northwestern School of Law, 10015 SW Terwilliger Blvd., Portland, OR 97219. *Environmental Law.* Vol. 6, No. 3, 1976. $3.00.

The proceedings of a law school symposium on the legal aspects of nuclear power.

Rolph, Elizabeth S. *Nuclear Power and Public Safety: A Study in Regulation.* Lexington, Mass.: Lexington Books, 1979. 213 pp. $17.95.

The regulatory history of commercial nuclear power provides an understanding of how regulation is a political process, taking into account public concern, and industry's pressure to proceed despite risks and uncertainties. Conflicting interests arise in regulatory agencies such as the Atomic Energy Commission with the dual mandates of protecting the public health and safety, and promoting nuclear power.

The Stanford University Institute for Energy Studies. *The California Nuclear Initiative.* Palo Alto, Calif.: Stanford University Press, 1976. 220 pp. $3.50.

An objective analysis and discussion of the issues of the campaign.

Tye, Lawrence S. *Looking But Not Seeing: The Federal Nuclear Power Plant Inspection Program.* Cambridge, Mass.: Union of Concerned Scientists, 1978. 54 pp. $3.50. (UCS)

Tye assesses the effectiveness of the Nuclear Regulatory Commission's program to protect the public from the risks of nuclear power plant accidents. He finds serious gaps in regulations, inadequate investigations and enforcement, and cases of falsification in industry documents.

U.S. Congress. *Nuclear Regulatory Legislation Through the 95th Congress, Second Session.* Washington, DC, 1979. S.N 052-070-04946-4. 467 pp. $5.00. (USGPO)

A compilation of all legislation pertaining to nuclear regulation and the Nuclear Regulatory Commission.

Safety and Accidents

Davis, Gloria. *Three Mile Island: The End or a Beginning?* York, Pa.: York Ski-Ad Service, 1979. 83 pp. $4.00.

The story of the accident at Three Mile Island is told by one who lived there and observed the results and repercussions, such as the realization that "we were had" by the industry and the government. The accident succeeded in capturing the attention of the people close by, and alerting the world to the danger of the technology and the utter callousness with which it has been foisted upon the public.

Edelhertz, Herbert, and Walsh, Marilyn. *The White Collar Challenge to Nuclear Safeguards.* Battelle Human Affairs Research Center. Lexington, Mass.: Lexington Books, 1978. 128 pp. $10.95.

This study addresses the potential problem presented by white collar employees, who, through guile rather than force, could breach nuclear safeguards to gain access to nuclear materials.

Environmental Action Foundation. *Accidents Will Happen: The Case Against Nuclear Power.* New York, N.Y.: Harper & Row, 1979. 352 pp. $2.50.

This collection of essays by energy experts and national leaders such as Ralph Nader, Dr. Helen Caldicott, Denis Hayes, and many others is packed with recent evidence on the hazards of nuclear power. It explains how nuclear power works—or doesn't work, what are the actual costs in economic well-being, public health, and environmental effects, and how alternative forms of energy can make nuclear power irrelevant.

Environmental Studies and Public Policy Group. *Meltdown at Montague.* Environmental Studies and Public Policy Group, Cole Science Center, Hampshire College, Amherst, MA 01002. 1977. 65 pp. $2.50. (ReSource)

A citizen's guide to the predictability of a meltdown at a nuclear power plant, the consequences of such an accident, and the value judgments involved.

Ferrara, Grace M., ed. *Atomic Energy and the Safety Controversy.* New York, N.Y.: Facts on File, 1978. 167 pp.

Many of the most important events and actions of the 1970's associated with the nuclear safety controversy are assembled here. Material is taken largely from the printed record compiled weekly by Facts on File. This useful reference covers safety, theft and sabotage, accidents, nuclear wastes, A-tests, and international issues.

Ford Daniel, and Kendall, Henry. *An Assessment of the ECCS Rulemaking Hearings.* San Francisco, Calif.: Friends of the Earth, 1974. 224 pp. $4.95. (FOE)
Explains how the 1972 hearings of the Atomic Energy Commission on the emergency core cooling systems failed to answer nuclear critics' worries about reactor accidents.

Ford, Daniel F.; Kendall, Henry W.; and Tye, Lawrence S. *Browns Ferry: A Regulatory Failure.* Cambridge, Mass.: Union of Concerned Scientists, 1976. 45 pp. $2.50.
A report on the UCS investigation of the accidental fire and subsequent safety system malfunctions that occured at the Browns Ferry nuclear power plant on March 22, 1975. Government files reveal serious compromises with basic safety requirements.

Ford, Daniel F., and Nadis, Steven J. *Nuclear Power: The Aftermath of Three Mile Island.* Cambridge, Mass.: Union of Concerned Scientists, 1980. $2.00. (UCS)
An analysis of the accident, and the economic and political implications for the future of the nuclear power industry.

Kemeny, John G. Chairman. *The Accident at Three Mile Island. The Need for Change: The Legacy of Three Mile Island.* Report of the President's Commission. New York, N.Y.: Pergamon Press, 1979. 201 pp. $15.00.
This report is also available from the U.S. Government Printing Office as S/N 052-003-00718-51. $5.50. (USGPO)
After a six month investigation of all factors surrounding the accident at Three Mile Island, the commission concluded that fundamental changes are necessary in the organization, procedures, practices, and attitudes of the Nuclear Regulatory Commission and the nuclear industry. However, the President's Commission could not agree upon a moratorium on nuclear power plant construction. The report includes an overview, an account of the accident, findings of its investigation, and recommendations regarding the NRC, the utility, personnel, health and safety, emergency planning, and the public's right to know.

Kendall, Henry, Study Director. *The Risks of Nuclear Power Reactors: A Review of the NRC Reactor Safety Study. WASH-1400. (NUREG-75/014).* Cambridge, Mass.: Union of Concerned Scientists, 1977. 210 pp. $6.25. (UCS)
After an outline of the history of reactor safety studies, the Union of Concerned Scientists presents a completely documented analysis of the methodology employed in WASH-1400, and concludes that its deficiencies lead to unrealistically low assessment of the risks. It calls upon the Nuclear Regulatory Commission to withdraw the study and to reassess the U.S. nuclear program objectively. Appendices include accidents, earthquake hazards, and data base inadequacies. See U.S. Nuclear Regulatory Commission, *Reactor Safety Study* for the document and subsequent NRC action.

Lanoue, Ron. *Evacuation Plans: The Achilles' Heel of the Nuclear Industry.* Critical Mass Energy Project, P.O. Box 1538, Washington, DC 20013. Second edition, 1978. Approx. 40 pp. $2.00. Also included in the CMEP Citizen Action Packet on Emergency Response Planning, $4.75.
Government planning for nuclear accidents is in a sorry state. This guide

can help you investigate local plans and bring public pressure for improvements. Includes the Nuclear Regulatory Commission's *Guide and Checklist for . . . Radiological Emergency Response Plans . . .*

Medvedev, Zhores A. *Nuclear Disaster in the Urals.* New York, N.Y.: Norton, 1979. 214 pp. $12.95.

A dissident Soviet scientist turns detective to uncover evidence indicating a terrible explosion in 1957, in a Soviet nuclear waste disposal area, which resulted in many deaths and widespread contamination. The report is contested by Soviet authorities and some members of the British and American nuclear establishment; however, some CIA documents seem to corroborate the story. (See also Friends of the Earth *ECO,* Vol X, No. 1 for a brief account of this incident.)

Pollard, Robert D., ed. *The Nugget File.* Union of Concerned Scientists, 1208 Massachusetts Ave., Cambridge, MA 02138. 1979. 95 pp. $4.95. (UCS)

This astonishing collection of excerpts from the government's special file on nuclear power plant "incidents", accidents, and safety defectrs was obtained by the Union of Concerned Scientists under the Freedom of Information Act.

Rogovin, Mitchell, director, with Frampton, George T., deputy director. *Three Mile Island: A Report to the Commissioners and to the Public.* Washington, DC: NRC Special Inquiry Group, 1980. NUREG/CR-1250. Vol. 1, A non-technical account of the accident, 183 pp. Vol. 2, Technical findings. (NRC) (NTIS)

An advisory panel, appointed by the Nuclear Regulatory Commission and headed by attorney Mitchell Rogovin, carried out an independent investigation of the accident at Three Mile Island and found that it came within 30 to 60 minutes of a meltdown. Recommendations include improvements in licensing, regulation, assessment of risks and health effects, operator training, and human factor engineering; more remote siting from population centers; and the requirement of workable evacuation plans as a pre-condition of operation.

Union of Concerned Scientists. *Testimony of Bridenbaugh, Hubbard and Minor Before the Joint Committee on Atomic Energy.* Cambridge, MA: Union of Concerned Scientists, 1976. 92 pp., $2.25.

An assessment of major nuclear safety problems by three experienced General Electric engineers who resigned in protest.

Union of Concerned Scientists. *UCS Petition before the Nuclear Regulatory Commission for Emergency and Remedial Action.* Cambridge, MA: Union of Concerned Scientists, 1977. 210 pp. $3.25.

Federal testing programs reveal that safety equipment in nuclear power reactors may fail when needed. UCS calls for a halt in construction and operation of nuclear power plants until compliance with applicable regulations can be demonstrated.

U.S. Atomic Energy Commission. *Theoretical Possibilities and Consequences of a Major Accident in Large Nuclear Power Plants.* WASH-740. *"The Brookhaven Report."* Washington, DC, 1957. 105 pp. (USGPO)

This AEC report was the first attempt to estimate the possible consequences of a serious nuclear accident. Although the plants were one-tenth the size of those today, the calculations found that 3,400 persons would be killed outright, 43,000 seriously injured, $7 billion worth of property damaged, and 150,000 square miles of land gravely affected.

U.S. Nuclear Regulatory Commission. *Reactor Safety Study. WASH-1400. "The Rasmussen Report."* NUREG-75/014. Washington, DC: Nuclear Regulatory Commission, 1975. (NTIS)

After three years of intensive study of nuclear reactor safety, the conclusion was reached that the chance of a serious accident was negligible, thus providing government and industry with reassurance for the public. However, on January 18, 1979, the NRC withdrew endorsement of the Executive Summary of WASH-1400, finding it no longer reliable. (See Kendall, Henry. *The Risks of Nuclear Power Reactors* for a critique of the *Reactor Safety Study*.)

Webb, Richard E. *The Accident Hazards of Nuclear Power Plants.* Amherst, MA: University of Massachusetts Press, 1976. 228 pp. $6.95.

Analyzes the possible types of reactor accidents and their probability, reviews the NRC's Reactor Safety Study, and describes fourteen accidents or near-accidents. It appears that nobody knows how dangerous reactors are, nor is anyone making much effort to find out.

Whitman, Lawrence E. *Fire Safety in the Atomic Age.* Chicago, Ill.: Nelson-Hall, 1980. 265 pp. $10.95.

Procedures for the handling of radiation fire safety problems are described, and for the training of fire departments and safety personnel, and pre-planning for specific situations. Radiation, contamination, transportation, nuclear power plants, and nuclear weapons are discussed at length.

Willrich, Mason, ed. *International Safeguards and Nuclear Industry.* Baltimore, MD: Johns Hopkins University Press, 1973. 307 pp. $15.00.

A collection of articles on the world wide nuclear industry, the possibilities for, and safeguards against, diversion of critical materials, and the political and social implications.

Willrich, Mason, and Taylor, Theodore B. *Nuclear Theft: Risks and Safeguards.* A report to the Ford Foundation. Cambridge, MA: Ballinger, 1973. 272 pp. $25.00.

Nuclear weapons are relatively easy to make, and the widespread use of nuclear energy makes materials available. The authors contend that effective safeguards can be developed, but cite facts that could lead to the opposite conclusion.

Uranium

Clergy and Laity Concerned. *Uranium Mining on Native Land.* Clergy and Laity Concerned, Human Rights and U.S. Power Program, 1322 18th St. NW, Washington, DC 20036. $2.00.

An introductory packet on the exploitation of Native American uranium reserves, the corporations involved, and the health effects on the population.

Elliott, Mary, ed. *Ground for Concern: Australia's Uranium and Human Survival.* Victoria, Australia: Penguin/Friends of the Earth, 1977. 235 pp. $4.95.

Contends that the moral decision for Australians would be to leave their uranium in the ground. This decision could affect the very survival of our species, due to the risks of thermonuclear war. The contributors combine scientific knowledge with social responsibility in their proposal for a nuclear-free world. Written in clear and non-technical language, it has a message for the entire world.

National Academy of Sciences, 2101 Constitution Ave., NW, Washington, DC 20418. *Mineral Resources and the Environment. Supplementary Report: Reserves and Resources of Uranium in the U.S.* 1975. 236 pp.

A survey of uranium reserves, resources, production, marketing, government-industry collaboration, and problems.

NIRS. *Resource Guide on Uranium.* Nuclear Information and Resource Service, 1536 16th St. NW, Washington, DC 20036. 1979. 4 pp. $.50.

Basic data on the uranium industry, organizational contacts, and bibliography.

Taylor, June H., and Yokell, Michael D. *Yellowcake: The International Uranium Cartel.* New York, N.Y.: Pergamon, 1980. 245 pp. $30.00.

The authors reveal the secret operations of the international uranium cartel from 1972 to 1976, and subsequent investigations. Background is also provided on the nuclear fuel cycle and the uranium industry.

Zimmerman, Charles F. *Uranium Resources on Federal Lands.* Lexington, Mass.: Lexington Books, 1979. 352 pp. $28.95.

The economics and market structure of U.S. uranium production are described, and the need for a federally legislated uranium leasing program pointed out.

SOLAR ENERGY

References

Aitken, Donald. *A Bibliography for the Solar Home Builder.* Office of Appropriate Technology, 1530 Tenth St., Sacramento, CA 95814. 1979. 38 pp. Single copies free to California residents; $1.00 out of state.

This excellent reference facilitates the choice of the books that will be most useful to the reader, whether a beginner or an expert. Categories include energy perspectives, alternative energy resources, solar home design, information for the home builder, books for the serious student, and journals.

Ann Arbor Science Task Group. *1977 Solar Energy & Research Directory.* Ann Arbor, MI: Ann Arbor Science Publishers, 1977. 386 pp. $24.00.

The names, addresses, products, services, and research areas are listed and cross-referenced for hundreds of individuals, organizations, and businesses concerned with solar and other alternate energy systems.

Bainbridge, David A. *The First Passive Solar Catalog.* The Passive Solar Institute, P.O. Box 722, Davis, CA 95616. 1978. 70 pp. $5.00.

This book is a useful aid in designing and building passive solar space heating and cooling systems, water heaters, and natural lighting systems. It gives details of different types of passive buildings, and provides access to passive solar components, consultants, and resources.

Bereny, Justin A. *Survey of the Emerging Solar Energy Industry.* National Solar Energy Education Campaign, 10762 Tucker St., Beltsville, MD 20705. 1977. 405 pp. $70.00.

A comprehensive overview of the solar energy industry, with names, addresses, and explanations. Describes in detail the various facets of the industry.

Centerline Corporation. *Calendar of Events for Solar Energy Related Activities.* Centerline Corporation, Dept. 115, 401 S. 36th St., Phoenix, AZ 85034.

Listings may be obtained by sending two stamps and an envelope.

Dierker, Janet. *A Directory of Federal Sources of Information on Solar Energy.* Center for Renewable Resources, 1001 Connecticut Ave. NW, 5th fl., Washington, DC 20036. 1978. 16 pp. $2.50.

An outline of government solar energy programs and sources of information, with names and addresses of contact persons and agencies.

International Association of Plumbing and Mechanical Officials. *Uniform Solar Energy Code.* International Association of Plumbing and Mechanical Officials, 5032 Alhambra Ave., Los Angeles, CA 90032. 1976. 102 pp. $7.00.

Definitions, materials, and construction are covered by this code, with the purpose of providing a safe and functional solar energy system with a minimum of regulations.

International Compendium. *International Compendium of Solar Energy/Energy Conservation Books and Services.* International Compendium, Dept. P., 10762 Tucker St., Beltsville, MD 10705. 1976. 44 pp. $2.00.

The 200 titles in this useful guide include books, plans, reports, studies, and periodicals, categorized by subject areas.

Martz, C.W., ed. *Solar Energy Source Book.* Solar Energy Institute of America, P.O. Box 9352, Washington, DC 20005, 1977. 712 pp. $12.00.

A looseleaf guide to manufacturers and organizations, with periodic updates to members.

McCabe, Mike. *Solar Energy: A Guide to Federal and State Programs and Information Sources.* Washington, DC: Environmental Study Conference, 1979. 18 pp. Free from your Congressperson.

Not all-inclusive, but well worth sending for.

National Solar Energy Education Campaign. *Solar Energy Books.* National Solar Energy Education Campaign, 10762 Tucker St., Beltsville, MD 20705. 1977. 118 pp. $4.50.

A catalog listing books and articles on solar energy in categories of general solar, home-owners/do-it-yourself, business/professional, alternate energy, energy conservation, and government activities.

Pesko, Carolyn, ed. *The Solar Directory.* Ann Arbor, Mich.: Ann Arbor Science Publishers, 1975. 624 pp. $20.00.

A comprehensive work, listing under many subtitles individuals, organizations, manufacturers and distributors, and describing research projects and legislation. Bibliographies and references.

Shurcliff, William A. *Informal Directory of the Organizations and People Involved in the Solar Heating of Buildings.* Third and final edition, June 1977. 243 pp. $9.00. (EARS) (TEA)

A selective directory covering 26 countries, with emphasis on the United States. Of value to architects, planners, builders, and home-owners.

Solar Age Magazine, eds. *Solar Age Catalog.* Solar Age Magazine, Solar Vision, Inc., Church Hill, Harrisville, NH 03450., 1977. 230 pp. $8.50. (EARS) (TEA)

This valuable sourcebook provides the background for purchasing and using solar energy equipment. Included are essays on solar design principles, product descriptions and comparisons, and resource lists.

Solar Energy Industries Association. *SEM 79: Solar Engineering Master Catalog.* Dallas, Tex.: Solar Engineering Publishers, 1979. 184 pp. $15.00. (from Solar Energy Industries Association, 1001 Connecticut Ave. NW, Suite 800, Washington, DC 20036.)

Information is readily accessible in this well organized and indexed directory of manufacturers, products, contractors, state energy organizations, and other resources.

Solar Energy Institute of America. *Solar Energy Source Book.* Solar Energy Institute of North America, 1110 Sixth St. NW, Washington, DC 20001. 1980 800 pp. $17.00.

All who are concerned with solar installations will find this a valuable resource, with lists of solar companies, products, and services, arranged both alphabetically and geographically, resumes of federal and state legislation, and bibliographies.

Solar Usage Now, Inc. *The 1978 SUN Catalog* (updated annually). Solar Usage Now, Inc., Box 306, Bascom, Ohio 44809. 224 pp. $2.00.

A full catalog of solar equipment and resources, including an extensive selection of books, plans, tools, materials, components, devices, slide sets, and educational kits for classroom use.

Southern California Solar Energy Association. *Western Regional Solar Energy Directory.* SCSEA Directory, 202 C Street, 11B. San Diego, CA 92101, 1978-79. 67 pp. $2.00.

Lists names and addresses of individuals, companies, and organizations in California, Arizona, Nevada, and Hawaii, who are involved in the solar energy industry.

U.S. Department of Energy. Division of Solar Technology. *Guide to Solar Energy Programs.* Washington, DC, 1978. 66 pp. $5.25. (NTIS)

An overview of the DOE's solar energy programs, grant proposals, and federal sources of energy information.

U.S. Department of Energy, Solar Energy Research Institute. *reaching up, reaching out: a guide to organizing local solar events.* Washington, DC, 1979. S/N 061-000-00345-2. 208 pp. $8.50. (USGPO) (EARS)

Based on a belief in the importance of community organization, this manual presents (1) examples of successful solar and energy conservation activities such as fairs and workshops; (2) an organizing primer; (3) a guide to selected resources including organizations, printed matter, and audio-visual materials. Lively illustrations, attractive format, and cross-indexing help to make this an invaluable reference.

Overviews and Oddments

Adzema, Robert. *The Great Sundial Cutout Book.* See ENERGY EDUCATION: BOOKS

Andrassy, Stella. *The Solar Food Dryer Book.* Dobbs Ferry, New York: Morgan & Morgan, 1978. 127 pp. $3.95.

Would you like to know how to use the sun to dry your food? Here are the directions for making a dryer and prserving vegetables, fruits, and herbs, plus a variety of unusual recipes. (Education)

Argue, Robert; Emanuel, Barbara; and Graham, Stephen. *The Sun Builders: A People's Guide to Solar, Wind, and Wood Energy in Canada.* Renewable Energy in Canada, 415 Parkside Dr., Toronto, Canada M6R 2Z7. 1978. 254 pp.

This guide to renewable energy now in use in Canada describes designs, problems, and successes of the pioneers in this field. Includes a consumers' guide, manufacturers' list, and resources.

Baer, Steve. *Sunspots.* Albuquerque, N. Mex.: Zomeworks Corporation, 1977. 115 pp. $4.00. (EARS) (TEA)

An intriguing approach to non-conventional solar energy applications.

Behrman, Daniel. *Solar Energy: The Awakening Science.* Boston, Mass.: Little, Brown, and Co., 1976. 408 pp. $12.50; or $10.50 from Wilderness Society Book Service, 40 Guernsey St., Stamford, CT 06904.

A study of the history and principles behind the use of solar energy. Both large and small scale applications are described, and future possibilities are assessed.

Bossong, Ken, ed. *The Solar Compendium.* Washington, DC: Citizens Energy Project, 1978. 160 pp. $6.00/$7.50. (CEP) (EARS)

This is a comprehensive guide for the solar activist, including articles on economics, the solar industry, technologies, politics, and the social and environmental impacts of solar systems.

Brinkworth, B.J. *Solar Energy for Man.* New York, N.Y.: Wiley, 1972. 250 pp. $8.95.

A comprehensive study of how solar energy can be collected and converted into heat, work, and electricity.

Buckley, Shawn. *Sun Up to Sun Down: Understanding Solar Energy.* See *ENERGY EDUCATION: BOOKS.*

California Public Policy Center. *Jobs from the Sun: Employment Development in the California Solar Energy Industry.* Solar Jobs, 304 S. Broadway #224, Los Angeles, CA 90013. 1978. 120 pp. $5/$10.

This study of the economic feasibility of solar energy in California has implications for the nation: new jobs can be created, tax savings gained, exported capital saved, and decentralized democratic government encouraged.

Cheremisinoff, Paul N., and Regino, Thomas C. *Principles and Applications of Solar Energy.* Ann Arbor, Mich.: Ann Arbor Science Publishers, 1978. 249 pp. $15.00.

This timely study of the feasibility of solar energy summarizes current technologies in a clear and readable form. Many systems and experiments are described and evaluated. Covers thermal solar energy applications, photovoltaic generation of electricity, wind, ocean thermal gradient power, and the chemical and biological conversion of solar energy.

Daniels, Farrington. *Direct Use of the Sun's Energy.* New York, N.Y.: Ballantine, 1964. 270 pp. $1.95. (EARS) (TEA)

Old but good introductory book, covering the entire range of the subject.

de Winter, F., and de Winter, J.W. *Description of the Solar Energy Research and Development Programs in Many Nations.* Energy Research and Development Administration, National Technical Information Service, Springfield, Va. 1976. 294 pp. $9.25. (NTIS)

Based in part on a conference of the International Solar Energy Society, this work contains descriptions of programs in 32 countries by UNESCO and other organizations.

Ewers, William. *Solar Energy: A Biased Guide.* Northbrook, Ill.: Domus. Revised, 1979. 100 pp. $4.95.

The author's intent is to increase public awareness of the potential of solar energy, and how it may be effectively utilized. This non-technical work includes many clear diagrams of solar applications, and an outline of the history of solar development. (Education)

Gunn, Anita. *A Citizen's Handbook On Solar Energy.* Public Interest Research Group, P.O. Box 19312, Washington, DC 20036. Revised 1977. 92 pp. $3.50 to individuals, $15.00 to business, institutions.

This manual reviews the economics and technologies of the six major solar research areas, furnishes information for citizen involvement on the local, state, and national level, lists experts who can be contacted, and includes a selected bibliography.

Halacy, Beth & Dan. *Solar Cookery.* See *ENERGY EDUCATION: RESOURCES*

Halacy, D.S., Jr. *The Coming Age of Solar Energy.* New York, N.Y.: Avon, 1973. 248 pp. $2.25. (EARS)

A popularly written historical survey of solar energy. Describes concepts and hardware for using the sun's energy. (Education)

Hayes, Denis. *Energy: The Solar Prospect.* Washington, DC: The Worldwatch Institute, 1977. 80 pp. $2.00. (EARS) (FOE)

This well-documented paper gives a global perspective on the potential for direct and indirect utilization of solar energy, and warns of the consequences of failure to convert to renewable energy sources.

Hayes, Denis. *The Solar Energy Timetable.* Washington, DC: Worldwatch Institute, 1978. 40 pp. $2.00. (FOE). (EARS)

Hayes presents a viable model proposal for a solar future, with the year 2025 as the goal for conversion to renewable resources. This will be possible only with a strong immediate commitment to the transition.

Hickok, F. *The Buy Wise Guide to Solar Heat.* St. Petersburg, Fla.: Hour House, 1976. 121 pp. $9.00.

A consumer's guide of what to buy, what to do, and what to beware of.

Hickok, Floyd. *Handbook of Solar and Wind Energy.* Boston, Mass.: Cahners Books, 1975. 125 pp.

Presents a time-table of probable development of solar and other non-fossil energy sources. Hickok believes that non-fossil energy will find its rightful place as fast as entrepreneurs find it a resource to be exploited, and predicts the decline of the utilities.

Hoke, John. *Solar Energy.* See *ENERGY EDUCATION: BOOKS*

Kendall, Henry W. and Nadis, Steven J. *Energy Strategies: Toward a Solar Future.* Cambridge, Mass.: Ballinger, 1980. 320 pp. $7.50. (UCS)

The Union of Concerned Scientists shows how the transition can be made to a solar energy economy and a solar society—a practical solution to the energy problem—and the only rational course for humanity.

Lyons, Stephen, ed. *SUN! A Handbook for the Solar Decade.* San Francisco, Calif.: Friends of the Earth/Solar Actions, Inc., 1978. 364 pp. $2.95. (FOE) (EARS)

Pioneers and innovators in the field explore energy policy, the solar resource, and the steps that can be taken now toward a solar future. They call for an International Solar Decade, when modern nations could put their energy plans on a sustainable foundation.

McDaniels, David. *The Sun: Our Future Energy Source.* New York, N.Y.: Wiley, 1979. 271 pp. $12.95.

Intended for use in an introductory course, this excellent college text emphasizes a qualitative understanding of the subject. Chapters cover growth in world energy usage, non-solar energy resources, the sun and the history of solar energy, and numerous methods for the utilization of solar energy.

McPhillips, Martin, and the editors of Solar Age Magazine. *The Solar Age Resource Book: The Complete Guidebook to the Dramatic Power of Solar Energy.* New York, N.Y.: Everest House, 1979. 242 pp. $9.95. (TEA)

The numerous ways in which solar energy can be captured, stored, and used are described in this guide, along with a rundown on equipment and systems, ideas for retrofitting, solving problems, and adapting to the site. Lists products and manufacturers.

McVeigh, J.C. *Sun Power: An Introduction to the Applications of Solar Energy.* New York, N.Y.: Pergamon Press, 1977. 180 pp. $8.00.
An analysis of all aspects of solar energy and its applications throughout the world. It includes thermal and small scale applications, photovoltaics, biological conversion systems, photochemistry, and wind power.

Metz, William, and Hammond, Allen. *Solar Energy in America.* Washington, DC: American Association for the Advancement of Science, 1978. 239 pp. $9.95.
Solar energy is democratic: it falls on everyone and can be put to use by individuals and small groups—a point that government planners seem to have trouble grasping. This well written and comprehensive text includes an account of each of the major renewable energy technologies, and a critical review of the government programs and policies behind them.

Mid-Peninsula Conversion Project. *Creating Solar Jobs: Options for Military Workers and Communities.* Mid-Peninsula Conversion Project, 867 West Dana, #203, Mountain View, CA 94041. 1978. 80 pp. $4.00.
The job skills of military workers can be utilized in new solar industries. Public policies are needed to facilitate community-oriented solar development and the transfer of workers from military production. The study is permeated with a sense of practicality, possibility, and exciting work-in-progress.

Popular Science Magazine, eds. *Solar Energy Handbook, 1978. A Complete Solar Sourcebook: Theory and Practice.* New York, N.Y.: Popular Science, 1978 $1.95.
This primer on the basics of solar heating and cooling contains a look back at the solar pioneers, a glimpse into the fascinating future, and practical home applications for the present. Includes plans, manufacturers list, and information on solar legislation.

Rankins, William III, and Wilson, David. *Practical Sun Power.* Black Mountain, N.C.: Lorien House, 1974. 52 pp. $4.00. (EARS)
A collection of plans for everything from cookers to greenhouses. (Education)

Rankins, William III, and Wilson, David. *The Solar Energy Notebook.* Black Mountain, N.C.: Lorien House, 1976. 56 pp. $4.00 (EARS)
A short, easily understood collection of solar energy facts and figures. Includes sections on the availability of equipment and climatological data. (Education)

Sands, Jonathan. *Practical Solar Heating Ideas with Sun-lite.* Manchester, N.H.: Kalwall Corporation, 1975. 44 pp. $2.50. (EARS)
Describes solar components and their applications. (Education)

Sands, Jonathan. *Solar Heating Systems.* Danbury, N.H.: Solar Systems, 1975. 46 pp. $3.00. (EARS)
Explains solar collector designs with clear diagrams. Includes basic solar facts for students. (Education)

SolarCal Council. *Toward a Solar California: The SolarCal Council Action Program.* California Energy Commission, 1111 Howe Ave., Sacramento, CA 95825. 1979. 63 pp.
Every state energy commission and local agency would do well to study this book, which outlines the advantages of solar energy, legislation, programs, solar potential, and recommended local, state, and federal actions.

Solar Lobby. *Blueprint for a Solar America.* Solar Lobby, 1001 Connecticut Ave. NW, 5th floor, Washington, DC 20036. 1979. 32 pp. $2.00.

Written by a coalition of citizens' groups—Solar Lobby, Common Cause, Conservation Foundation, Environmental Action, Environmental Policy Center, Natural Resources Defense Council, and the Sierra Club—the *Blueprint* proposes a series of programs for achieving at least 25% of U.S. energy from renewable resources by the year 2000.

Solar Lobby. *1980 Counter Budget.* Solar Lobby, 1001 Connecticut Ave. NW, Washington, DC 20036. 1979. 33 pp. $2.00.

This critique of the national budget calls for a doubling of solar outlays, recommendations for specific solar proposals, appropriate solar legislation, and the choice of cost-effective energy options that foster decentralization of both energy and political power.

The Skylight Book: Capturing the Sun and the Moon. A Guide to Creating Natural Light. Philadelphia, Pa.: Running Press, 1977. $4.95.

A beautifully illustrated book filled with ideas on building skylights.

U.S. Department of Energy. Program Evaluation Branch. Solar Energy Research Institute. *Annual Review of Solar Energy (for 1977)* Washington, DC, 1978. SERI/TR-54-066. 166 pp. $9.00. (NTIS)

Solar is a significant energy option for the near future, and a major candidate for the inexhaustible energy system of the next century. Solar programs are discussed, with impacts, problems, and factors affecting progress, and a synopsis of major solar technologies provided.

U.S. Executive Office of the President. Council on Environmental Quality. *Solar Energy: Progress and Promise.* Washington, DC, 1978. S/N 041-011-00036-0. 52 pp. $2.30. (USGPO)

Solar energy in its many forms is our best hope for energy independence. This report discusses economic and policy questions, progress in solar energy development, and a strategy for implementing solar energy. It suggests that a reasonable solar goal would be 25% solar by the year 2000.

Waugh, Albert E. *Sundials: Their Theory and Construction.* New York, N.Y.: Dover, 1973. 228 pp. $3.50.

All about sundials, from the mathematical and astronomical background to simple directions for construction, is contained in this book. Also describes dial furniture, and explains how to determine time in different locations. (Education)

Williams, Robert H., ed. *Toward a Solar Civilization.* Cambridge, Mass.: MIT Press, 1978. 251 pp. $12.50.

Specialists and policy analysts explore the potential for innovation in solar technology, and diverse strategies to reflect regional differences in the solar resource. Institutional obstacles, and the need to eliminate energy waste are also considered.

In A Category By Itself

Augustyn, Jim. *The Solar Cat Book.* Illustrations by Hildy Paige Burns. Berkeley, Calif.: Ten Speed Press, 1979. 96 pp. $3.95.

In this delightful mix of fact and fantasy, we discover the solar wisdom known to cats since the beginning of time. The humorous text and clever drawings explain both people's and cats' techniques for utilizing direct and

indirect forms of solar energy. Don't miss this book! It's the cat's MEOW*
(*Moral Equivalent Of War.) (Education)

Legal and Political Issues

American Bar Foundation. *Proceedings of the Workshop on Solar Energy and the Law,*
Chicago, Ill.: American Bar Foundation, 1975. 29 pp. $3.00. (EARS)
A discussion of legal issues related to use of solar energy.

Broyles, J.; Gunn, A.; Leibovitz, H.; Rhodes, D.; and Shirley, L., eds. *Citizens'*
National Solar Program: State Reports on Barriers and Strategies to Renewable Energy
Development. Center for Renewable Resources, 1001 Connecticut Ave. NW,
5th fl. Washington, DC 20036. 1978. 693 pp. $20.00. 27-page summary,
$4.50.
A state-by-state analysis of projects and potentials for the development of
renewable energy, plus useful resources on funding and information sources.

Citizens' Solar Program: State Reports on Barriers and Strategies to Renewable
Energy Development. Washington, DC: Center for Renewable Resources,
1978. 693 pp. $20.00.
A state-by-state analysis, including the *Citizens' National Solar Platform; Sources*
of Funds for Solar Activists; A Directory of Federal Sources of Information on Solar Energy; A
Survey of Model Programs; State and Local Solar/Conservation Porjects; and a list of
contacts.

Hayes, Gail Boyer. *Solar Access Law: Protecting Access to Sunlight for Solar Energy Systems.*
Environmental Law Institute. Cambridge, Mass.: Ballinger, 1979. 303 pp.
$18.50.
Legislators, urban planners, attorneys, teachers, and solar home owners
will find valuable information in this volume on legal strategies to assure solar
energy system owners that they will receive sunlight on their collectors. The
focus is on urban and suburban areas.

Keyes, John. *The Solar Conspiracy.* Dobbs Ferry, N.Y.: Morgan, 1974. 174 pp. $3.95.
An expose of what the author feels to be a criminal conspiracy of the
corporate giants to steal the sun from you.

Kraemer, Stanley F. *Solar Law: Present and Future, With Proposed Forms.* New York,
N.Y.: McGraw-Hill, 1978. 364 pp. $35.00.
The legal issues surrounding the use of solar power are analyzed, including
easements, zoning, air pollution, and building codes. Recommendations for
future measures are proposed.

Okagaki, Alan. *Solar Energy: One Way to Citizen Control.* Washington, DC: Center for
Science in the Public Interest, 1976. 124 pp. $6.00. (EARS)
This study shows that all communities can attain a high degree of energy
self-sufficiency by developing and controlling local resources.

Reece, Ray. *The Sun Betrayed: A Study of the Corporate Seizure of U.S. Solar Energy*
Development. Boston, Mass.: South End Press, 1979. 234 pp. $5.50.
A tight case is presented for the thesis that big corporations and big
government are strangling the newborn solar industry in its crib. The author
finds the official U.S. energy policy is to sit on solar energy until fossil fuel
profits have peaked; to encourage only capital-intensive and centralized solar
options; to minimize corporate risk at taxpayers' expense; and to confine
energy decisions to Washington.

Thomas, William A.; Miller, Alan S.; and Robbins, Richard L. *Overcoming Legal Uncertainties About Use of Solar Energy Systems.* Chicago, Ill.: American Bar Foundation, 1978. 80 pp. $5.00. (EARS)
 What are the legal barriers to the use of solar energy systems, and how can they be overcome? This report suggests new legislation to guarantee essential rights and to induce private and public investments.

U.S. Department of Energy. Solar Energy Research Institute. *Solar Energy Legal Bibliography: Final Report.* SERI/TR-62-069. Washington, DC, 1979. S/N 061-000-00302-9. 160 pp. $4.75. (USGPO).
 A summary of the legal and policy content of 160 solar publications, including research reports, government documents, law reviews, etc., concerned with legal barriers and incentives to solar energy development.

U.S. Department of Energy, Department of Commerce, and the National Bureau of Standards. *State Solar Energy Legislation of 1977. A Review of Statutes Relating to Buildings.* Washington, DC, 1979. $13.00. (NTIS)
 A summary of acts involving tax incentives, sun rights, standards, solar loans, and state research.

Western SUN. *Capturing the Sun's Energy: Opportunities for Local Governments.* Western Solar Utilization Network, c/o SolarCal, 1111 Howe Ave., Sacramento, CA 95825. 1979. 45 pp. $2.50.
 Public policy options available to local decision-makers are outlined, with descriptions of innovative actions and ordinances by cities and counties.

Solar Homes and Design

Adams, Robert W. *Adding Solar Heat to Your Home.* Blue Ridge Summitt, Pa.: TAB Books, 1979. 280 pp. $7.95. (EARS)
 A solar-powered heating system can be retrofitted to your home to supplement or replace an existing heating system by following the clear instruction in this guide.

American Institute of Architects Research Group. *Solar Dwelling Design Concepts.* Washington, DC: U.S. Government Printing Office, #023-000-00334-1. 1976. 146 pp. $3.00. (EARS) (USGPO)
 A resource manual for use by designers, builders, community leaders, local officials, and homeowners.

American Institute of Architects Research Corporation. *Solar Heating and Cooling Demonstration: A Descriptive Summary of HUD Solar Residential Demonstrations, Cycle 1.* Washington, DC: USGPO #023-00338-4. 1976. 59 pp. $2.25.
 Fifty-three projects are described, including climatic data, physical characteristics, energy conservation features, and the solar energy system components. See below, Troutman.

American Institute of Architects Research Corporation. *A Descriptive Summary of HUD Solar Residential Demonstrations, Cycle 2.* Washington, DC: USGPO, 1977. $2.30 (USGPO)
 Projects are described, including building elevations and schematic drawings of each solar system. See below, Troutman.

American Institute of Architects Research Corporation. *A Survey of Passive Solar Buildings.* Washington, DC: American Institute of Architects, 1979. 176 pp. $5.00. (EARS)

Hundreds of examples are illustrated, with floor plans and photographs of buildings employing passive solar heating concepts.

Anderson, Bruce. *Solar Energy: Fundamentals in Building Design.* New York, N.Y.: McGraw-Hill, 1977. 374 pp. $23.95. (EARS) (TEA)
Geared to the professional architectural designer and engineer wishing to implement solar energy in buildings of all scales. Authoritative and practical.

Anderson, Bruce, and Riordan, Michael. *The Solar Home Book.* Harrisville, N.H.: Brick House, 1976. 304 pp. $9.50. (EARS) (TEA)
An outstanding and unified treatment of energy conservation, passive solar design, and the more complex active solar energy systems. Aimed at homeowners, tradespeople, and designers, it also includes small scale projects and retrofitting existing homes.

Bainbridge, David; Corbett, Judy; and Hofacre, John. *Village Homes: Solar House Designs. A Collection of 43 Energy-Conscious House Designs.* Emmaus, Pa.: Rodale, 1979. 188 pp. $6.95.
This 70 acre solar subdivision in Davis, California, with bike paths, greenbelt, orchards, and vegetable gardens, uses 50% less energy than its conventional counterparts, and demonstrates that solar homes do not have to be expensive or ugly. Basic concepts, plans, details, and prices are given for 43 homes, including both passive and active designs.

Barnaby, Charles S.; Caesar, Philip; Wilcox, Bruce; and Nelson, Lynn. *Solar for Your Present Home.* California Energy, Resources, Conservation, and Development Commission, 1111 Howe Ave., Sacramento, CA 95825. 1978. 160 pp. $4.29
This guide is concerned with the uses of solar that are practical now, especially in existing houses. Includes basic information, worksheets, tables, and charts. Several editions cover specific areas, such as the San Francisco Bay Area.

Canon, Austin. *Solar Self-Help Book.* Southwest Research and Information Center, P.O. Box 4524, Albuquerque, NM 87106. 1978. 40 pp. $4.00.
Solid information about insulation, passive solar design, greenhouses, heat storage, and energy conservation, provided in an easy-to-read and humorous manner.

Carlson, B. *Solar Primer One.* Whittier, Calif.: SOLARC, 1975. 101 pp. $8.95.
Presents basic solar applications and building design: written by architects.

Cassiday, Bruce. *The Complete Solar House.* New York, N.Y.: Dodd, Mead, 1977. 212 pp. $8.95. Also, New York, N.Y.: Warner, 1977. 287 pp. $2.50.
An introductory look at the use of solar energy in the home, presenting successful applications in ordinary residences, both new and old. The challenge of solar to architecture is discussed, and a chapter on solar electricity is included. Excellent photography. Not a "how-to" manual.

Crowther, Richard, et al. *Sun Earth.* Denver, Colo.: Crowther/Solar Group, 1977. 232 pp. $10.00. (EARS)
This is a survey of architecture and its relation to the natural environment. It includes cost-effective concepts for the use of free natural energy sources, and information on the design of passive solar energy systems.

Daniels, George. *Solar Homes and Sun Heating.* New York, N.Y.: Harper & Row, 1976. 178 pp. $11.95. (EARS)

How to plan for solar heating in a new home or add it to an existing structure. Ten systems are described for laymen, with instructions and references.

Davis, Chester, and Davis, Martha. *People Who Live in Solar Houses And What They Say About Them.* New York, N.Y.: Popular Library, 1979. 224 pp. $2.25.
This cross-country tour takes a look at solar houses in actual operation and interviews the owners. Includes details on how the systems work, construction specifications, costs, and environmental factors.

Davis, Norah Deakin, and Lindsey, Linda. *At Home in the Sun. An Open House Tour of Solar Homes in the United States.* Charlotte, Vt.: Garden Way, 1979. 236 pp. $9.95. (EARS)
Not only do we find a variety of solar home diagrams, plans, and photographs, but we are introduced to the people and their way of solar living.

Davis, William B. *Living With the Sun.* Dallas, Tex.: Solar Book Corporation, 1976. 163 pp. $6.00. (EARS)
A guide for home owners and professionals for the use of solar energy in residential space heating. Includes a number of ASHRAE tables.

Foster, William M. *Homeowner's Guide to Solar Heating and Cooling.* Blue Ridge Summit, Pa.: Tab Books. 1976. 196 pp. $4.95. (EARS)
An introduction to basic economics, various systems, and applications.

Frank, Ruth F. *Something New Under the Sun: Building Connecticut's First Solar Home.* Harrisville, N.H.: Brick House, 1979. 160 pp. $8.95. (TEA)
The experiences involved in building a solar home are related, from the first plans to finding builders and setting a realistic budget. The Franks find that they have not only saved money but have enriched their lives.

Franta, Gregory E., and Olson, Kenneth R. *Solar Architecture.* Ann Arbor, Mich.: Ann Arbor Science Publishers, 1979. 331 pp. $18.00.
Examples and case studies illustrate fundamentals of building design in relation to climate, energy and resource conservation, and alternate energy sources. Addresses undergrounding, cost-effectiveness, solar and other energy systems, and greenhouses, as well as the broader issues of environmental education and energy policy.

Gropp, Louis. *Solar Houses: 48 Energy Saving Designs.* A House and Garden Book. New York, N.Y.: Pantheon, 1978. 160 pp. $8.95. (EARS)
A look at new solar houses across the nation—and the people that live in them. It is clear that architectural style and elegance need not be sacrificed. Both active and passive systems are described and illustrated. Appendices include a summary of solar legislation.

Heshong, Lisa. *Thermal Delight in Architecture.* 104 pp. $5.95. (TEA).
Designers whose thermal sensibilities go beyond simple engineering efficiencies can explore the potential for using thermal qualities as an expressive element of architectural space—as in the hearth, the sauna, and the bath.

Hudson Home Guides, eds. *Practical Guide to Solar Homes.* New York, N.Y.: Bantam/Hudson, 1978. 140 pp. $10.95.
Thirty solar and energy-conserving home plans are described, suitable for areas across the country. Also included are planning guides, addresses of manufacturers, recommended equipment, and a list of blueprints that may be

purchased.

Joint Venture and Friends. *Here Comes the Sun. 1981: Solar Multi-Family Housing.* Boulder, Colo.: Joint Venture, 1975. 98 pp. $12.00. (EARS)

Discusses solar mechanical heating systems; energy conservation in building design; and higher density housing as a way of changing the environment for a healthier life on the planet. Includes floor plans and models.

Lucas, Ted. *How to Use Solar Energy in Your Home and Business.* Pasadena, Calif.: Ward Ritchie, 1977. 315 pp. $7.95.

Provides detailed plans and photographs for a wide variety of solar applications, including solar cells and windmills. Appendices.

Massdesign. *Solar Heated Houses for New England and Other North Temperate Climates.* (Revised Edition). Cambridge, Mass.: Massdesign, Architects and Planners, Inc., 1976. 68 pp. $7.50.

Examines different types of solar heating systems for single family houses.

Mazria, Edward. *The Passive Solar Energy Book: A Complete Guide to Passive Solar Home, Greenhouse, and Building Design.* Emmaus, Pa.: Rodale, 1979. 435 pp. $10.95. (EARS)

Mazria demystifies the technology of passive design and application, and makes this information accessible to the beginner as well as the professional. He includes the basics of passive solar systems, design pattenrs, and criteria for choosing systems suited to one's particular situation.

Mazria, Edward. *The Passive Solar Energy Book.* Expanded Professional Edition. Emmaus, Pa.: Rodale, 1979. 687 pp. $24.95. (hardbound). (EARS)

In addition to the topics covered in the shorter version, the professional edition contains 13 appendices for predicting precisely a building's energy effectiveness, solar radiation calculators, and additional charts and illustrations.

Montgomery, Richard H., with Budnick, Jim. *The Solar Decision Book: A Guide for Heating Your Home with Solar Energy.* New York, N.Y.: Wiley, 1978. 300 pp. $12.95.

Clear directions, diagrams, and tables assist the home owner and contractor in studying energy needs and costs, selecting alternative energy sources, planning, financing, and installing solar equipment. A complete reference work.

Nicholson, Nick. *Harvest the Sun: Solar Construction in the Snow Belt.* Ayer's Cliff, Quebec, Canada: Ayer's Cliff Center for Solar Research, 1978. 256 pp. $9.95. (EARS) (TEA)

Novel devices have been developed to utilize the sun's energy in northern climates. Easy-to-follow, detailed plans are accompanied by fine photographs.

Nicholson, Nick, and Davidson, Bruce. *The Nicholson Solar Energy Catalog and Building Manual.* Frenchtown, N.J.: Renewable Energy Publications, Ltd. 1977. 172 pp. $9.50. (EARS)

One of the first books dealing with solar applications at a northern latitude and with a severe winter climate. It is based upon the design and construction of 10 solar homes in Quebec, Canada.

Rahders, Richard R., *Your House Can Do It: The Passive Approach to Free Heating and Cooling.* Santa Cruz, Calif.: Thatcher and Thompson, 1979. 169 pp. $12.00.

Beginning with ancient history, the author examines passive designs and shows how they can be applied to new and old houses: a here-and-now approach to living in accord with the natural processes. Includes a chapter on energy politics and the present mismanagement.

Reynolds, John S. *Solar Energy for Pacific Northwest Buildings.* Center for Environmental Research, School of Architecture, University of Oregon, Eugene, OR 97403. 1976. 70 pp. $7.00.
    General solar information is presented, with a focus on homes in the Pacific Northwest.

Reynoldson, George, et al. *Let's Reach for the Sun. Thirty Original Solar Home Designs.* Bellevue, Wash.: Space/Time Designs, 1978. 143 pp. $9.95.
    The challenge of designing solar homes that are both functional and beautiful is met with this series of unique plans. Complete house plan packages may be ordered from the publishers.

Scully, Dan; Prowler, Don; and Anderson, Bruce. *The Fuel Savers: A Kit of Solar Ideas for Existing Homes.* Harrisville, N.H.: Cheshire, 1978. 64 pp. $2.75. (TEA) (EARS)
    A practical do-it-yourself guide to low cost solar retrofits, using simple tools and materials—a wealth of ideas adaptable to almost any home.

Shurcliff, William A. *Solar Heated Buildings—A Brief Survey.* Thirteenth and final edition, January 1977. 306 pp. $12.00.
    A detailed and accurate survey of 319 solar homes and buildings, including descriptions of operating principles, costs, and problems.

Shurcliff, William A. *Solar Heated Buildings of North America: 120 Outstanding Examples.* Harrisville, N.H.: Brick House, 1978. 296 pp. $8.95. (TEA) (EARS)
    A detailed and illustrated description is provided for a wide variety of installations, including houses, office buildings, schools, churches, apartments, and greenhouses, employing both active and passive systems.

Sunset Magazine, eds. *Sunset Homeowners' Guide to Solar Heating, Space Heating and Cooling, Hot Water Heaters, Pools, Spas, and Tubs.* Menlo Park, Calif.: Lane, 1978. 96 pp. $2.95. (EARS)
    Basic principles are simplified, and guidelines provided for planning a solar system to meet your needs. Excellent color photographs and drawings illustrate active, passive, and retrofit applications.

Szokolay, S.V. *Solar Energy and Building.* New York, N.Y.: Wiley, 1977. 174 pp. $18.50.
    Analyzes solar energy problems and solutions, and reviews solar houses, including plans and performance data.

Troutman, Curt; Maier, Peter; and Stanton, Thomas. *Clouded Progress: An Evaluation of the HUD Residential Solar Energy Program.* Center for Study of Responsive Law, P.O. Box 19367, Washington, DC 20036. 1977. 61 pp. $5/$10.
    The U.S. Department of Housing and Urban Development solar program is examined, and suggestions made for its improvement. See above, American Institute of Architects.

U.S. Department of Housing and Urban Development. *The First Passive Solar Home Awards.* Franklin Research Center. Washington, DC, 1979. S/N 023-000-00517-4. 226 pp. $6.95. (USGPO) (EARS)
    One hundred and sixty-two award-winning projects are described, and

information provided on the selection of the best type of solar project for a given area, materials, calculating solar gain, and marketing passive solar homes.

U.S. Department of Housing and Urban Development. *Solar Dwelling Design Concepts.* Washington, DC, 1978. S/N 023-000-00334-1. 146 pp. $2.30. (USGPO)
Designers, home builders, and community leaders will find this a useful resource for applications of solar heating and cooling.

U.S. Department of Housing and Urban Development. *A Survey of Passive Solar Buildings.* Washington, DC, 1978. S/N 023-000-00437-2. 177 pp. $3.75. (USGPO)
The state-of-the-art in passive solar design is documented, with definitions and descriptions for a number of applications.

Van Dresser, Peter. *Home Grown Sundwellings.* The Lighting Tree, Box 1837 Santa Fe, NM 87501, 1977. 133 pp. $5.95. (EARS)
A study of model homes constructed to test principles of passive solar house heating and low technology design.

Watson, Donald. *Designing and Building a Solar Home: Your Place in the Sun.* Charlotte, Vt.: Garden Way Publishing, 1977. 282 pp. $8.95. (EARS)
This book makes the solar home a workable, energy-efficient reality for today. The graphic presentation clarifies passive and active solar heating systems, cooling, and house design. Costs of different systems are compared.

Wells, Malcolm, and Spetgang, Irwin. *How to Buy Solar Heating . . . Without Getting Burnt.* Emmaus, Pa.: Rodale Press 1978. 262 pp. $6.95. (EARS) (TEA)
This lively consumer's guide takes much of the mystery out of choosing, financing, and installing solar heating equipment.

Wells, Malcolm, and Spetgang, Irwin. *Your Home's Solar Potential.* Barrington N.J.: Edmund Scientific Company, 1976. 60 pp. $9.95.
A "do-it-yourself" survey and questionnaire to determine your home's solar suitability.

Wright, David. *Natural Solar Architecture: A Passive Primer.* New York, N.Y.: Van Nostrand-Reinhold, 1978. 256 pp. $7.95. (EARS)
The natural approach to solar architecture requires minimal expenditure of commercial energy, and little equipment. The building itself collects, stores, and distributes the sun's energy. Unusual diagrams, checklists, and handwritten text make this a most useful reference for architect or homebuilder.

Solar Technology

American Physical Society. *Solar Photovoltaic Energy Conversion.* American Physical Society, 333 E. 45th St., New York, NY 10017. 1979. $5.00.
This report, prepared by the American Physical Society under a contract with the U.S. Department of Energy, stresses the need for more basic research, and does not expect the growth of a solar photovoltaic industry until the 1990's.

Ametek, Inc./Power Systems Group. *Solar Energy Handbook: Theory and Applications.* Radnor, Pa.: Chilton, 1979. 179 pp. $18.50.

This is a tool for architects, contractors, home owners, and businessmen concerned with solar energy, and is intended to bridge the gap between theoretical texts and consumer manuals. Includes formulas, tables, and maps.

ASHRAE *Handbook*. See below, Jordan.

Backus, Charles E. *Solar Cells*. New York, N.Y.: Institute of Electric and Electronics Engineers, Inc., 1976. 504 pp. $12.45.
　　Technical papers on solar cell theory, fabrication, and applications.

Bailey, Robert L. *Solar-Electrics Research and Development*. Ann Arbor, Mich.: Ann Arbor Science Publishers, 1980. 550 pp. $29.50.
　　Offers perspectives on the complex issues involved in photovoltaics, wind, energy storage, and solar electric systems, and identifies the technical barriers.

Beckman, William; Klein, Sanford; and Duffie, John. *Solar Heating Design by the F-Chart Method*. N.Y., N.Y.: Wiley-Interscience, 1977. 200 pp. $15.95. (EARS)
　　Information on economic sizing of systems, estimates of heating loads, and thermal performance of flat plate collectors.

Bennett, Robert. *Sun Angles for Design*. Bala Cynwyd, Pa.: Bennett, 1978. 78 pp. $6.00. (EARS)
　　A set of 25 sun angle charts, with an explanation of how to use them in solar site analysis and architecture.

Braden, Spruille III. *Graphic Standards of Solar Energy*. Boston, Mass.: CBI Publishing Company, 1977. 212 pp. $22.25.
　　Unique graphics make this a useful desk-and-drafting-table companion for architects and builders. All phases of solar energy design are covered in sections on energy conservation, solar energy systems, and climatic factors.

Calthorpe, Peter. *The Farallones Institute Solar Study: A Comparison of Four Passive and Hybrid Space Heating Systems*. The Farallones Institute, 15290 Coleman Valley Rd., Occidental, CA 95465. 1978. 35 pp. $3.50.
　　Four cabins and their location and climate are described, and the comparactive collector efficiency of each system is calculated and discussed.

Campbell, Stu, with Taff, Doug. *Build Your Own Solar Water Heater*. Charlotte, Vt.: Garden Way, 1978. 124 pp. $7.95. (TEA) (EARS)
　　One of the best manuals on solar water heating: easy to understand, yet including basic facts, charts, and illustrations.

Crowther Solar Architects. *Sun Path Indicator*. 1979. $3.00. (EARS)
　　Essentially a sun dial, this simple cardboard instrument can tell the time of day and year at which that sun angle will occur.

Dean, T.S. *Thermal Storage*. Phila, Pa.: Franklin Institute, 1978. 61 pp. $8.95.
　　Practical technical information on the design and use of thermal storage systems is provided in this monograph.

Duffie, John A., and Beckman, William A. *Solar Energy Thermal Processes*. New York, N.Y.: John Wiley and Sons, 1974. 386 pp. $20.25. (EARS)
　　A detailed summary of the literature on solar applications. with diagrams, tables, and references. An advanced textbook.

Edwards, Donald K. *Solar Collector Design*. Philadelphia, Pa.: Franklin Institute, 1977. 64 pp. $8.95.

Of interest to the builder, householder, and serious student, this primer gives an overview of collector development and theory, and calculations and drawings for various systems.

Eklund, Ken, et al. *The Solar Water Heater Workshop Manual.* Ecotope Group, 2332 East Madison, Seattle, WA 98112. 1979. 82 pp. $5.75.
The authors provide a step-by-step description of how to build a solar water heater, and how to organize a workshop on this topic.

Field, Richard. *Design Manual for Solar Heating of Buildings and Domestic Hot Water.* SOLPUB Company, Box 9209 College Station, TX 77840. 1979. $7.95.
Worksheets and information provide the basis for the do-it-yourself designer to determine the specifications of a solar unit suited to his/her locale.

Fleck, Paul A. *Solar Energy Handbook.* Pasadena, Calif.: Time-Wise Publications, 1975. 92 pp. $3.95. (EARS)
A collection of data needed by the designer and serious experimenter for constructing solar devices.

Foster, William F. *Build-It Book of Solar Heating Projects.* Blue Ridge Summit, Pa.: TAB Books, 1977. 195 pp. $7.95.
Four solar heating systems are described, with materials and components, basic climatic information, and requisite skills listed.

Institute of Electrical and Electronic Engineers. *Thirteenth IEEE Photovoltaic Specialists Conference.* June, 1978. Institute of Electrical and Electronic Engineers, 345 E. 47th St., New York, NY 10017. 1346 pp.
Two hundred and fifty research papers describe the development of photovoltaics as a large-scale power source. This potentially important technology will be competitive for certain applications by the end of the 1980's.

International Solar Energy Society. *Proceedings of the Second National Passive Solar Conference,* March 1978, University of Pennsylvania. International Solar Energy Society, American Section, P.O. Box 1416, Killeen, TX 76541. $14/$50.
Vol. 1, 269 pp. Passive design in buildings and greenhouses.
Vol. 2, 421 pp. Components, hot water systems.
Vol. 3, 261 pp. Policy, education, and economics.

International Solar Energy Society. *Proceedings of the Third National Passive Solar Conference.* January 1979, San Jose, California. International Solar Energy Society, American Section, P.O. Box 1416, Killeen, TX 76541. 925 pp. $19/$65.
The emphasis in these papers is on the design of homes and buildings made comfortable by natural energy and simple means, and creativity in solar energy applications.

International Solar Energy Society, and the Solar Energy Society of Canada, Inc. *Sharing the Sun! Solar Technology in the Seventies.* Beltsville, Md.: Solar Science Industries, Inc., 1976.
This ten-volume set includes the proceedings of the joint conference in Winnipeg, Canada, August 15-20, 1976. Approximately 350 papers document the status of solar energy conversion technology.
Vol. 1. *International and U.S. Programs; Solar Flux.* 389 pp.
Vol. 2. *Flat Plate Collectors; Focusing Collectors.* 387 pp.
Vol. 3. *Cooling Methods; Heating and Cooling; Heat Pumps.* 405 pp.

Vol. 4. *Passive Systems; Retrofit Systems; Simulation; Design Methods.* 424 pp.

Vol. 5. *Thermal Energy Systems; Ocean Thermal.* 548 pp.

Vol. 6. *Photovoltaics.* 348 pp.

Vol. 7. *Agricultural and Industrial Process Applications; Bioconversion; Wind.* 391 pp.

Vol. 8. *Solar Storage; Solar Heat for Buildings and Water Heaters.* 371 pp.

Vol. 10. *Business and Commercial Implications.* 269 pp.

Jordan, R.C., and Liu, B.Y.H., eds. *Applications of Solar Energy for Heating and Cooling of Buildings.* American Society of Heating, Refrigerating and Air Conditioning Engineers: ASHRAE, 345 47th St., New York, NY 10017. 1976. 206 pp. $9.00.

A technical handbook for engineers with detailed data on components, solar systems, solar radiation, and other factors in the application of solar energy. ASHRAE has developed standards for energy efficient building design.

Karaki, Susumu, and Wilbur, Paul J. *Solar Cooling.* Philadelphia, Pa.: Franklin Institute, 1977. 48 pp. $8.95.

Solar powered cooling systems for air conditioning and refrigeration are described. The most promising are the absorption cooler, and a heat engine that drives a vapor compression refrigerator. Technical information, diagrams, and calculations are presented.

Keyes, John H. *Consumer Handbook of Solar Energy, for the United States and Canada.* Dobbs Ferry, New York: Morgan, 1979, 273 pp. $10.95.

This handbook includes tables for the calculation of solar needs, output of solar systems, costs and payback time, and home heat loss; also, data to assist in the evaluation of solar equipment.

Keyes, John. *Harnessing the Sun to Heat Your House.* Dobbs Ferry, N.Y.: Morgan, 1975. 202 pp. $3.95. (EARS)

A basic introduction to solar heating applications, including the solar furnace. Includes data from the *Climatic Atlas of the U.S.*

Kreider, Jan, and Kreith, Frank. *Solar Heating and Cooling: Engineering, Practical Design, and Economics.* New York, N.Y.: McGraw-Hill. Revised, 1977. 342 pp. $31.50. (EARS)

This is a how-to-do-it handbook, describing systems and providing data needed on materials, climate, and economics.

Landa, Henry C. *Solar Energy Calculations and Programs for Pocket Programmable Electronic Calculators.* Milwaukee, Wis.: Film Instruction Company of America, 1978. 62 pp. $4.00. (EARS)

A manual of solar energy systems calculations, with programs for depreciation, furnace size, heat loss, surface insolation, water heating, and other factors.

Landa, H.C., et al. *The Solar Energy Handbook.* 4th ed. Milwaukee, Wis.: Film Instruction Company of America, 1976. 154 pp. $9.00. (EARS)

A compilation of theory, practical applications, and technical data.

Libby-Owens-Ford Company. *Sun Angle Calculator.* Libby-Owens-Ford Company, 811 Madison Ave., Toledo, OH 43695. $5.00.

A handy device—a circular slide rule—for determining the position of the sun, angle of incidence, and other factors.

Lucas, Ted. *How to Build a Solar Heater: A Complete Guide to Building and Buying Solar Panels, Water Heaters, Pool Heaters, Barbecues, and Power Plants.* New York, N.Y.: Mentor, 1975. 238 pp. $4.95. (EARS)

Using examples of working models, this guide tells how to select the right devices, how they work, and how they can be built.

Mazria, Edward, and Winitzky, David. *Solar Guide and Calculator*. Center for Environmental Research, School of Architecture and Allied Arts, University of Oregon, Eugene, OR 97403. 1976. 20 pp. $4.25. (EARS)
Sun angles and available heat energy may be calculated by this simplified method.

Merrigan, Joseph A. *Sunlight to Electricity—The Prospects for Solar Energy Conversion by Photovoltaics*. Cambridge, Mass.: Massachusetts Institute of Technology Press, 1975. 163 pp.
Surveys the prospects of U.S. energy requirements, resources, magnitude of solar energy potential, principles of photovoltaics, and economic obstacles.

NSF-RANN Workshop on Solar Collectors for Heating and Cooling of Buildings. New York, N.Y.: National Science Foundation—Research Applied to National Needs. 1974. 507 pp.
These proceedings describe solar collectors, manufacturers' experience, materials, models, testing, and standards in federal programs.

Olgyay, Victor, and Olgyay, Aladar. *Solar Control and Shading Devices*. Princeton, N.J.: Princeton University Press, 1957. 201 pp. $8.95. (EARS)
Despite its age, this is a uniquely valuable approach to the study of climate, the seasons, latitude, calculation of solar energy, shading devices, and the role of vegetation. Examples from many corners of the world.

Palz, Wolfgang. *Solar Electricity: An Economic Approach to Solar Energy*. Paris; UNESCO, 1978. 312 pp. $46.00. (UNIPUB)
The latest achievements in the field of solar energy are described, including direct use of solar heat, thermodynamic conversion into mechanical and electrical energy, and solar cells, which convert light directly into electricity. An excellent text for students at all levels.

Paul, J.K. *Solar Heating and Cooling: Recent Advances*. Park Ridge, N.J.: Noyes Data Corporation, 1977. 485 pp. $48.00.
175 patents are described and illustrated in this summary of patent literature from 1970-1977.

Patton, Arthur R. *Solar Energy for Heating and Cooling of Buildings*. Park Ridge, N.J.: Noyes Data Corporation, 1975. 328 pp. $24.00.
Research for the American Institute of Architects. Gives details of low temperature solar thermal processes; describes experimental buildings and current research; addresses for materials and references.

Schwartz, Morris Sokol, ed. *Harvesting the Sun's Energy*. Fullerton, Calif.: Design III Printing, 1975. 653 pp. $8.00.
A compendium of valuable technical information.

Sayigh, A.A.M., ed. *Solar Energy Engineering*. New York, N.Y.: Academic Press, 1977. 506 pp. $39.75.
Technical selections on the conversion and storage of solar energy, photovoltaics, desalination, economics, and other topics are intended for advanced engineering students and professionals.

Shurcliff, William A. *New Inventions in Low Cost Solar Heating; 100 Daring Schemes, Tried and Untried*. Harrisville, N.H.: Brick House, 1979. 293 pp. $12.00. (TEA) (EARS)

The emphasis is on bold new schemes which open up new avenues in solar design, cut costs, and improve performance. Describes passive, active, and combination systems that are simple and inexpensive, including storage systems and greenhouses.

Shurcliff, William A. *Thermal Shutters and Shades.* Harrisville, N.H.: Brick House, 1980.
Many ideas for reducing heat loss are contained in this survey of all types of shutters, shades, and window insulation.

Sinha, Evelyn, and McCosh, Bonnie. *Solar Energy Technology—State of the Art.* Ocean Engineering Information Service, P.O. Box 989. La Jolla, CA 92038, 1975. 63 pp.
Contains 547 abstracts from professional journals and reports for the period of 1969 to 1975.

Solarex Corporation. *Making and Using Electricity from the Sun.* Blue Ridge Summit, Pa.: TAB Books, 1979. 143 pp. $5.95. (EARS)
The operation, applications, and potential of the solar cell is explained, along with experiments to perform and projects to construct.

Stewart, John W. *How to Make Your Own Solar Electricity.* Blue Ridge Summit, Pa.: TAB Books, 1979. 168 pp. $5.95. (EARS)
You can design and construct a photovoltaic energy conversion system to produce your own electricity from the sun. Information is provided on solar arrays, storage systems, components, and the economics of photovoltaics.

Sussman, Art, and Frazier, Richard. *Handmade Hot Water Systems.* Garcia River Press, Box 527, Point Arena, CA 95468. 1978. 91 pp. $4.95. (EARS)
A do-it-yourself handbook for designing and building wood and solar hot water systems, with a chapter on swimming pools and hot tubs.

Turner, Robert A. *High Temperature Thermal Energy Storage.* Philadelphia, Pa.: Franklin Institute Press, 1977. 101 pp. $8.95.
High temperature thermal storage systems are compared, including storage in pressurized and unpressurized fluids, in stationary solids, in moving solids, and in phase change materials.

Turner, Rufus P. *Solar Cells and Photocells.* Indianapolis, Inc.: Howard W. Sams and Company, Inc., 1975. 96 pp. $3.95. (EARS)
Intended for experimenters, technicians and science fair participants. Gives schematics for operating circuits.

United Nations. *Solar Distillation as a Means of Meeting Small Scale Water Demands.* New York, N.Y.: United Nations Department of Economic and Social Affairs, 1970. 86 pp. $6.00. (UNIPUB)
This study describes the technology, costs, potential scope, installation, and operation of solar stills and energy-source systems.

United Nations. *Technology for Solar Energy Utilization.* United Nations, 1978. 164 pp. $10.00. (UNIPUB)
Technical papers cover the conversion of solar into mechanical or electrical energy, through collectors, refrigeration, distillation, dryers, cookers, and other devices. Information is provided on the utilization of solar energy in developing countries.

U.S. Congress. Office of Technology Assessment. *Application of Solar Technology to Today's Energy Needs.* Washington, DC, 1978. Vol. I., 525 pp. S/N 052-003-

00539-5. Vol. II., 756 pp. S/N 052-003-00608-1. (USGPO)

Volume I reviews a range of solar energy systems designed to produce thermal and electrical energy directly from sunlight with units small enough to be located on or near the buildings served. It also examines the technology and the impact of decentralized solar energy on the way society evolves. Volume II presents detailed information about calculation techniques and the results of systems analysis.

U.S. Department of Commerce. *Solar Heating and Cooling of Residential Buildings.* Washington, DC, 1977. (USGPO)

Volume I. *Design of Systems.* S/N 003-011-00084-4. 569 pp. $8.25.

Volume II. *Sizing, Installation, and Operation of Systems.* S/N 003-011-00085-2. 375 pp. $7.00.

These volumes comprise a course to train home designers and builders.

U.S. Department of Energy. *Energy Storage Systems: Program Overview.* Washington, DC, 1978, S/N 061-000-00195-6. 91 pp. $2.75. (USGPO)

The aim of the Energy Storage Program is to develop reliable and inexpensive systems for use in transportation, heating and cooling of buildings, industry, and utilities.

U.S. Department of Energy. *Fundamentals of Solar Heating.* Washington, DC, 1978. 175 pp. $4.50. (USGPO) (EARS)

Active solar collectors systems and associated systems are treated in detail.

U.S. Department of Energy. *Introduction to Solar Heating and Cooling Design and Sizing.* Washington, DC, 1978. S/N 061-000-00152-2. 502 pp. $6.75. (USGPO)

Written for contractors, architects, engineers, and builders, this manual describes the practical aspects of solar heating and cooling systems, applications in specific geographical areas, and economic benefits.

U.S. Department of Energy. *Photovoltaic Program.* Washington, DC, 1978. S/N 061-000-0087-9. 221 pp. $4.00. (USGPO)

An overview and abstracts of projects in the DOE's program to investigate the possibilities of producing electricity by photovoltaics.

U.S. Department of Energy. *SOLCOST*

For a minimal processing fee, this computer service of the U.S. DOE helps consumers make decisions about solar energy system installations and costs. Forms and instructions are contained in two booklets:

Space Heating Handbook with Service Hotwater and Heat Loads Calculations. Washington, DC, 1978. S/N 061-000-00148-4. 19 pp. $1.20. (USGPO)

Solar Hot Water Handbook. Washington, DC, 1978. S/N 061-000-00137-9. 15 pp. $1.00. (USGPO)

University of New Mexico. *Solar Thermal Energy Utilization, 1957-1970.* University of New Mexico, Technology Application Center, Albuquerque, NM 87131. 2 vols. $35.00.

Abstracts of approximately 4000 books, papers, and articles on all aspects of solar energy utilization.

Ward, Dan; Karaki, Susumu; and Lof, George. *Sizing, Installation, and Operation of Systems for the Solar Heating and Cooling of Residential Buildings.* Washington, DC: USGPO, 1977. 460 pp. $8.75. (EARS)

Directed toward the architect, engineer, and builder, this detailed manual covers almost all aspects of solar energy design and installation.

Williams, J. Richard. *Solar Energy Technology and Applications.* Ann Arbor, Mich.: Ann Arbor Science Publishers, revised 1977. 184 pp. $6.95.

This text is both a state-of-the-art book and a how-to-do-it book, introducing the various techniques for utilizing solar and alternative energy sources. These sources can be utilized economically to provide an inexhaustible and non-polluting resource for all time.

Winn, Byron; Karaki, Susumu; and Lof, George. *Design of Systems for the Solar Heating and Cooling of Residential Buildings.* Washington, DC: USGPO, 1977. 610 pp. $10.50. (EARS)

A manual to train home designers and builders, covering the fundamentals of solar hydronic and air systems, calculations, storage systems, and controls.

Yellott, John. *Solar Energy Utilization for Heating and Cooling.* Harrisville, N.H.: Total Environmental Action, 1974. 20 pp. $2.00. (EARS) (TEA)

An introduction to the technical and engineering aspects of solar energy use.

The Solar Greenhouse

Clegg, Peter, and Watkins, Derry. *The Complete Greenhouse Book: Building and Using Greenhouses from Cold Frames to Solar Structures.* Charlotte, Vt.: Garden Way, 1978. 280 pp. $8.95. (EARS) (TEA)

This complete, non-technical guide covers history, planning, construction, materials, horticulture, pests, solar design, and window greenhouses in an attractive, large format volume.

Dekorne, James. *The Survival Greenhouse.* El Rito, N.Mex.: Walden Foundation, 1975. 165 pp. $7.95. (EARS)

The story of an endeavor to create a self-sustaining eco-system, a basic food-producing greenhouse capable of supplementing the diet of a small family.

Fisher, Rick, and Yanda, Bill. *The Food and Heat Producing Greenhouse: Design, Construction, Operation.* Santa Fe, N.M.: John Muir Publications, 1976. 161 pp. $6.00. Distributed by Bookpeople, 2940 Seventh St., Berkeley, CA 94710. (TEA)

Everything you ever wanted to know about greenhouses, from a desert agricultural project to a simple lean-to. If you want to make the sun a practical part of your life today, this book will tell you how.

Fontanetta, John, and Heller, Al. *Building and Using a Solar Heated Geodesic Greenhouse.* Charlotte, Vt.: Garden Way, 1979. 200 pp. $8.95.

A low-cost solar-heated dome greenhouse can be built by following these complete directions, which also tell how to use it for horticulture, aquaculture, and as an auxilliary source of home heat and hot water.

Hayes, John, and Gillett, Drew, eds. *Proceedings of the Conference on Energy-Conserving, Solar-Heated Greenhouses.* Marlboro, Vt.: Marlboro College, 1979. 282 pp. $9.00.

This well-illustrated series of state-of-the-art papers contains excellent background material and actual case histories.

Huke, Robert, and Sherwin, Robert Jr. *A Fish and Vegetable Grower for All Seasons.* Norwich, Vt.: Norwich Publications, 1977. 125 pp. $4.95. (EARS).

You can buy or build your own greenhouse to use for horticulture, aquaculture, or a combination of the two.

Kasprzak, Rick. *The Passive Solar Greenhouse and Organic Hydroponics: A Primer*. R.L.D. Publications, P.O. Box 1443, Flagstaff, AZ 86002. 1977. 79 pp. $5.80.

A manual for the design and construction of a passive solar greenhouse, and for methods of hydroponic gardening.

Magee, Tim; Oberton, Carol; and Stewart, Liz. *A Solar Greenhouse Guide for the Northwest*. Ecotope Group, 2332 E. Madison, Seattle, WA 98112. 1978. 92 pp. $5.00.

This well illustrated guide provides practical directions for the construction and operation of solar greenhouses in the Northwest.

McCullagh, James C. *The Solar Greenhouse Book*. Emmaus, Pa.: Rodale Press, 1978. 314 pp. $8.95. (EARS)

A comprehensive book, providing detailed information for the design, construction, and crop production in a variety of solar greenhouses, for every climate and every need.

Nearing, Helen, and Nearing, Scott. *Building and Using Our Sun-Heated Greenhouse*. Charlotte, Vt.: Garden Way, 1977. 148 pp. $6.95. (EARS)

By means of a clear text and excellent photographs, the Nearings tell how to build and use a sunheated greenhouse to produce vegetables all year round, even in chilly New England.

Nicholls, Richard. *The Handmade Greenhouse: From Windowsill to Backyard*. Philadelphia, Pa.: Running Press. 1975. 127 pp. $4.95.

Offers designs for the construction and operation of different types of greenhouses with tips on tools and materials.

Pierce, John H. *Greenhouse Grow How: A Reference Book*. Seattle, Washington: Scribner. 1977. 242 pp. $19.95. (EARS)

All you need to know about greenhouses is contained in this unique and beautifully illustrated volume—design, construction, operation, management of air and moisture, soil, and pest control.

TRANSPORTATION

Ayres, Robert U., and McKenna, Richard P. *Alternatives to the Internal Combustion Engine: Impacts on Environmental Quality.* Published for Resources for the Future. Baltimore, Md.: Johns Hopkins University Press, 1972. 324 pp. $12.00.

A comprehensive treatment of existing and potential power plants and fuels for motor vehicles. Comparisons are made with regard to performance, costs and environmental pollution.

Bendixson, Terence. *Without Wheels: Alternatives to the Private Car.* Bloomington, Inc.: Indiana University Press, 1975. 256 pp. $10.00.

Here is what new technology can do to improve present modes of transportation, to design new ones, and to create patterns of settlement and styles of life that reduce the need to travel.

Brown, Lester R.; Flavin, Christopher; and Norman, Colin. *The Future of the Automobile in an Oil Short World.* Washington, DC: Worldwatch Institute, 1979. 64 pp. $2.00. (FOE) (EARS)

A compact version of *Running on Empty* by the same authors.

Brown, Lester R.; Flavin, Christopher; and Colin, Norman. *Running on Empty: The Future of the Automobile in an Oil Short World.* New York, N.Y.: Norton, 1979. 116 pp. $7.95.

The uncertain outlook for fuel supplies demands an all-out effort to develop alternative fuels and more efficient automobiles. Society is faced with complex political, economic, and personal choices as the future of the automobile begins to dim and we face the spectre of an economic system harnessed to a decaying albatross.

Dark, Harris Edward. *Auto Engines of Tomorrow: Power Alternatives for Cars to Come.* Bloomington, Ind.: Indiana University Press, 1975. 192 pp. $8.95.

A survey of the possible automotive power plants of the future, and some far-out ideas in auto engineering.

Dark, Harris Edward. *The Wankel Rotary Engine.* Bloomington, Ind.: Indiana University Press, 1974. 145 pp. $6.95.

This book traces the history of the automobile engine, and tells how changes in the interest of clean air have lowered its efficiency. It considers alternatives to the piston engine, with details on the development of the Wankel engine in the Mazda car.

Environmental Action Foundation and National Wildlife Federation. *The End of the Road: A Citizen's Guide to Transportation Problem-Solving.* Environmental Action Foundation, 1346 Connecticut Ave. NW, Washington, DC 20036. 1977. 159 pp. $3.50.

This is an analysis of the financial and political aspects of transportation planning, national legislation in this field, and the energy, economic, and social costs of various modes of transportation. Also tells what citizens can do to help solve these problems.

Hackleman, Michael. *Electric Vehicles.* Culver City, Calif.: Peace Press, 1977. 202 pp. $7.95. An Earthmind Publication.

The author is an advocate of small vehicles, for economy, range and less weight. Several types of electric vehicles are described, and construction plans include every detail of mechanical power, electric power, batteries, and framework. Resources for materials are included.

Hudson, Mike. *The Bicycle Planning Book.* London: FOE Ltd., 1978. 154 pp. $4.95. (FOE)

A revival is now under way for this energy-efficient and non-polluting means of transportation. Careful local planning will contribute to its success.

Hudson, Mike. *Way Ahead: The Bicycle Warrior's Handbook.* London: FOE Ltd., 1978. 59 pp. $2.50. (FOE).

Here is a field manual for starting a bicycle campaign: how to lay out routes, lobby for your proposals, and fit bicycle planning into your community.

Jerome, John. *The Death of the Automobile.* New York, N.Y.: Norton, 1972. 288 pp. $6.95.

The standard U.S. car is an ecological, engineering, and economic disaster. After considering the total costs of the automobile from highway taxes and repair bills to pollution and social problems, the author concludes that it is not worth the price. Unless Detroit can adapt, its products will go the way of the dinosaur.

Mass Transit and Energy Conservation. NTIS: PB-246-232/AS. 1975. $3.50. (NTIS)

This study discusses trends, efficiencies, and energy conservation potentials in urban transportation.

National Research Council, National Academy of Science. *Energy Use in Transportation: Potential for Cooperative Research.* A report to the Office in International Programs, U.S. Department of Transportation, Washington, DC, 1975. 142 pp.

A report on the status of transportation research and governmental policies in the U.S. and Europe.

Shonka, D.B., Loebl, A.S. and Patterson, P.O. *Transportation Energy Conservation Data Book, Edition 2.* ORNL-5320. Oak Ridge National Laboratory, 1977. 573 pp. $13.75. (NTIS)

A statistical compendium of all major modes of transportation, presenting data on energy use, efficiency, impact of government activities, supply and cost of energy, and general demographic and economic characteristics.

Sikorsky, Robert. *How To Get More Miles per Gallon: An Indispensable Glove-Compartment Guide for Every Car Owner in America With Tips to Save You Gasoline and Money.* New York, N.Y.: St. Martin's Press, 1978. 111 pp. $2.95.

Tips on every angle of car maintenance and driving technique reveal what people can actually do to conserve fuel.

Sittig, Marshall. *Automotive Pollution Control Catalysts and Devices.* Park Ridge, N.J.: Noyes Data Corporation, 1977. 323 pp. $39.00.

Technical developments in engine design, catalytic converters, mechanical devices, and new fuels and additives for the reduction of emissions.

Southerland, Thomas C., Jr., and McCleery, William. *The Way to Go: The Coming*

Revival of U.S. Rail Passenger Service. 1973. New York, N.Y.: Simon & Schuster, 256 pp. $8.95.

The authors tell the story of railroads in the United States and abroad, and look forward to a new era in public transportation that will bring benefits to the commuter, the traveler, and the ecology as well.

U.S. Department of Energy. *Three State-of-the-Art Individual Electric and Hybrid Vehicle Test Reports.* Washington, DC, 1978. S/N 061-000-00199-9. 535 pp. $6.75. (USGPO)

Data are presented on the Fiat 850T Electric Van, The Ripp Electric Passenger Car, and the Volkswagen Taxi Hybrid Passenger Vehicle.

Wakefield, Ernest H. *The Consumer's Electric Car.* Ann Arbor, Mich.: Ann Arbor Science Publishers, 1977. 136 pp. $9.95.

The future electric car is described, from theory to on-road operation.

Wildhorn, Sorrell, et al. *How to Save Gasoline: Public Policy Alternatives for the Automobile.* Cambridge, Mass.: Ballinger, 1975. 352 pp. $18.50.

Public and industry react at government hearings on conservation measures; price increases appeared to be the best near-term way to gasoline savings, with greater long-term savings through improvements in technology and weight reduction.

UTILITIES

Berlin, Edward, and Cicchetti, Charles J. *Perspective on Power: Study of the Regulation and Pricing of Electrical Power.* Cambridge, Mass.: Ballinger Publishing Co., 1974. 204 pp. $7.95.
 A study of the changes taking place in the power industry, with suggestions for policy reform.

Cornell University. *An Organizer's Notebook on Public Utilities and Energy for New York State.* Cornell University, Human Affairs Program. 410 College Ave., Ithaca, NY 14853. 300 pp. $15.00.
 A useful guide to citizen action against a utility or an oil company.

Critical Mass Energy Project. *Nuclear Power and Utility Rate Increases.* Critical Mass Energy Project, Box 1538, Washington, DC 20013. $1/$10.
 This study finds that utilities with large nuclear investments receive higher rate hikes than non-nuclear-dependent utilities.

Doyle, Jack. *Lines Across the Land.* Environmental Policy Institute, 317 Pennsylvania Ave. SE, Washington, DC 20003. 1979. 760 pp. $12.50/$30.00.
 This massive study of rural electric cooperatives finds that they are becoming increasingly involved in the construction of nuclear and coal-fired generating stations and large scale transmission projects, fighting environmental regulations, and resisting the development of effective energy conservation and renewable energy programs.

Environmental Action Foundation. *A Citizen's Guide to the Fuel Adjustment Clause.* Washington, DC: Environmental Action Foundation, 1975. 52 pp. $2.50. (EARS)
 An aid to challenging utility abuses.

Environmental Action Foundation. *How to Challenge Your Local Electric Utility: A Citizen's Guide to the Power Industry.* Washington, DC Environmental Action Foundation, 1976. 100 pp. $3.50. (EARS)
 How electrical power plants affect us, and what can be done about it.

Environmental Action Foundation. *Phantom Taxes in Your Electric Bill.* Washington, DC: Environmental Action Foundation, 1974. 24 pp. $2.50. (EARS)
 Discusses the nature of tax breaks which benefit the utilities.

Environmental Action Foundation. *Taking Charge: A New Look at Public Power.* Washington, DC: Environmental Action Foundation, 1976. 100 pp. $3.50. (EARS)
 Lists the accomplishments of the nation's 3000 municipally owned utilities and rural electric coopeartives in such areas as energy conservation, solar energy development, and rate structure reform.

Environmental Action Foundation. *Utility Scoreboard.* Washington, DC: Environmental Action Foundation, 1978. 52 pp. $3.50.

This statistical survey of the top 100 utilities in the United States in 1976 uncovers many interesting facts regarding excess generating capacity and its cost to consumers; overcharging customers; unpaid taxes; political spending and opposition to safe energy legislation; and air and water pollution by the utilities.

Institute for Local Self-Reliance. *How to Research Your Local Utility.* Washington, DC: Institute for Local Self-Reliance, 1980. $4.00.

A working knowledge of the economics and politics of electric utility operations is provided in this guide, with directions for analyzing options, and case studies from around the country.

Mitchell, Bridger M.; Manning, Willard G. Jr.; and Acton, Jan Paul. *Peak-Load Pricing: European Lessons for U.S. Energy Policy.* Cambridge, Mass.: Ballinger, 1977. 244 pp. $16.50.

The theory of peak-load pricing of electricity is presented, with examples of its practical application in Europe and its implications for American energy policy.

National Consumer Information Center. *Handbook for Consumer Advocates: Electric Utility Rate Proceedings.* National Consumer Information Center, 3005 Georgia Ave. NW, Washington, DC 20001. 500 pp. $12.00.

Attorneys and others who wish to become familiar with the regulatory process in order to seek utility reforms will find this a valuable reference.

Newkirk, Ross T. *Environmental Planning for Utility Corridors.* Ann Arbor, Mich.: Ann Arbor Science Publishers, 1979. 200 pp. $30.00.

Computer-based planning is applied to the environmentally sound placement of continuous utility corridors and environmental impact assessment methodology. For engineers, regional planners, and utility companies.

Seattle City Light. *Energy 1990.* Seattle City Light, 1015 Third Ave., Seattle, WA 98104. $4.00.

The outcome of this study was Seattle's decision to opt for energy conservation over nuclear power plants. It is a useful guide for anyone challenging energy growth projections for their community.

Scott, David L. *Financing the Growth of Electric Utilities.* New York, N.Y.: Praeger, 1976. 142 pp. $17.50.

An overview of the industry is followed by an examination of the financial requirements and funding of U.S. electric utilities, and projections through 1990.

Vogt, Lawrence J., and Conner, David A. *Electrical Energy Management.* Lexington, Mass.: Lexington Books, 1977. 128 pp. $12.00.

A consideration of energy management incentives, electrical load surveys, load management techniques, and programs for energy conservation.

White, Ronald H. *The Price of Power Update: Electric Utilities and the Environment.* Council on Economic Priorities, 84 Fifth Ave., New York, NY 10011. 1977. 430 pp.

Energy planners and utility executives need to reconsider the present rapid growth energy policies, and move toward more diversified programs. Problems to be faced include fuel shortages, rising costs, pollutants and emission control technologies, siting, public health and safety, and environmental degradation.

Young, Louise. *Power Over People*. England: Oxford University Press. 1974. 224 pp. $4.95. (EARS)

Tells of the dangers of high-voltage transmission lines, and the conflicting interests of the electric power companies and communities.

WATER POWER

Energy from Running Water, Tides, Waves, and Thermal Gradients; Offshore Energy Systems

Goldberg, Edward. *The Health of the Oceans.* UNESCO. 1976. 172 pp. $9.25. (UNIPUB)

The author reviews the problems of marine pollution, including radioactivity, oil spills, toxic chemicals, and pollution monitoring strategies.

Gray, T.J., and Gashus, O.K. *Tidal Power.* Proceedings of an International Conference on the Utilization of Tidal Power, Halifax, Nova Scotia, May 1970. New York, N.Y.: Plenum Press, 1972. 630 pp.

Reviews the many advantages and complexities involved in large tidal projects, reports on pilot projects, and surveys the economic and envvironmental effects.

Hagen, Arthur W. *Thermal Energy from the Sea.* Park Ridge, N.J.: Noyes Data Corporation, 1976. 150 pp. $24.00.

Provides a condensed data base to aid in proof-of-concept experiments and continued research and development on the technical feasibility and economic viability of generating either electricity or hydrogen by harnessing the temperature gradients in the sea.

Hamm, Hans. *Low Cost Development of Small Water Sites.* Mt. Rainier, Md.: Volunteers in Technical Assistance. 50 pp. $2.95. (TEA)

A handbook for determining the power generation potential of your water source, constructing a small dam, and selecting water wheels, turbines, and other equipment.

International Bibliography on Water Resources. UNIPUB, Box 433, Murray Hill Station, New York, NY 10016. 1977. 24 pp. Free.

Knight, H. Gary; Nyhart, J.D.; and Stein, Robert E. *Ocean Thermal Energy Conversion: Legal, Political, and Institutional Aspects.* Lexington, Mass.: Lexington Books, 1977. 272 pp. $19.95.

Many questions relating to Ocean Thermal Energy Conversion are answered by this discussion of the technical background, economic assessment, international legal and political aspects, environmental impact, and domestic regulation of this new source of energy.

McGuigan, Dermot. *Harnessing Water Power for Home Energy.* Charlotte, Vt.: Garden Way, 1978. 101 pp. $4.95. (EARS) (CEP)

A wide range of new and old water power systems are available to fit every set of conditions and just about every pocket book. Initial costs may be high, but maintenance is low and pay-back rapid. Most people with flowing water on their land can now benefit from this source of power. Waterwheels, turbines, and generators are described, and resources listed.

Noyes, Robert, ed. *Offshore and Underground Power Plants.* Park Ridge, N.J.: Noyes Data Corporation, 1977. 309 pp. $42.00.
Based for the most part on federally-funded studies, this work explores the potential, costs, technologies, and environmental considerations of nuclear and fossil-fuel fired power plants located offshore or underground. It also describes the production of power from the ocean by harnessing waves, wind, tides, currents, salinity gradients, and thermal gradients.

Ross, David. *Energy from the Waves.* New York, N.Y.: Pergamon Press, 1979. 121 pp. $8.25.
The historical background and current research and development in the field of utilizing wave energy are described in this non-technical account, which also discusses the environmental and political implications of the technology.

Saila, Saul B., ed. *Fisheries and Energy Production.* Lexington, Mass.: Lexington Books, 1975. 320 pp. $16.50.
Twelve research reports investigate the potential environmental damage to aquatic life due to the effects of electric power production.

Smith, Norman. *Man and Water.* Great Britain: Charles Scribner's Sons, 1975. 239 pp. $12.95.
This volume tells how man's way of life has been conditioned by hydro-technology. It presents the history of irrigation, land reclamation, water supply, and the varied forms in which water power has been utilized.

U.S. Congress. *Energy From the Ocean.* Washington, DC, 1978. S/N 052-070-04495-1. 433 pp. $4.25. (USGPO)
The energy resource potential of the ocean is described in chapters on ocean thermal energy conversion, waves, tides, ocean currents, winds, salinity gradients, bioconversion, deep ocean oil and gas, offshore geothermal, and hard mineral energy resources.

U.S. Congress, Office of Technology Assessment. *Coastal Effects of Offshore Energy Systems: An Assessment of Oil and Gas Systems, Deepwater Ports, and Nuclear Power Plants off the Coast of New Jersey and Delaware.* Washington, DC, 1976. S/N 053-004-00345-1. 288 pp. $4.45. (USGPO)
This study assesses the social, political, institutional, environmental, and economic effects of these systems. Problems and benefits are discussed, as well as the need for future planning and setting priorities. Comments of public participants at hearings are included.

U.S. Department of Energy. *Ocean Thermal Energy Conversion (OTEC): Power Cycle and Components.* Washington, DC, 1978. S/N 061-000-00028-3. 36 pp. $1.50. (USGPO)
The objectives and strategies of the OTEC program are described, with background and implementation information.

WIND ENERGY

Technology and Applications

Beedell, Suzanne. *Windmills.* New York, N.Y.: Charles Scribner's Sons, 1975. 143 pp. $12.00.

An interesting text and outstanding photographs describe the history, structure, and modern use of various types of windmills in Europe and America.

Cheremisinoff, Nicholas P. *Fundamentals of Wind Energy.* Ann Arbor, Mich.: Ann Arbor Science Publishers, 1978. 170 pp. $8.95.

An overview of the potential of wind as an energy source, with consideration of the history, modern applications, performance, design, site selection, storage systems, and environmental problems.

Clews, Henry. *Electric Power from the Wind.* Maine: Solar Wind Publications, 1973. 40 pp. $2.00.

A basic, introductory, non-technical publication dealing with domestic-scale wind electric plants. It includes a price list of commercial units.

Coonley, Douglas. *An Introduction to the Use of Wind.* Harrisville, N.H.: Total Environmental Action, 1975. 22 pp. $2.00. (TEA)

A brief outline of wind energy use principles.

Coonley, Douglas R. *Wind: Making it work for You.* Philadelphia, Pa.: Franklin Institute Press, 1978. 99 pp. $7.95. (TEA)

This introductory book discusses the nature of wind, passive and active wind design, and the effects of wind upon architecture. Useful for the home experimenter and secondary students.

Dennis, Landt. *Catch the Wind.* New York, N.Y.: Four Winds Press, 1976. 114 pp. $7.95.

A look at the uses of windpower in the past, the problems of today, and the possibilities for the future. An excellent introduction for both children and adults. (Education)

Eldridge, Frank. *Wind Machines.* Prepared for the National Science Foundation, Washington, DC, 1976. 78 pp. $3.00. (EARS) (USGPO)

This is one of the best overviews of the subject. It describes the history, potential, applications, performance, and system design of wind machines.

Eldridge, Frank R. *Wind Workshop #2.* McLean, Va.: The Mitre Corporation, 1975. #038-000-00258-9. 536 pp. $7.40. (USGPO)

Wind energy machines: design, operation, economics, and applications in the U.S. and abroad. Technical. Sponsored by ERDA and the National Science Foundation.

Energy Task Force. *Windmill Power for City People.* The Energy Task Force of New York City's Lower East Side. Washington, DC: USGPO #059-000-00001-2. 1977. 65 pp. $2.60. (USGPO)

This handbook documents experiences with the first urban wind installation, including calculations and diagrams.

Golding, E.W. *The Generation of Electricity by Wind Power.* National Energy Book Service, 143 Maple Road, Surbiton, Surrey, KT64BH, United Kingdom, 1976. 344 pp. $9.00.

Gives comprehensive details on all aspects of wind machines: history, energy available, sites, structure, generators, and economics.

Fraenkel, Peter. *Food From Windmills.* Intermediate Technology Development Group in London. ISBS, P.O. Box 555, Forest Grove, OR 97116. 1975. 70+ pp. $7.95.

The practical use of windmills at the village level is demonstrated by this irrigation project in Ethiopia.

Hackelman, Michael A. *The Homebuilt, Wind-Generated Electricity Handbook.* Earthmind, 5246 Boyer Rd., Mariposa, CA 95338. 1975. 194 pp. $7.95. (EARS) (TEA)

Practical information on the restoration of discarded wind generators, and designing and installing towers, wind machines, and generating equipment.

Hackelman, Michael A. *Wind and Windspinners.* Earthmind, 5246 Boyer Rd., Mariposa, CA 95338. 1974, with 1975 update newsletter. 140 pp. $7.50. (EARS) (TEA)

Here are complete instructions for making a wind-electric system yourself, covering theory, planning, construction, and operation, as well as necessary sources and references.

Inglis, David R. *Wind Power and Other Energy Options.* Ann Arbor, Mich.: University of Michigan Press, 1978. 298 pp. $8.50.

Inglis compares nuclear and wind power, and finds that wind is the economically feasible and socially desirable option. Wind could be implemented immediately if sufficient market is guaranteed to warrant large-scale production.

Justus, C.G. *Winds and Wind System Performance.* Philadelphia, Pa.: Franklin Institute Press, 1978. 120 pp. $8.95.

A description of aspects of wind characteristics that should be considered in performance evaluation, design, siting, and operation of wind energy systems.

Kovarik, Tom; Pipher, Charles; and Hurst, John. *Wind Energy: The Generation, Storage, and Conversion of Wind Power for Practical Use.* Chicago, Ill.: Domus, 1979. 150 pp. $6.95.

The tale of wind power, past, present, and future begins this book, which proceeds to define wind characteristics, provide criteria for site selection, and describe new technologies for producing and storing wind power.

McGuigan, Dermot. *Harnessing Wind for Home Energy.* Charlotte, Vt.: Garden Way, 1978. 134 pp. $4.95. (EARS) (CEP)

Small scale wind energy systems can be installed at many various sites. Here is how to plan and build a wind system to meet your needs.

Noll, Edward M. *Wind/Solar Energy for Radio-Communications and Low-Power Electronic/*

Electric Applications. Indianapolis, Ind.: Howard W. Sams and Company, Inc., 1975. 208 pp. $7.95. (EARS)

Simple, practical plans for solar and wind generator installations.

NSF-RANN Wind Energy Conversion Research: Recent Publications. Bulletin No. 3. Washington, DC: National Science Foundation, June 1975.

A bibliography with abstracts.

Park, Jack. *Simplified Wind Power Systems for Experimenters.* Box 4301, Sylmar, CA 91342: Helion, 1975. 80 pp. $6.00. (EARS) (TEA)

A "cookbook" for planning and designing a wind-powered energy system. Many clear diagrams and technical details.

Park, Jack, and Schwind, Dick. *Wind Power for Farms, Homes, and Small Industry.* Mountain View, Calif.: Nelson Engineering and Research, Inc., 1978. 163 pp. $9.25. (NTIS #RFP-2841/1270/78/4)

This thorough and useful book on wind energy from the consumer's point of view considers wind turbines, site selection, system components, and costs.

Putnam, Palmer C. *Power from the Wind.* New York, N.Y.: Van Nostrand Reinhold, 1948. 224 pp. $11.95. (EARS) (TEA)

An oldie, but a classic and still-relevant study of basic principles and applications. It tells the story of a great experiment, the Smith-Putnam Wind-Turbine, a 175-foot, 1250-kilowatt unit on Grandpa's Knob, Vermont.

Reynolds, John. *Windmills and Watermills.* New York, N.Y.: Praeger, 1970. 196 pp. $8.95.

The fascinating history of mills and milling machinery is delineated in this generously illustrated volume. There are examples, old and new, from all parts of the world. Present day possibilities of wind and water power are described in their social context.

Simmons, Daniel M. *Windpower.* Park Ridge, N.J.: Noyes Data Corporation, 1975. 300 pp. $24.00.

Outlines the steps in harnessing, storing, and utilizing wind power. Developments in the United States and abroad are described, and commercially available wind machines are listed.

Sullivan, George. *Windpower For Your Home. The First Complete Guide That Tells How to Make the Wind's Energy Work For You.* New York, N.Y.: Cornerstone, 1978. 127 pp. $4.95.

You can obtain light, heat, and power from your own wind-electric system. This guide offers advice on choosing the right location, plans, components, and estimating costs.

Syverson, C., and Symons, J. *Wind Power.* North Mankato, Minn.: Syverson Consulting Co., 1974. 19 pp. $2.50.

A good technical introduction to domestic-scale wind electric plants, with information on system components, demand analysis, and sample calculations.

Torrey, Volta. *Wind Catchers, American Windmills of Yesterday and Tomorrow.* Brattleboro, Vt.: Stephen Greene Press, 1976. 226 pp. $12.95. (EARS)

The story of windmill progress in America, and the potential of windmills as an energy source in the future. Describes designs and capabilities, from home-built installations to the large NASA and ERDA projects.

University of New Mexico. *Wind Energy Utilization: A Bibliography with Abstracts.*

University of New Mexico, Technology Application Center, Albuquerque, NM 87131. Sponsored by NASA, ERDA, and NSF. TAC W 75-700. 1975. 496 pp.

A compilation of wind information from around the world, from 1944 to 1974, arranged under subject headings and cross indexed. It indicates that much of wind research was accomplished during the early years of this century.

Windworks. *Wind Energy Bibliography.* Windworks, P.O. Box 329, Rt. 3, Mukwanago, WI 53149. 72 pp. $3.00. (EARS)

An annotated bibliography covering wind behavior and measurement, windmills, aerodynamics, storage, conversion, hydrogen production, and catalogs.

CITIZEN ACTION

Resources

Alderson, George, and Sentman, Everett. *How You Can Influence Congress: The Complete Handbook for the Citizen Lobbyist.* New York, N.Y.: Dutton, 1979. 360 pp. $9.95. (FOE)

    This is a complete operating manual for the citizen lobbyist and every individual concerned with influencing legislation. Congresspersons can be reached—through letters, visits, organizations, media, and campaigns—and this book will tell you how.

Anderson, Joanne Manning. *For The People: A Consumer Action Handbook.* Introduction by Ralph Nader. Reading, Mass.: Addison-Wesley, 1977. 379 pp. $5.95.

    Although portions of this handbook are concerned with consumer action in the areas of health care and grocery products, the energy activist will find useful suggestions in the sections on energy conservation, fighting for lower utility bills, working with the media, and changing legislation.

Caldwell, Lynton K., Hayes, Lynton R., and MacWhirter, Isabel M. *Citizens and the Environment. Case Studies in Popular Action.* Bloomington, Indiana: Indiana University Press, 1976. 480 pp. $17.50 & $6.95.

    Describes 68 cases in which friends of the environment have come into conflict with government, industry, and other power blocs.

League of Women Voters Education Fund. *Citizens: The Untapped Energy Source.* A Community Guide. League of Women Voters, 1730 M St. NW, Washington, DC 20036. 1980. 8 pp. $.50, plus $.50 handling per order.

    Detailed directions for planning energy education projects include how to get organized, examples of activities, audio-visual media, publicity, and additional resources.

League of Women Voters Education Fund. *Federal Environmental Laws and You.* League of Women Voters, 1730 M St. NW, Washington, DC 20036. 1978. 12 pp. $.75, plus $.50 handling per order.

    The principal provisions of the major environmental laws are explained in plain English, with suggestions as to how the environmentalist can influence decisions made under these laws.

Massachusetts Public Interest Research Group. *Energy Teach-ins: Organizing for a Brighter Future.* MassPIRG, 233 N. Pleasant St., Amherst, MA 01002. 1977. 95 pp. $2.00.

    A systematic guide, with all of the necessary details for planning, funding, organizing, publicizing, and presenting a teach-in.

McFarland, Andrew S. *Public Interest Lobbies: Decision-Making on Energy.* American Enterprise Institute for Public Policy Research, 1150 17th St. NW,

Washington, DC 20036. 1976. 141 pp. $3.00.

The energy positions of seven groups are examined: Common Cause, the Nader organizations, League of Women Voters, the Sierra Club, Consumers Union, Energy Policy Task Force, and Americans for Energy Independence. These widely varied groups perform roles of initiating new proposals, communicating opinions to the public, and balancing the special interests that control many governmental policies.

Robertson, James, and Lewallen, John. eds. *The Grass Roots Primer*. San Francisco, Calif.: Sierra Club Books, 1975. 192 pp. $7.95.

A practical book for people who want to do something effective to prevent the piecemeal destruction of Earth's natural environment. Interviewed activists offer specific steps a grassroots environmental group can take to gain victory. References.

Ross, Donald K. *A Public Citizen's Action Manual*. Introduction by Ralph Nader. New York, N.Y.: Grossman, 1973. 237 pp. From Citizen Action Group, 2000 "P" St. NW, Washington, DC 20036. $1.95.

Although this book focuses mainly on consumer issues, including the cost of unnecessary electric lighting, it has many practical suggestions for making the government responsive, and for mobilizing citizen action on all issues.

Smith, Dorothy. *In Our Interest: A Handbook for Citizen Lobbyists in State Legislatures*. Madrona Publishers, 2116 Western Ave., WA 98121. 1979. $4.95.

Advice on strategy and problems is offered by this guidebook for citizens' participation in the state legislative process.

U.S. Department of Energy, Solar Energy Research Institute. *reaching up, reaching out: a guide to organizing local solar events*. Washington, DC, 1979. S/N 061-000-00345-2. 208 pp. $8.50. (USGPO) (EARS)

Based on a belief in the importance of community organization, this manual presents (1) examples of successful solar and energy conservation activities such as fairs and workshops; (2) an organizing primer; (3) a guide to selected resources including organizations, printed matter, and audio-visual materials. Lively illustrations, attractive format, and cross-indexing help to make this an invaluable aid to all grassroots energy activists. (See also U.S. DOE, Solar Energy Research Institute—SERI—under GOVERNMENT AGENCIES.)

Fundraising

Citizens' Energy Project. *How to Apply to a Foundation*. Citizens' Energy Project, 1110 Sixth St. NW, #300, Washington, DC 20001. 1978. 5 pp. $.75. (CEP)
Ideas for preparing grant proposals.

The Collaborators. P.O. Box 5429, Charlottesville, VA 22903.
Publications of interest to community planners include:
The Funding Process: Grantsmanship and Proposal Development, $6.95.
Community Involvement for Classroom Teachers, $2.95.
Creating Interagency Programs, $3.95.
Basic Steps of Planning, $1.00.

Flanagan, Joan. *The Grass Roots Fundraising Book: How to Raise Money in Your Community*. Chicago, Ill.: Swallow Press, 1977. 219 pp. $5.75. Available from The Youth Project, 1555 Connecticut Ave. NW, 5th fl., Washington, DC 20036, and The Institute for Local Self-Reliance, 1717 18th St. NW,

Washington, DC 20009.

Beginners and experienced groups will find scores of ideas and step-by-step instructions in this guide. It includes bibliographies, film sources, and even tips on how to handle all the money that you will raise.

The Foundation Center, 1001 Connecticut Ave., NW, Washington, DC 20036.

The Foundation Directory and the *Foundation Grants Index*, from the Columbia University Press, are available in many university libraries.

Grantsmanship Center, 1031 South Grand Ave., Los Angeles, CA 90015. *Grantsmanship Center News.* Bimonthly, $15.00/yr.

Information and assistance for non-profit and public agencies in obtaining grants, fund raising, lobbying, and developing management skills.

Grubb, David, and Zwick, David. *Fundraising in the Public Interest.* Center for Study of Responsive Law, P.O. Box 19367, Washington, DC 20036. 1976. 186 pp. $5.00.

A beginner's manual covering money-raising techniques from canvassing to bikeathons.

Gunn, Anita. *Sources of Funds for Solar Activities.* Center for Renewable Resources, 1001 Connecticut Ave. NW, 5th floor, Washington, DC 20036. 1979. 130 pp. $5.00.

Foundations and federal agencies that may be interested in funding solar projects are listed, and a step-by-step procedure for grant application is outlined.

Leibert, Edwin, and Sheldon, Bernice. *Handbook of Special Events for Nonprofit Organizations: Tested Ideas for Fund Raising and Public Relations.* Taft Products, 1000 Vermont Ave. NW, Washington, DC 20005. 224 pp. $13.45.

Citizen groups can organize concerts, parties, sports events, festivals, and many other activities to heighten public awareness of issues as well as to raise funds.

McGraw-Hill Guide to Federal Energy Assistance. Available from Elizabeth Ness, Dept. "C", 457 National Press Building, Washington, DC 20045. 1979. 252 pp. $47.00.

Energy producers, consumers, researchers, and consultants will find federal programs offering free assistance identified, described, and cross-indexed. It is based upon the *Catalog of Federal Domestic Assistance* published annually by the U.S. Office of Management and Budget.

NIRS *Resource Guide on Grassroots Fundraising.* Nuclear Information and Resources Service, 1536 16th St. NW, Washington, DC 20036. 1979. 4 pp. $.50.

Ideas and resources to help energy activists secure funds.

Playboy Foundation. *Network of Change-Oriented Foundations.* Playboy Foundation, 919 N. Michigan Ave., Chicago, IL 60611.

ENERGY EDUCATION

References

Beacon Press. *Seed Catalog*. Beacon Press, 15 Beacon St., Boston, MA 12108. Approx. 350 pp. $5.95.

Here are seeds of information—materials, ideas, devices, organizations—with emphasis on the simpler, less expensive teachings tools.

Citizens' Energy Project. 1110 Sixth St. NW, Suite 300, Washington, DC 20001.

The *CEP Catalog* includes many books and articles on energy that would be valuable as background material for the teacher, or for classroom reference. Most of the material is designed for the general reader and could be handled by secondary students.

Clark, Rusty. *4-H Energy Bibliography National Intern Report*. Order from Gary Deverman, National 4-H Council, 7100 Connecticut Ave., Washington, DC 20015.

Energy education materials are listed in three major categories: printed materials; visual aids, and programs, kits, curricula, and activities. Includes adult background material, student material, the 4-H energy curriculum matrix, and materials from the U.S. Department of Agriculture.

Conservation Education Association. *Environmental Conservation Education, A Selected Annotated Bibliography*. Interstate Printers and Publishers, Inc., Danville, IL 61832. 1974, with 1976 supplement.

Material is divided by grade level, with a publisher's directory.

New Mexico Solar Energy Assocation. *Educational Materials Bibliography*. New Mexico Solar Energy Assocation, P.O. Box 2004, Santa Fe, NM 87501. 1978. 4 pp. $.50.

A well-selected list for a variety of ages.

Rain Magazine, eds. *Rainbook: Resources for Appropriate Technology*. New York, N.Y.: Schocken, 1977. 251 pp. $7.95. (EARS)

Access to information on all aspects of the appropriate use of our environment, with names and descriptions of hundreds of organizations and publications. See *APPROPRIATE TECHNOLOGY: REFERENCES*.

Saterstrom, Mary H., ed. *Educators' Guide to Free Science Materials*. Educators Progress Service, Inc., Randolph, WI 53956. 18th Edition, Aug. 1979. approx. 300 pp. $15.35.

Revised annually, this guide describes hundreds of audio-visual and printed materials available from government, industry, and public interest groups. Guides in other curriculum areas are also published.

Schaffer, Dale E., Library Consultant, 437 Jennings Ave., Salem, OH 44460.
Sources of Free Teaching Materials. $3.95.
Free Posters, Charts, and Maps. $2.95.
Well-researched guides to supplementary teachings materials.

Scherner, Sharon, ed. *The Energy Education Bibliography.* Energy and Man's Environment, 0224 SW Hamilton, Portland, OR 97201. 1979. 45 pp.
An annotated listing of energy and conservation materials, including texts, references, activity guides, games, etc. from government, universities, industry, and public interest groups. (Industry oriented.)

U.S. Department of Energy. *Activities of the DOE in Energy Education.* 1978. S/N 061-000-00146-8. 66 pp. $2.40. (USGPO)
A description of government programs and services.

U.S. Department of Energy. *Energy Education Materials Inventory.* Vol. 1. May, 1978. S/N 061-000-00183-2. 293 pp. $5.25. (USGPO)
A compilation of resources for educators, grades 1 through 12.

U.S. Department of Energy, Office of Public Affairs. *Selected DOE Publications.* U.S. DOE, Office of Public Affairs, Washington, DC 20585. 1978. 19 pp. Free.
A list of free DOE publications, booklets of general interest, curriculum materials, fact sheets, and films. These materials are ordered through the Department of Energy/Technical Information Center, P.O. Box 62, Oak Ridge, TN 37830.

U.S. Department of Energy, Solar Energy Research Institute. *National Solar Energy Education Directory.* Washington, DC, 1979. S/N 061-000-00210-3. 279 pp. $4.75. (USGPO)
A survey of all solar energy-related programs and courses currently being offered by more than 700 U.S. post-secondary educational institutions. Individual state directories are available free from the National Solar Heating and Cooling Information Center, P.O. Box 1607, Rockville, MD 20850.

U.S. Office of Education.* *A Selected Guide to Federal Energy and Education Assistance.* U.S. Office of Education, Energy and Education Action Center, Rm 514, Reporters' Building, 300 7th St. SW, Washington, DC 20202. 1978 (or update). 18 pp. Free.
An outline of federal grants and programs for curriculum development, student assistance, teacher training, facilities improvement, and research.

U.S. Office of Education.* *A Selected Bibliography of Energy and Education Materials.* U.S. Office of Education, Energy and Education Action Center, Rm. 514 Reporters' Building, 300 7th St. SW, Washington, DC 20202. 8 pp.
A listing of curriculum materials and resources for further information.

U.S. General Service Administration, Consumer Information Center, Pueblo, CO 81009.
A free catalog lists many free and inexpensive booklets on saving energy and money in the home, food, health care, gardening, and transportation.

Wagner, Beth, ed. *Solar Energy Education Bibliography for Elementary, Secondary, and College Students.* Center for Renewable Resources, 1001 Connecticut Ave. NW, 5th floor, Washington, DC 20036. 1979. 44 pp. $2.50.

*Note: Energy education has been transferred to the Education and Training Division, Office of Consumer Affairs, M.S. 7E-054, Department of Energy, Washington, DC 20585.

This reference guide covers all renewable energy sources, describing hundreds of solar publications and audio-visual materials suitable for classroom use.

War Resisters League. *Childrens' Reading List.* WRL, 339 Lafayette St., New York, NY 10012. $.50.

An informal list of recommended reading for children: over 200 books that are neither sexist, racist, nor militarist.

Woodbury, Marda. *Recommended Materials in Environmental Education.* Ecology Center, 2179 Allston Way, Berkeley, CA 94704. 1977. 24 pp. $.50.

Resources are listed and described in these categories: overviews, energy, urban ecology, classroom recycling, pollution, natural history, plants, gardening, outdoor recreation, and fiction.

Resources for Teachers

The Bolton Institute. *Energy Conservation Youth Training Program Manual.* The Bolton Institute, Inc., Suite 302, 1835 K Street NW, Washington, DC 20006. 1975. 300 pp.

Detailed plans for a conservation workshop are presented, plus a most comprehensive list of references and resources.

Brace, Judith; White, Ralph R.; and Bass, Stephen C. *Teaching Conservation in Developing Nations.* Sponsored by the National Audubon Society, 950 Third Ave., New York, NY 10022, and the Peace Corps, 806 Connecticut Ave. NW, Washington, DC 20525. Washington, DC, 1977. 251 pp. $1.50. S/N 056-000-00018 (USGPO)

Guidelines are provided for the establishment of an environmental education center, and the incorporation of environmental education into schools, health centers, agricultural extension centers, and other community services. Specific directions for activities and projects are given.

Center for Environmental Education. *Environmental Education Report.* Center for Environmental Education, 2100 M St. NW, Washington, DC 20036. Monthly, $25.00/yr.

A highly recommended resource.

Center for Environmental Learning. *Teachers' Environmental Resource Unit—Energy & Power.* Center for Environmental Learning, 705 Avocado Ave., Cocoa, FL 32922. 40 pp. $1.10.

Background material on conservation and all sources of energy.

Channing L. Bete Company, Inc. *Scriptographic Booklets.* Channing L. Bete Company, Inc., Greenfield, MA 01301. Catalog describes content and gives quantity prices.

This series of booklets has easily understood texts and clear graphics which appeal to students. Topics include sources of energy, conservation, environment, pollution, safety, health, and related subjects. The emphasis is on technological solutions to increase the energy supply; however, some of the booklets are quite useful.

Coon, Herbert L., and Alexander, Michele Y. *Energy Activities for the Classroom.* ERIC Center for Science, Mathematics, and Environmental Education, College of Education, Ohio State University, 1200 Chambers Rd., Columbus, OH 43212. 148 pp. $4.50.

Activities are planned to enable students of grades K-12 to develop basic concepts concerning fossil and alternative sources of energy, energy use patterns, and the need for conservation.

Cousteau Society. *Dolphin Log.* A section of the *Calypso Log.* Cousteau Society, 777 Third Ave., New York, NY 10017. Bimonthly, $15.00/yr.
A newsletter for young people about our water planet and its resources, including energy. Posters.

Creative Recycling Center. *Put Your Garbage to Work.* Creative Recycling Center, 4614 Liberty Ave., Bloomfield, Pittsburgh, PA 15224. 53 pp. plus 24" x 35" poster. $3.50.
Identifies household waste, and suggests activities to reuse, recycle, and return wasted items.

Design Alternatives, Inc. *Energy Education Guidebook,* Community Services Administration, Office of Energy Programs, 1200 19th St. NW, Washington, DC 20506. 1979.
A guide for local agencies undertaking energy education programs.

Ecology Center of Ann Arbor. *Discover Energy Series.* Ecology Center of Ann Arbor, 417 Detroit St., Ann Arbor, MI 48104. 150 pp. $10.00.
A comprehensive curriculum guide on all aspects of energy for grades 7-12.

Education Commission of the States. *Energy Knowledge and Attitudes.* Report 08-E-01. Education Commission of the States, Suite 700, 1860 Lincoln St., Denver, CO 80295.
This survey of what various age groups know about energy can be used to help plan lessons.

Energy and Man's Environment, 0224 SW Hamilton, Suite 301, Portland, OR 97201.
Curriculum development and teacher training programs. Publications include: *K-12 Activity Guide, Glossary, Energy Films Index,* and *Energy Education Bibliography.* (Funded by electric utilities.)

Environmental Action Coalition, 156 5th Ave., Suite 1130, New York, NY 10010.
Publications include teaching packets, books, and *Eco-News* for young people.

Environmental Action Coalition. *It's Your Environment: Things to Think About—Things to Do.* Edited by Shirley Koehler. New York, N.Y.: Charles Scribner's Sons, 1976. 206 pp. $4.95.
Geared to elementary and junior high school students, this guide includes information, illustrations, and activities covering basics such as waste, energy, pollution, and overpopulation. Recommended for children of *all* ages.

ERIC. *Current Issues in Environmental Education II.* ERIC Center for Science, Mathematics, and Environmental Education, Ohio State University, 1200 Chambers Rd., Columbus, OH 43212. 1976. 192 pp.
Selected papers on topics such as urban environmental education and community action.

Friend, Gil, and Morris, David. *Kilowatt Counter.* Milaca, Minn... Alternative Sources of Energy, 1976. 36 pp. $2.00. (EARS).
A consumer's guide to energy concepts, quantities, and uses. Especially suited for secondary teachers.

Fritsch, Albert. *Lifestyle Index 77.* Washington, DC: Center for Science in the Public

Interest, 1977. 32 pp. $2.00. (CEP)

The simplest way yet devised to show citizens how much energy they use in everyday life, and where they can cut back. Charts and tables on all aspects of energy consumption make this an excellent classroom tool.

Geothermal World Corporation. 18014 Sherman Way, #169, Reseda, CA 91335. Educational and audiovisual materials, and other publications.

Halacy, Beth, and Halacy, Dan. *The Solar Cookery Book.* Culver City, Calif.: Peace Press, 1978. 108 pp. $6.95. (EARS)

Here is a book that tells how to harness the sun's energy to prepare food: complete plans and instructions for an inexpensive solar oven and reflector cooker, as well as recipes.

Halacy, D.S., Jr. *Solar Science Projects.* New York, N.Y.: Scholastic Book Service, 1974. 96 pp. $.85.

Seven simple and interesting solar energy projects that you can build. Excellent for educational and demonstration projects. Grade 7 to 12.

Harty Sheila. *Hucksters in the Classroom: A Review of Industry Propaganda in Schools.* Center for Study of Responsive Law, P.O. Box 19365, Washington, DC 20036. 1979. 190 pp. $10/$20.

Before sending away for any more free educational materials, read this three-year Nader study of corporate responsibility and industry's efforts to reach young audiences, especially in the areas of nutrition, economics, energy, and the environment. Harty urges closer evaluation of industry materials, and the increased use of alternative resources for balance.

Interstate Energy Conservation Leadership Project, Colorado Department of Education. *A Teacher's Handbook on Energy.* Also, an *Energy Conservation Materials Package.* Colorado Department of Education, 201 East Colfax Ave., Denver, CO 80203.

Teaching aids, classroom activities, graphics and resources on energy.

Massachusetts Audubon Society. *The Energy Crisis—Aids to Study.* Massachusetts Audubon Society, Hatheway Environmental Education Institute, Environmental Education Curriculum Materials Center, South Great Road, Lincoln, MA 01773. 23 pp. $.60.

A bibliography of books, articles, and teaching aids.

Michigan Association of School Administrators. *Energy Conservation—Guidelines for Action.* Michigan Association of School Administrators, 421 West Kalamazoo, Lansing, MI 48933. 58 pp. $.75.

Curriculum guidelines and background information.

Minnesota Environmental Sciences Foundation, Inc. *The Hydrocarbon Civilization.* Minnesota Environmental Sciences Foundation, Inc., 5400 Glenwood Ave., Minneapolis, MN 55422.

Energy activities for students of grades 10 to 12, involving interdisciplinary skills.

National Association of Independent Schools. *Interdependence: A Handbook for Environmental Education.* National Association of Independent Schools, 4 Liberty Square, Boston, MA 02109. (1979) 45 pp. $4.00.

A description of 56 environmental education programs at independent schools around the country.

National Audubon Society, Educational Services Division, 950 Third Ave., New

York, NY 10022.
Offers materials for use in environmental education.

National Science Teachers Association. *Energy and Education.* National Science Teachers Association, 1742 Connecticut Ave. NW, Washington, DC 20009. Supported in part by the U.S. Department of Energy. Bimonthly. Free.
News of energy education, new developments in alternative energy technologies, book reviews, resources, teaching materials, and conference announcements.

National Science Teachers Association, 1742 Connecticut Ave., NW, Washington, DC 20009. Set of three books, 1975. $9.00.
Energy-Environment Source Book. Vol. 1, 97 pp.; Vol. 2, 173 pp. $4.00. Information on energy and its interaction with society and the environment; and the extraction, conversion, and use of energy. Written for teachers' reference. Includes many graphs and tables.
Energy-Environment Mini-Unit Guide. 220 pp. $3.00. A series of lesson plans for grades K-12.
Energy-Environment Materials Guide. $2.00. Energy bibliographies for teachers and for students of various grade levels.

National Science Teachers Association. *Project for an Energy-Enriched Curriculum.* Available from the Department of Energy/Technical Information Center, P.O. Box 62, Oak Ridge, TN 37830.
Fact sheets and classroom packets for grades 1-12. Titles are listed in the *Selected Bibliography of Energy and Education Materials,* U.S. Office of Education.

National Wildlife Federation. *Energy: Selected Resource Materials for Developing Energy Education/Conservation Programs.* NWF, Education Servicing Section, 1412 16th St. NW, Washington, DC 20036. Single copies free.
A listing of over 60 publications available at little or no cost. A list of *Conservation Education Publications* is also available.

Norton, Thomas, W., Hunter, Donald C., and Cheng, Roger J. *Solar Energy Experiments for High School and College Students.* Emmaus, Pa.: Rodale, 1977. 144 pp. $5.95. (EARS)
A manual comprising nineteen experiments and eight classroom-type activities of varying difficulty and covering the important aspects of solar energy utilization.

Park Project on Energy Interpretation. *Energy Activity Guide.* National Recreation and Park Association, 1001 North Kent St., Arlington, VA 22209. 24 pp. Free.
Colorfully illustrated articles and activities on energy sources.

Posthuma, Frederick E. *Energy and Education: Teaching Alternatives.* Washington, DC: National Education Association, 1978. $5.95.
A sampler of readings in energy education, including some helpful classroom materials; the nuclear and solar sections are weak, however.

Schipper, Lee. *Explaining Energy: A Manual of Non-Style for the Energy Outsider Who Wants in!* LBL 4458. Lawrence Berkeley Laboratory, and Energy Resources Group, University of California, Berkeley, CA 94720. 72 pp. $6.00. (NTIS)
A manual for teachers and others who explain energy. It outlines the basics of energy systems and controversial issues, and includes many attention-getting graphics as well as other aids and resources. An especially useful reference.

Sierra Club. *Teaching Packet on Environmental Education.* Sierra Club, Informational Services, 530 Bush St., San Francisco, CA 94108. $3.00.

A collection of booklets and brochures on environmental problems, and resources lists for books, films, exhibits, and other materials.

Solar Energy Institute of North America, 1110 Sixth St. NW, Washington, DC 20001.

Offers educational materials including pamphlets, workbooks, lesson plans, kits, and audio-visual aids.

Solar Usage Now, Inc. *The SUN Catalog.* Solar Usage Now, Inc., Box 306, Bascom, OH 44809. Updated annually. $2.00.

Among many other solar products and books, this catalog lists kits for teaching basic solar concepts, slide sets, film strips, and other curriculum materials.

Teacher Works, 2136 NE 20th Ave., Portland, OR 97212.

A national grassroots teacher exchange of curriculum materials.

Stapp, William, and Liston, Mary Dawn. *Environmental Education: A Guide to Information Sources.* Detroit, Mich.: Gale Research Corporation, 1975.

Lists instructional aids, government services, private organizations, periodicals, and sources of funding.

Stephenson, Lee. *Energy Manual for Parks: A Handbook for Interpreters and Naturalists.* National REcreation and Park Association, 1601 N. Kent St., Arlington, VA 22209, 1976. 180 pp. $3.00.

Although intended as a resource in park interpretive programs, this is an outstanding reference for all teachers as well as for the general reader. Natural and human energy systems are explained in relation to the total environment. Alternative energy sources are described, and the need for conservation is stressed. Excellent graphics and references.

Terry, Mark, and Witt, Paul. *Energy and Order: A Lesson Plan.* San Francisco, Calif.: Friends of the Earth, 1976. 42 pp. $3.00. (FOE) (EARS)

A handbook for secondary school teachers that acquaints students with the ways in which energy works, and how it is connected to the world we live in.

Thomas Alva Edison Foundation, Cambridge Office Plaza, Suite 143, 18380 West Ten Mile Road, Southfield, MI 48075. Single copies free.

A series of booklets describing electrical, chemical, and energy conservation experiments for grades 4 to 10.

U.S. Department of Energy. *Solar Energy Project.* Washington, DC, 1979. 8 books, S/N 061-000-00228-6 through S/N 061-000-00235-9. 650 pp. $19.60 total. (USGPO)

Teacher's Guide, background information, and activities, grades 7-12, for solar projects related to biology, earth science, chemistry, and physics.

U.S. Department of Health, Education, and Welfare. *How to Use ERIC, Educational Resources Information Center, Ohio State University.* 1978. HE 19.208: Ed 8/2. S/N 017-080-01828-4. 20 pp. $1.00. (USGPO)

A booklet describing the operations, services, and reference tools of this national information center for more effective educational programs.

U.S. Forest Service. *Teaching Materials for Environmental Education.* Washington, DC: U.S. Government Printing Office, 1973. $.95. (USGPO)

University of Tennessee Environment Center. *Ideas and Activities for Teaching Energy Conservation, Grades 7-12.* Tennessee Energy Authority, Suite 250, Capitol Hill Building, Nashville, TN 37219. 1977. 225 pp.

Includes an overview of energy issues and facts; student activities in science, social studies, and language arts; and resource lists.

University of Tennessee Environment Center. *Energy Conservation in the Home: An Energy Education/Conservation Curriculum Guide for Home Economics Teachers.* Prepared for ERDA. University of Tennessee Environment Center and College of Home Economics, Knoxville, Tenn., 1977. 325 pp.

Lesson plans and activities teach conservation in the home, considering the house, environmental control, food, clothing, appliances, and basic energy principles.

University of Tennessee Environment Center. *A Teacher's Guide for Energy Conservation.* Jonathan Wert, Environment Center, University of Tennessee, South Stadium Hall, Knoxville, TN 37916. 100+ pp.

A compilation of activities and teaching procedures that can be adapted to a wide range of learners.

University of Wisconsin. *The Household Energy Game.* Sea Grant College Program, University of Wisconsin, 1800 University Ave., Madison, WI 53706.

The "game" involves putting together a personal energy budget, and then finding ways to modify the budget to conserve energy, save money, and help the environment.

Wagner, Beth, ed. *Solar Energy Education Packet for Elementary and Secondary Students.* Center for Renewable Resources, 1001 Connecticut Ave. NW, Washington, DC 20036. 1979. 64 pp. $3.75. (EARS)

Any science teacher will find this book an excellent source of easy projects, basic information, and additional resources.

Washington State Office of Environmental Education. *Energy, Food, and You: An Interdisciplinary Guide for Elementary Schools.* Washington State Office of Education, c/o Shoreline School District Administration Building, NE 158th & 20th Aves., NE, Seattle, WA 98155. 1977. 292 pp. $5.00. Also available for secondary levels.

A wealth of information and activities for exploring renewable and non-renewable energy sources, natural energy flows, hidden energy and environmental costs, and ways to use energy and resources more efficiently.

Zero Population Growth, Inc. 4080 Fabian Way, Palo Alto, CA 94303.

Offers a resource kit, study guide, bibliographies, and other publications.

Books for Young People

Adzema, Robert, and Jones, Mablen. *The Great Sun Dial Cutout Book.* New York, N.Y.: Hawthorn, 1978. 120 pp. $9.95. (EARS)

What a great idea! A fascinating account of ancient myths and sun lore, with a description of sundials and how they work; then a section with pull-out, easy-to-assemble sundial cutouts that enable you to follow the path of the sun for yourself.

Alternative Energy Resources Organization, 435 Stapleton Building, Billings, MT 59101. *AERO's Sun Fun Coloring Book.* 1978. 13 pp. $.50.

A fun learning tool for kids which illustrates solar, geothermal, wind, and wood energy. Additional titles are available in this series.

Augustyn, Jim. *The Solar Cat Book.* Berkeley, Calif.: Ten Speed Press, 1979. 96 pp. $3.95.

In this delightful mix of fact and fancy, youngsters (and oldsters too) will discover the solar wisdom known to cats since the beginning of time. It's the cat's MEOW.* (*Moral Equivalent of War.)

Barling, John. *John Barling's Solar Fun Book: 18 Projects for the Weekend Builder.* Harrisville, N.H.: Brick House, 1979. 104 pp. $7.95. (TEA)

These projects were developed as the author taught applications of solar energy to junior high school students. Step-by-step instructions, photos, and drawings explain how these solar home appliances can be built using inexpensive recycled and new materials.

Bergaust, Erik, ed. *The Illustrated Nuclear Encyclopedia.* New York, N.Y.: Putnam, 1971. 125 pp. $4.89.

A glossary of words and terms, as well as essays, tables, and illustrations. Includes a bibliography by grade level. Suitable for school libraries.

Berger, Melvin. *Energy From the Sun.* New York, N.Y.: Crowell, 1976. 34 pp. $5.95. (EARS)

A children's book which explains how almost all of the energy on earth begins with the sun. Ages 5 through 9.

Brandt, Barbara, and Lee, Roger. *Solar Energy: Putting the Sun to Work.* Solar Booksmith, 21 Burnside Ave., Somerville, MA 02144. $3.50.

A great workbook for children and their friends: the solar story is presented in a simple text and colorful illustrations which explain energy, fuels, electricity, and solar energy.

Branley, Franklyn M. *Solar Energy.* New York, N.Y.: Crowell, 1975 11 pp. $3.95.

A good juvenile introduction to solar energy: how the sun works and how we can use its energy. Grades 5-8.

Buckley, Shawn. *Sun Up to Sun Down: Understanding Solar Energy.* New York, N.Y.: McGraw-Hill, 1979. 166 pp. $6.95.

Here is a book to simplify solar technology for the student or general reader. Clear explanations, with familiar examples and line drawings demonstrate basic concepts.

Cox, John. *OVERKILL: Weapons of the Nuclear Age.* New York, N.Y.: Crowell, 1978. 208 pp. $7.95.

The case for disarmament is presented for the junior and senior high school student. War is not a "natural" function, but is derived from social, economic, and political factors. The author explains counterforce, deterrence, weapons systems, and arms limitation strategies.

Croall, Stephen. *The Anti-Nuclear Handbook.* New York, N.Y.: Pantheon, 1978. 133 pp. $2.95.

This documentary comic book traces the history of nuclear weapons and nuclear power with cartoon and text. Explains the atomic bomb; the "peaceful atom"; problems with the nuclear fuel cycle; social, political and economic aspects; and the alternative of a soft energy future. Not a handbook!

Educomics. *Last Gasp Comics.* Educomics, P.O. Box 212, Berkeley, CA 95701.

$1.25. Bulk rates available.

Up-to-date, reliable information in cartoon form on the major problems of nuclear energy and how it affects our lives. Good for secondary students.

Gordam, Jonathan W. *Solar Concepts: A Background Text and Teachers' Notes*. Maine Audubon Society, 118 U.S. Rt. 1, Falmouth, ME 04105. 1979. Two volumes: text, 127 pp.; notes, 135 pp. $6.50 each, or $12.00 set.

A basic text for junior or senior high schools or vocational education, covering renewable and non-renewable energy sources, history of solar energy use, potential of various solar applications, and both active and passive solar systems.

Hoke, John. *Solar Energy*. New York, N.Y.: Franklin Watts., revised, 1978. $4.90.

The development of solar energy technology is outlined, including space heating, solar cells, and biofuels. Projects for junior and senior high school students are described.

Israel, Elaine. *The Great Energy Search*. New York, N.Y.: Messner, 1974. $5.30.

This book for young readers covers the subject from fossil fuels to solar energy and leans toward a pro-environmentalist viewpoint. The author confronts political issues, and points out the roles of industry and government. Grades 4-6.

Metos, Thomas H., and Bitter, Gary G. *Exploring With Solar Energy*. New York, N.Y.: Messner, 1978. $6.97.

An intermediate text, which presents an overview, history, current applications, and future potential of solar energy, with instructions for experiments and models.

Pringle, Lawrence. *Nuclear Power From Physics to Politics*. New York, N.Y.: Macmillan, 1979. 133 pp. $7.95.

Pringle, a well-known writer of environmental books for young people, traces the development of nuclear power from early peacetime uses to the recent upsurge of public concern after the Three Mile Island accident. He explains the basic operations and the hazards of the nuclear fuel cycle, and explores the social, political, economic, and ethical questions which must be faced if we are to ensure a safe energy future for the world.

Ross, Michael Elsohn. *Cycles, Cycles, Cycles*. Illustrated by the author. Yosemite Natural History Association, Box 545, Yosemite National Park, CA 95389. 1979. $2.95 + $.75 postage.

All about cycles: apple cycles, bug cycles, water cycle, calcium cycle, and the decomposition cycle. Ages 6-10.

Ross, Michael Elsohn. *What Makes Everything Go?* Illustrated by the author. Yosemite Natural History Association, Box 545, Yosemite National Park, CA 95389. 1979. 94 pp. $2.95 + $.75 postage.

A simple text and humorous drawings bring the energy story to beginning readers, ages 6-10. Ross connects basic energy concepts with youngsters' everyday life. A similar book on solar energy is forthcoming.

Spetgang, Tilly, and Wells, Malcolm. *Tilly's Catch-A-Sunbeam Coloring Book: The Story of Solar Heat Even Grown-ups Can Understand*. Cherry Hill, N.J.: Solar Service Corporation, 1975. 32 pp. $1.50. (EARS) (TEA)

A delightful and highly educational booklet on solar energy for children in the elementary grades. A lesson plan for teachers is included.

Tanner, Thomas. *Of Democracy, Truth, and Courage: Studies of Environmental Action.* National Audubon Society, Educational Services Division, 950 Third Ave., New York, NY 10022. Package includes a 67 page Student Edition (with spirit masters) and an Instructor's Guide. 1976. $24.95.

For high school and college students, these materials include six case studies of conservation battles, and show the role of public interest groups in the governmental decision-making process. One activity involves ERDA's energy budget.

Many books in other sections may also be of use, especially the following:

Andrassy, Stella. *The Solar Food Dryer.* See *SOLAR ENERGY: OVERVIEWS*

Ewers, William. *Solar Energy.* See *SOLAR ENERGY: OVERVIEWS*

Halacy, D.S. *Coming Age of Solar Energy.* See *SOLAR ENERGY: OVERVIEWS*

Rankins, William III. *Practical Sun Power.* See *SOLAR ENERGY: OVERVIEWS*

Rankins, William III. *Solar Energy Notebook.* See *SOLAR ENERGY: OVERVIEWS*

Sands, Jonathan. *Practical Solar Heating.* See *SOLAR ENERGY: OVERVIEWS*

Sands, Jonathan. *Solar Heating Systems.* See *SOLAR ENERGY: OVERVIEWS*

Waugh, Albert. *Sundials.* See *SOLAR ENERGY: OVERVIEWS*

Mandeville, Michael. *Solar Alcohol.* See *BIOMASS: ALCOHOL FUELS*

Fritsch, Albert. *The Contrasumers.* See *ENERGY CONSERVATION: OVERVIEWS*

Fritsch, Albert. *99 Ways to a Simple Lifestyle.* See *APPROPRIATE TECHNOLOGY: TOOLS*

Rothschild, John. *Home Energy Guide.* See *ENERGY CONSERVATION: SAVING ENERGY IN THE HOME*

U.S. DOE. *Tips for Energy Savers.* See *ENERGY CONSERVATION: SAVING ENERGY IN THE HOME*

AUDIO-VISUAL MATERIALS

References

Education Film Library Association. 43 West 61st St., New York, NY 10034. Film information and programming advice.

Environment Information Center, Inc. *The Energy Index*. New York, N.Y.: Environment Information Center, Inc. Updated annually. Includes section on energy films and film distributors.

Garey, Diane, and Hott, Larry. *Reel Change: A Guide to Films on Appropriate Technology*. Soft Aware Associates. San Francisco, Calif.: Friends of the Earth, 1979. 54 pp. $3.50. (FOE)
Eighty films are reviewed, ranging from documentaries to explicit lessons on sources of renewable energy and appropriate technology. Includes a helpful subject index, a list of distributors, and tips on ordering films.

Mobilization for Survival. *Audio-Visual Guide, 1978-1980*. Mobilization for Survival, 3601 Locust Walk, Philadelphia, PA 19104. 1979. 39 pp. $2.00.
This carefully researched and well organized guide describes films, slides, and video-tapes on ecology, nuclear and alternative energy, multinational corporations, liberation struggles, militarism, and related topics. Prices and distributors are listed.

Nuclear Information and Resource Service. *NIRS Resource Guide on Films, Videotapes, and Slideshows*. Nuclear Information and Resource Service, 1536 16th St. NW, Washington, DC 20036. 1979. 4 pp. $.50.
A listing of the best audio-visual resources on nuclear power, with ordering information.

Scherner, Sharon et al., eds. *The Energy Films Index: An Educator's Guide to Current Energy Films*. Energy and Man's Environment, 0224 SW Hamilton, Suite 301, Portland, OR 97201.
An annotated listing of films from producers, educational institutions, government, and industry, with distributors' addresses and ordering information. (Industry oriented.)

U.S. Department of Energy. Solar Energy Research Institute. *reaching up, reaching out: a guide to organizing local solar events*. Washington, DC, 1979. S/N 061-000-00345-2. 208 pp. $8.50. (USGPO) (EARS)
In addition to suggestions for organizing activities, this manual includes descriptions of many films and slides. See *CITIZEN ACTION* for further information on this publication.

U.S. General Services Administration, National Archives and Records Service, National Audiovisual Center, Washington, DC 20409. *Environment/Energy Conservation Information List.*

Describes films, slide sets, and other audio-visual materials available for purchase or rental from this agency.

U.S. National Audio-Visual Center. *A Reference List of Audio-Visual Materials Produced by the U.S. Government.* Washington, DC, 1978. S/N 052-003-00497-6. 396 pp. $5.75. (USGPO)

A compilation of over 6000 audio-visual materials produced by 175 federal agencies: films, video formats, slide sets, audio tapes, and multi-media kits covering many subject areas including education.

Film Distributors

A detailed description of films is beyond the scope of this bibliography.
Please consult the above references, or write to the distributors listed here.

ACI Productions
35 W 45th Street
Eleventh Floor
New York, NY
10036

American Film
House, Inc.
566 Ann St.
Birmingham, MI
48009

American Institute
of Architects
Audio Visual
Librarian
1735 New York
Avenue
Washington, DC
20006

Arthur Mokin
17 W 60th Street
New York, NY
10023

Association Films
410 Great Road
Littleton, MA 01460

Barr Films
3490 E Foothill Blvd.
Pasadena, CA 91107

Bitter Root
551 River St.
Missoula, Montana
59801

Bullfrog Films
Oley, PA 19547

California
Earthwork/
Newsreel Media
Center
3410 19th St.
San Francisco, CA
94110
Multinationals

Campaign for
Political Rights
201 Massachusetts
Ave. NE
Washington, DC
20002

Caterpillar Films
Library
1687 Elmhurst Road
Elk Grove, IL 60007

Churchill Films
662 N Robertson
Blvd.
Los Angeles, CA
90069

Citizens Energy
Council
P.O. Box 285
Allendale, NJ 07401
"Danger! Radio-
active Wastes"

Corinth Films
410 E. 62nd St.
New York, NY
10021
"Linus Pauling."

Danamar Film
Productions
275 Kilby
Los Alamos, NM
87544

Document Assoc.
43 Britain Street
Ontario, Canada

Earth Energy Media
Box 188
Santa Barbara, CA
93102

Encyclopedia
Britannica
Educational Corp.
Preview Library
1822 Pickwick Ave.
Glenview, IL 06011

Farm Film
Foundation
1425 H Street, NW
Washington, DC
20005

Film Counselor, Inc.
500 5th Avenue
New York, NY
10036

Film Library
Cornell University
55 Judd Falls Road
Ithaca, NY 14853

Films, Inc.
1144 Wilmette
Wilmette, IL 60091

Goodyear Tire and
Rubber Co.
Public Relations Film
Library
1144 E Market St.
Akron, OH 44316

Green Mountain
Post Films
Box 177
Montague, MA
01351
Nuclear power &
citizen opposition.

Handel Film Corp.
8730 Sunset Blvd.
W. Hollywood, CA
90069

Keep America
Beautiful
99 Park Avenue
New York, NY
10016

Kirby Brumfield
Energy
Productions
Suite 322, Governor
Bldg.
408 SW 2nd Street
Portland, OR 97204

Lumen-Bel
Fred James
303 W 11th Street
New York, NY
10014

MacMillan Films
866 3rd Avenue
New York, NY
10022

McDonnell Douglas
Films and Television
Service
3855 Catewood Blvd
(36-16)
Long Beach, CA
90846

McGraw-Hill Text
Films
1221 Avenue of the
Americas
New York, NY
10020

Metabasis
6701 Seybold Road
Madison, WI 53719

Montage Educational
Films
P.O. Box 33992
Seattle, WA 98133

Monumental Films,
Inc.
2160 Rockrose at
Malden Ave.
Baltimore, MD
21211

National Film Board
of Canada
1251 Avenue of the
Americas
16th Floor
New York, NY
10020

National Solar
Heating and Cool-
ing Information

Center
P.O. Box 1607
Rockville, MD 20850
Toll free call:
800/523/2929

National Training
Fund
1900 L Street, NW
Suite 405
Washington, DC
20036

New Mexico People
& Energy
Research Project
810 Vassar NE
Albuquerque, NM
87106

New Time Films
1501 Broadway,
Ste. 1904
New York, NY
10036
"Paul Jacobs & the
Nuclear Gang."

New Western
Energy Show
226 Power Block
Helena, MT 59601

Public Television
Library
Public Broadcasting
System
475 L'Enfant Plaza
SW
Washington, DC
20024

Pyramid Films
Box 1048/2801
Colorado Ave.
Santa Monica, CA
90404

Ram Films
200 Lovers Lane
Steubenville, OH
43952

Ramsgate Films
704 Santa Monica
Blvd.
Santa Monica, CA
90401

Reynolds Metal Co.
Motion Picture
Service
P.O. Box 27003
Richmond, VA
23261

Time Life
Multimedia Distri-
bution Center
100 Eisenhower Dr.
Paramus, NJ 07652

Unit 1 Film
Producers
540 West 114th St.
New York, NY
10025

United Auto
Workers
8000 E Jefferson
Detroit, MI 48217

U.S. Army Corps of
Engineers
Modern Talking
Picture Service
2323 New Hyde
Park Road
New Hyde Park, NY
11040

U.S. Army Engineer
District
San Francisco Bay
Delta Hydraulic
Model
2100 Bridgeway
Sausalito, CA 94965

U.S. Dept. of Energy
Film Library
P.O. Box 62
Oak Ridge, TN
37803

Office of Consumer
Affairs
U.S. Dept. of Energy
Room 8G-082,
Forrestal Bldg.
Washington, DC
20585

Bureau of Mines
U.S. Department of
the Interior
Motion Pictures
4800 Forbes Avenue
Pittsburgh, PA
15213

University of Calif.
Educational Media
Service
Berkeley, CA 94720

Educational Media
Center
University of Colo.
Stadium Building
Boulder, CO 80309

Audio Visual Library
Service
University of Minn.
3300 University Ave.
St. Paul, MN 55414

Xerox Education
Publications
245 Long Hill Rd.
Middletown, CT
06457

Drama

Garde, Anne, and Leprohon, Angie. *The Energy Show*. New Western Energy Show,
842 5th Ave., Helena, MT 59601. 1978. 42 pp. $3.00.
Here is an entertaining way to inform youngsters—and adults—about
energy. The book includes script, songs, and set descriptions for presentations
to schools, organizations, or outdoors as a traveling show.

Great Atlantic Radio Conspiracy, 2743 Maryland Ave., Baltimore, MD 21218.
A radio collective producing taped shows on utility rip-offs, alternative
energy, nuclear power, and related environmental and political issues.

Games

Ampersand Press. 2603 Grove St., Oakland, CA 94612.
Card games:
Predator—for understanding the food web. $5.00 postpaid
Pollination—interdependence of flowers and their animal pollinators. $6.50
postpaid
AC-DC—basic electric circuitry. $5.50 postpaid
Puzzle:

Science Participoster, 24" x 36". $4.70 postpaid
A giant crossword puzzle with terms from the physical and biological sciences.

Animal Town Game Company, P.O. Box 2002, Santa Barbara, CA 93120.
Educational family and classroom boardgames about Mother Nature, conservation, whales, self-sufficiency, and human values. $12.00 and up. Free catalog.

Andrea Asaro, 813 Lawrence Rd., Lawrenceville, NJ 08648.
Nuke: The Race to Nuclear Power. $8.95. Have fun while you learn about the construction of nuclear power plants, the regulatory process, the permits required, the pitfalls, and the potential for bankruptcy.

Cliff Humphrey, Box 3895, Modesto, CA 95352.
Recycle. A board game, age 12 and up. $11.00

Sekunon Industries, 1823 Oxford St., Rockford, IL 61103.
Meltdown. $8.00. Includes game board, tokens, dice, and cards, for ages 8 to adult. Simulates the perils and promise of nuclear energy, demands quick decisions and a bit of luck.

Soft-Aware Associates, Inc., P.O. Box 93, Hadley, MA 01035.
Nature's Energy Game. $14.00. Includes game board, markers, dice, and cards, for ages 8 to adult. Players travel to rugged environments, cope with natural disasters, and learn how Mother Nature plays the Energy Game.

Maps

American Nuclear Society, 555 N. Kensington Ave., La Grange Park, IL 60525.
Fact Sheet No. 1: Commercial Nuclear Power Stations in the United States, Operable, Under Construction, or Ordered. A 23" x 35" map of the United States, with data on nuclear power stations. Updated annually, August 1. Free while supply lasts.
Fact Sheet No. 2: Commercial Nuclear Power Stations Around the World. Operable, Under Construction, or Ordered. A 23" x 44" world map, with data on nuclear power stations. Updated annually, September 1. Free while supply lasts.

U.S. Geological Survey. *National Atlas Separate Sales Editions.*
Customers east of the Mississippi River: Branch of Distribution, Central Region, U.S. Geological Survey, 1200 South Eads Street, Arlington, VA 22202.
Customers west of the Mississippi River: Branch of Distribution, Central Region, U.S. Geological Survey, Box 25286, Federal Center, Denver, CO 80225.
Most of these maps are 19" x 28", and cost $1.50. *The National Energy Transportation Maps* describe the movement of fossil and nuclear fuels by highways, pipelines, railroads, and waterways across the country. Other *National Atlas Maps* show sunshine, evaporation, average temperatures, vegetation, population distribution, etc. A complete list of titles is available.

War Resisters League, 339 Lafayette St., New York, NY 10012.
Nuclear America, color, 17" x 22". $1.00. (Bulk rates available). Shows nuclear weapons and nuclear power facilities, including all steps in the nuclear fuel cycle. Name and description of each facility is on reverse side. Revised June 1979.

Posters

Alternative Energy Resources Organization. 435 Stapleton Building, Billings, MT 59101.
   A set of four posters showing renewable energy systems. $3.75.

Citizens' Energy Project, 1110 Sixth St., NW, Suite #300, Washington, DC 20001.
   Community Self-Reliance. June 1979, four colors, 22" x 30". $3.50. Depicts an Appropriate Technology Community basking under the sun; side panels show close-ups of community self-reliance projects; the reverse side lists books and organizations concerned with these issues.

Creative Recycling Center. 4614 Liberty Ave., Bloomfield, Pittsburgh, PA 15224.
   A black and white poster to be colored in, depicting 80 objects made from petroleum. $2.00.

Environmental Action Foundation, 724 Dupont Circle Building, Washington, DC 20036.
   Love Your Mother, a color poster of Mother Earth, 2' x 3'. $1.50

Environmental Education Group, 18014 Sherman Way, #169, Reseda, CA 91335.
   Geothermal: Clean and Abundant Power from the Earth. A 24" x 36" wall chart with text and pictures explaining geothermal resources and technologies.

Institute of Environmental Sciences, 940 E. Northwest Highway, Mt Prospect, IL 60056.
   Solar Energy. A set of eleven full color 22" x 34" wall charts. $4.50.

Pollution Probe. *The Unfinished Agenda.* Pollution Probe, 43 Queens Park, CR East, Toronto, Canada, M5S 2C3. $2.00.
   A 34" x 22" action poster, printed on both sides, with information on hundreds of environmental concerns from energy to food additives. Useful for home or classroom.

Rain Magazine, 2700 NW Irving, Portland, OR 97210. A set of two posters, line drawing, black on white, great for coloring. $3.00 shipped folded, or $4.00 in mailing tube, each. These are also available from EARS.
   Urban Ecotopia. 22" x 33"
   Suburban Ecotopia, 22" x 30"

ReSource, Inc. P.O. Box 127, Astor Station, Boston, MA 02133.
   Ionizing Radiation 18" x 24", black on buff figure showing where radioactive isotopes concentrate in the body. $.75.

Soft-Aware Associates, Inc., P.O. Box 93, Hadley, MA 01035. A set of two posters, 22" x 34", full color, with comprehensive energy text on the reverse side. $3.50 each, or $6.00 for the set of two, including postage. These posters are also available from MassPIRG, 233 N. Pleasant St., Amherst, MA 01002.
   1. *Nuclear Power Plants: A Shocking Harvest.* Depicts health, economic, and environmental effects.
   2. *Plant for the Future: Harvest the Sun.* Shows the many alternatives to nuclear power.

Syracuse Peace Council, 924 Burnet Ave., Syracuse, NY 13203.
   People's Energy Calendar, $4.00. Includes useful information on safe energy issues and organizations.

Total Environmental Action, 24 Church Hill, Harrisville, NJ 03450.
History Chart of Solar Domestic Water Heating. 14" x 36" two color chart. $2.00.
History Chart of Solar Heated Buildings. 16" x 36" two color chart. $2.00.

U.S. Congress. *Energy History of the U.S., 1776-1976.* Washington, DC, 1975.
S/N 052-010-00459-0. $2.05. (USGPO)
A colorful 48" x 36" wall chart, with a 24 page booklet.

Windworks, P.O. Box 329, Rt. 3, Mukwanago, WI 53149.
Wind Energy, a 24" x 31" color poster of wind devices and technical data.
$3.00.

Slide Shows

(usually with script and cassette) Please write for prices and availability.

Butti, Ken. 511-A Strand St., Santa Monica, CA 90405.
Full Circle. The evolution and present uses of solar technology.

Diana Wyllie, 3 Park Road, Baker Street, London NW1 6XP, England.
An international series of three tape/slide sets, all for $79.00 incl. air mail.
1. *Harnessing the Atom;*
2. *Radioactivity and the Nuclear Fuel Cycle.*
3. *Fast Breeders and the Nuclear Economy.*
Other sets available on energy, waste and recycling, pollution, and
population.

Earthmind, 4844 Hirsch Rd., Mariposa, CA 95338.
Wind Power Slide Shows. Send $.50 and a stamped, self-addressed envelope for
list of slide shows and publications on wind and appropriate technology.

Ecotope Group. 2332 East Madison, Seattle, WA 98112
Home Energy Conservation
Infiltration, and Ways to Beat It. Reducing heat loss in the home.
The Solar Greenhouse. Principles and construction of various types.

New England Coalition on Nuclear Pollution, Inc., Box 637, Brattleboro, VT
05301.
Nuclear Power Slide Show.

New England Solar Energy Association. P.O. Box 541, Brattleboro, VT 05301.
Passive Solar Energy, I. Direct gain, sunspace, thermosiphon.
Passive Solar Energy, II. Trombe wall, roof pond, and hybrid systems.

New Mexico People and Energy Research Project, 810 Vassar NE, Albuquerque,
NM 87106
People and Energy in the Southwest. The effects of energy development on the
Navajo Nation and other residents of New Mexico.

New Mexico Solar Energy Assocation, P.O. Box 2004, Santa Fe, NM 87501.
Passive Solar slide shows: six sets, including general principles, specific
devices, and attached greenhouses.

Packard-Manse Media Project. P.O. Box 450, Stoughton, MA 02072.
Slideshows, filmstrips, and tapes. Titles include:
The Last Slideshow. The nuclear issue and human needs.
I Have Three Children of My Own. Dr. Helen Caldicott on the health hazards of
nuclear power.

Guess Who's Coming to Breakfast. Multinational corporations.
Banking on South Africa. Human consequences.
Medical Implications of Nuclear Power and Weapons. Dr. Helen Caldicott. (tape)

Solar Energy Educational Service, Inc. P.O. Box 307, Eaton, CO 80615.
Solar Energy: five programs, including solar collectors, manufactured and owner-built solar systems, large-scale systems, and greenhouses.

Solar Sustenance Team. Rt. 1, Box 107 AA, Sante Fe, NM 87501
Solar Greenhouse: seven sets of slides covering design, construction, horticulture, problems, and applications.

Southwest Research and Information Center, P.O. Box 4524, Albuquerque, NM 87106.
New Mexico Uranium Industry
Nuclear Waste Disposal. Includes the Waste Isolation Pilot Plant planned for New Mexico.

Total Environmental Action, 24 Church Hill, Harrisville, NH 03450
Passive Solar Slide Show: An Introduction to Passive Solar Heating and Cooling Systems. 54 slides & tape. $75.00.
Solar Information Kit. Slides, plans, booklet. $50.00.

Visual Information Project, Box 40602 Washington, DC 20016
Atomic Power and the Arms Race. The two crucial issues are linked.

Zomeworks Corporation, P.O. Box 712, Albuquerque, NM 87103.
Passive Solar Design and Construction.

Videocassettes

Earth Energy Media, Box 188 Santa Barbara, CA 93102.
Medical Implications of Nuclear Energy, with Dr. Helen Caldicott. Available as ¾" or ½" videocassettes, or 16 mm film.

Solarvision, Inc. *Solar Visions/Solar Video.* Solarvision, Inc., Box A, Hurley, NY 12443.
A series of videotape programs exploring solar energy applications.

UNITED STATES GOVERNMENT ENERGY-RELATED AGENCIES

References

National Referral Center, Science and Technology Division, Library of Congress. *Federal Government: A Directory of Information Resources in the United States.* Washington, DC, 1974. 416 pp. $4.25. (USGPO)
   Provides names, addresses, and services, arranged by Department and indexed, covering all subjects. All federal organizations are included except a few who requested omission, or provided inadequate information.

Office of the Federal Register. *Federal Register.* General Services Administration, Office of the Federal Register, National Archives and Records Services, Washington, DC. Published Monday through Friday, $50.00/yr. (USGPO)
   The *Federal Register* makes available to the public the regulations and legal notices issued by Federal agencies, including Presidential proclamations and executive orders.

Office of the Federal Register. *United States Government Manual.* Washington, DC, 1979/80. Updated annually. S/N 022-003-00982-5. $6.75. (USGPO)
   Lists all government offices and programs, with addresses, personnel, and services available.

U.S. Congress, Joint Committee on Printing. *Congressional Record.* Washington, DC. Printed each day that one or both Houses are in session. $85.00/yr. (USGPO)
   The public proceedings and debates of each House of Congress are reported in full.

Washington Information Directory. Congressional Quarterly, Inc., 1414 22nd St., NW, Washington, DC 20036. 800 pp. $18.00.
   Access to Congressional committees, staffs, media, and organizations.

Agencies

ACTION—c/o VISTA, 806 Connecticut Ave., NW, Washington, DC 20525.
   Promotes use of solar technologies in other nations through Peace Corps

volunteers.

Community Services Administration, 1200 19th Street NW, Washington, DC 20506.
Home weatherization programs for low income families.

Department of Agriculture, 14th and Independence Ave. SW, Washington, DC 20250.
Conducts solar programs for farms, such as crop drying, greenhouses, space heating, food processing, and the production of alcohol from farm wastes.

Department of Commerce, 14th St. betw. Constitution Ave. & E St. NW, Washington, DC 20230.
Office of Energy Programs. Concerned with policy and the development of new energy resources such as biomass and energy conservation.

National Technical Information Service, (NTIS), U.S. Department of Commerce, 5285 Port Royal Rd., Springfield, VA 22161.
The central source for the public sale of government-sponsored research. A *General Catalog* may be obtained by writing to NTIS. It lists bibliographies and services available, including *Weekly Government Energy Abstracts,* $75.00/yr. Files include over one million titles of scientific, technical, and engineering information, available on paper or microfiche. Inquire at EPA and DOE information centers for NTIS microfiche libraries.

Department of Energy.
This agency has the responsibility for research on conventional and new sources of energy, policy development, and informational services.
Office of Consumer Affairs. Rm 8G031 Forrestal, DOE, Washington, DC 20585.
The Energy Consumer. Bimonthly, free. Solar & energy conservation programs.
Education and Training Division, Office of Consumer Affairs, M.S. 7E-054, DOE, Washington, DC 20585.
Energy information for teachers; academic and community energy education.

Office of Public Affairs, U.S. Department of Energy, Washington, DC 20585.
General information and educational material.

Office of Conservation and Solar Applications, U.S. Department of Energy, 20 Massachusetts Ave., NW, Washington, DC 20545.
Promulgates the use of solar technologies which are presently feasible; has prepared a solar energy curriculum.

Department of Energy Regional Offices:
Region I, 150 Causeway St., Boston, MA 02114.
Region II, 26 Federal Plaza, Rm 3200, New York, NY 10007.
Region III, 1421 Cherry St., 10th fl., Philadelphia, PA 19102.
Region IV, 1655 Peachtree St. NE, Atlanta, GA 30309.
Region V, 175 West Jackson Blvd., Rm A-333, Chicago, IL 60604.
Region VI, P.O. Box 35228, 2626 West Mockingbird Lane, Dallas, TX 75235.
Region VII, 324 East 11th St., Kansas City, MO 64106.
Region VIII, P.O. Box 26247, Belmar Branch, 1075 S. Yukon St., Lakewood, CO 80226.

Region IX, 333 Market St., San Francisco, CA 94105.
Region X, Rm. 1992 Federal Building, 915 Second Ave., Seattle, WA 98174.

Solar Energy Research Institute, 1536 Cole Blvd., Golden, CO 80401.
SERI is the Department of Energy's center for solar research and development, responsible for evaluating new programs, and overcoming technical and economic barriers to the widespread utilization of solar energy. Publication list includes free brochures and bibliographies.
There are four *Regional Solar Energy Centers:*
> *Mid-American Solar Energy Complex,* 1256 Trapp Rd., Eagan, MN 55121.
> *Northeast Solar Energy Center,* 70 Memorial Dr., Cambridge, MA 02142.
> *Southern Solar Energy Center,* Exchange Place, Suite 1250, 2300 Peachford Rd., Atlanta, GA 30338.
> *Western Solar Utilization Network,* 921 SW Washington, Suite 160, Portland, OR 97205.

Department of Health, Education, and Welfare.
Office of Consumer Affairs. 330 Independence Ave. SW, Washington, DC 20201.
Consumer programs include solar projects.
Office of Education. * Energy and Education Action Center, Room 514 Reporters Building, 300 7th St. SW, Washington, DC 20202.
Materials and programs for educators.

Department of Housing and Urban Development, 451 7th St. SW, Washington, DC 20410.
Projects and publications on energy conservation and community development; concerned with the development of a residential solar market.

Department of the Interior.
Bureau of Mines, 2401 E St. NW, Washington, DC 20241.
Research, publications, and films on mineral resource technology, health and safety, and environmental impact.
Bureau of Reclamation, Washington, DC 20240
Publications and films, especially on the generation of hydroelectric power.
U.S. *Geological Survey.* East: 1200 South Eads St., Arlington, VA 22202; West: Box 25286, Bldg 41, Federal Center, Denver, CO 80225.
Maps of energy resources and transportation.

Environmental Protection Agency, 401 M St. SW, Washington, DC 20460.
Programs include energy from biomass, solid waste management, and community planning. Many free pamphlets are available on environmental problems, such as pollution, toxic substances, and the impact of energy on the environment. Regional Information Centers have libraries with NTIS material on microfiche.

Environmental Study Conference, 3334 House Annex 2, Washington, DC 20515.
This Congressional organization monitors environmental and energy issues, and publishes reports and the *ESC Weekly Bulletin.* Send S.A.S.E. for publication list.

Executive Office of the President, Council on Environmental Quality, 722 Jackson Pl. NW, Washington DC 20006.

---

*Note: Energy education has been transferred to the Department of Energy: Education and Training Division, Office of Consumer Affairs, M.S. 7E-054, DOE, Washington, DC 20585.

Conducts studies and makes reports on a wide variety of energy and environmental issues; several are favorable to solar development. Send for list of publications, which are available from CEQ or USGPO.

Federal Trade Commission, Pennsylvania Ave. at 6th St. NW, Washington, DC 20580.
Investigates problems of utility involvement in solar development, solar patent rights, and consumer warranties.

General Accounting Office, Document Handling and Information Services Facility, P.O. Box 6015, Gaithersburg, MD 20760. *Monthly List of Reports,* free.
The GAO is Congress's "watchdog", and reviews executive branch programs with pro and con views on controversial issues, in layperson language.

General Services Administration, Consumer Information Center, Pueblo, CO 81009.
A free catalog is issued four times a year, and is available from the above address or from the USGPO. The Center is a clearinghouse for free and inexpensive materials on energy conservation and other areas of consumer interest.

House Committee on Science and Technology, House Office Building, Washington, DC 20215.

House Environment, Energy and Natural Resources Subcommittee, House Office Building, Washington, DC 20515.

National Aeronautics and Space Administration, 400 Maryland Ave. SW, Washington, DC 20546.
In addition to research in the areas of flight and space exploration, NASA studies wind energy, photovoltaics, and space power satellites.

National Bureau of Standards, Office of Energy Conservation, Washington, DC 20234.
Energy Conservation Publications List.

National Center for Appropriate Technology, P.O. Box 3838, Butte, MT 59701.
NCAT addresses the need for small scale technologies and ways in which low income individuals and communities can become self-sufficient. It gathers and disseminates information, provides technical and program support, and makes grants for projects. Brochure and publication list available. Funded by Community Services Administration.

National Referral Center, Science and Technology Division, Library of Congress, 10 First St., SE, Washington, DC 20540.
Selected Information Resources on Energy. Free. A guide to government agencies and other information-gathering organizations, including trade associations.
A list of available *LC Science Tracer Bullets and Computer Printouts of Topic Area Resource People.* Free. These are bibliographies and resource lists on specific topics.

National Science foundation, 1800 G. St., NW, Washington, DC 20550.
Supports basic and applied research, and science education programs.

National Solar Heating and Cooling Information Center, P.O. Box 1607, Rockville, MD 20850. Call toll-free: Pennsylvania, (800) 462-4983; other Continental U.S., (800) 523-2929.

A complete, one-stop facility for all information, domestic and foreign, technical and non-technical, on any aspect of solar heating and cooling. Funded by DOE and HUD.

Nuclear Regulatory Commission (NRC). 1717 H St., NW, Washington, DC 20555.

National and regional offices issue free press releases, and provide documents rooms where the public may examine materials. Contact the NRC in Washington for the address of the Regional Office in your area.

Oak Ridge Associated Universities Institute, Box 117, Oak Ridge, TN 37830.
Energy research and education.

Oak Ridge National Laboratory, P.O. Box X, Oak Ridge, TN 37830.
Monthly *Energy Abstracts,* inventories of *Current Energy Research,* and other publications and services.

Senate Committee on Energy and Natural Resources, Senate Office Building, Washington, DC 20510.

Small Business Administration, 1441 L St. NW, Washington, DC 20416.
Low interest loans to small solar firms.

Superintendent of Documents, U.S. Government Printing Office (USGPO), Washington, DC 20402.

For access to over 24,000 publications, request the free *Subject Bibliography Index* which lists over 270 free subject bibliographies, such as energy conservation, atomic energy and nuclear power, education, environment, films, consumer information, waste, transportation, and publications of the FPC, NASA, and NSF.

Also, you may request Form 3848 (R2-77) to place your name on a mailing list for *Selected U.S. Government Publications,* 10 issues/yr., free.

For direct service, there are Government Bookstores located in the following cities: Atlanta, GA.; Birmingham, Ala.; Boston, Mass.; Cleveland, Ohio; Columbus, Ohio; Dallas, Tex.; Denver, Colo.; Detroit, Mich.; Houston, Tex.; Jacksonville, Fla.; Kansas City, Kans.; Los Angeles, Calif.; Milwaukee, Wis.; Philadelphia, Pa.; Pueblo, Colo.; San Francisco, Calif.; Seattle, Wash.; and Washington, D.C.

Technical Information Center, P.O. Box 62, Oak Ridge, TN 37830.
Government energy research and publications. Educators materials.

Your Congressman, House Office Building, Washington, DC 20515. and
Your Senator, Senate Office Building, Washington, DC 20510.
Can provide certain congressional records.

Your State Energy Office.

ORGANIZATIONS, PERIODICALS, AND CATALOGS

References

Barkas, J.L. *The Help Book*. New York, NY: Scribner's, 1979. 667 pp. $9.95.

An annotated directory of over 5,000 U.S. programs, organizations, and agencies offering assistance: federal, state, citizen, and non-profit organizations. This is a remarkably useful resource for the citizen activist, libraries, and social service agencies, with information in 52 areas such as citizen action, health, environment, media, emergencies, consumer affairs, and civil rights.

Citizens' Energy Project. *Citizens' Energy Directory, Second Edition*. Simpson, Jan, and Bossong, Ken, eds. Citizens' Energy Project, 1110 Sixth St. NW, #300, Washington, DC 20001. 1979. 195 pp. $10/$15. (CEP)

This is an essential reference book for the energy activist. It describes in detail some 600 safe energy organizations in the United States, in order by state; organizations are also listed by type and by the area of interest; important publications are also listed. The information is here, and is accessible.

Commission for the Advancement of Public Interest Organizations. *Periodicals of Public Interest Organizations: A Citizen's Guide*. Commission for the Advancement of Public Interest Organizations, 1875 Connecticut Ave. NW, Suite 1013, Washington, DC 20009. 1979. 57 pp. $4/$5/$15.

This important reference describes organizations which deal with alternative solutions to public problems, and help citizens become more involved in community and national actions. Publications are arranged in categories and indexed. The attractive format includes a reduced reproduction of the front page of each periodical.

Gale Research Company. *Encyclopedia of Associations. 13th Edition*. Detroit, MI: Gale Research Company, 1979. Updated annually. Vol. 1. *National Organizations of the United States*. 477 pp. $80.00. Vol. 2. *Geographic and Executive Index*. $65.00. Vol. 3. *New Associations and Projects: Periodical Supplements*. $75.00.

Data and descriptions are provided for thousands of international, national, and regional groups, in categories, and indexed. It is usually available in libraries.

Lower, Eric, ed. *Energy Atlas: A Who's Who Resource to Information*. Fraser/Ruder and

Finn, 1701 K St. NW, Washington, DC 20006. $25.00.

Who's got the action in energy within governmental and non-governmental organizations. Publications and periodicals are also listed.

National Wildlife Federation. *Conservation Directory.* National Wildlife Federation, 1412 16th St. NW, Washington, DC 20036. 1980 (updated annually). 290 pp. $4.00.

Descriptions of organizations, agencies, and officials concerned with natural resource use and management are arranged by state. Foreign groups and other references are also included.

Park Project on Energy Interpretation. *Energy - Who's Doing What?* National Recreation and Park Association, 1601 N. Kent St., Arlington, VA 22209. 1976. 43 pp. Free.

A list and description of some 200 U.S. citizen and non-profit groups, and companies involved in energy-related activities.

Public Affairs Clearing House. *Energy: A Guide to Organizations and Information Resources in the United States.* Public Affairs Clearing House, P.O. Box 10, Claremont, CA 91711. Second edition, 1978. 221 pp. $20.00.

Data is provided on more than 1000 organizations, arranged in subject areas, with sections on federal, state, and local agencies, utilities, trade associations, research centers, information clearing houses, and citizen groups.

Rain Magazine, eds. *Rainbook: Resources for Appropriate Technology.* New York, NY: Schocken, 1977. 251 pp. $7.95. (EARS)

This resource includes names and descriptions of hundreds of organizations and publications. See *APPROPRIATE TECHNOLOGY: REFERENCES.*

Sunspark Press. *Guide to Alternative Periodicals.* Sunspark Press, P.O. Box 91, Greenleaf, OR 97445. 1977. 76 pp. $3.00.

Hundreds of publications are described in this guide. Items range from newsletters to magazines, in categories such as conservation, alternative energy, appropriate technology, and social, political, and economic change.

Synerjy: A Directory of Energy Alternatives. P.O. Box 4790, Grand Central Station, New York, NY 10017. Published semi-annually, in January and July. $9.00/yr. $5.00/single copy.

A listing, by category, of books and periodicals, facilities, current research, and manufacturers. Issues are cumulative for one year. Entries are not repeated, hence reference to previous editions is necessary.

U.S. Department of Energy, Solar Research Institute. *Reaching Up, Reaching Out: A Guide to Organizing Local Solar Events.* Washington, DC, 1979. S/N 061-000-00345-2. 208 pp. $8.50. (USGPO) (EARS)

In addition to suggestions for organizing activities, this manual includes an extensive list of citizen groups and government agencies among many other resources. See *CITIZEN ACTION* for further description of this publication.

Organizations, Periodicals, and Catalogs

The following groups are engaged in education, research, publication, litigation, lobbying, or citizen action related to energy and the environment. Most of these groups will send a brochure or publication list upon request. A self-addressed, stamped envelope (S.A.S.E.) would be appreciated. Some publications have a sliding scale for subscription rates; the regular rate is quoted here. Please check before ordering publications; the frequency and price of subscriptions and publications often change, and organizations may move or disband.

Akwesasne Notes. Mohawk Nation via Rooseveltown, NY 13683. 5 issues/yr., $5.00.
   The best Native American newspaper reports on sovereignty, self-sufficiency, and energy exploitation of Indian lands. Late Winter Feb. 1979 issue deals with Native Americans and the nuclear fuel cycle; $1.00.

Alcohol Renewable Resource Center, 1110 Sixth Ave. NW, Suite 3, Washington, DC 20001. *Alcohol Renewable Resource Center News.* Monthly, 4 pp. $6.50/yr.
   National and international research, development, and commercialization of alcohol fuels, and political updates.

Alliance to Save Energy. 1925 K St. NW, Suite 507, Washington, DC 20006. *Conservation Energy!* Monthly, $15.00/yr.
   Research, education and advocacy in the field of conservation and energy efficiency, with focus on industry, agriculture, transportation, residences, and commerce.

Alternate Architecture: The Energy Management Journal. Dove Publications, 660 Newport Center Dr., Suite 1220, Newport Beach, CA 92660. Bimonthly, $10.00/yr.
   Contains many new ideas to utilize alternate energy sources and dispose of wastes.

Alternative Energy Collective, Inc. 2600 Dwight Way, 204, Berkeley, CA 94704. *Newsletter.* $10.00/yr.
   Education, research, workshops, exhibits, consultation. Booklet: *Steps to Energy Self-Reliance,* $1.00.

Alternative Energy Resource Organization. 435 Stapleton Building, Billings, MT 59101. *AERO Sun-Times.* Monthly, $10.00/yr.
   Education and action in the areas of solar and wind technology. Publications and audio-visual resources. Producers of *The New Western Energy Show.*

Alternatives: Perspectives on Society and the Environment. c/o Trent University, Peterborough, Ontario, Canada, K9J 7B8. Quarterly, $4.00 Canada, $5.00 U.S.
   This journal, oriented toward a conserver society, presents a discussion of energy policy, resource use, pollution, and the environment.

Alternative Sources of Energy Magazine. Route 2, Box 90-A, Milaca, MN 56353. Bimonthly, $15.00/yr.
   A communication network for people concerned with the development of alternative technologies for a decentralized society. The magazine contains practical information on the construction and use of alternative energy equipment in many areas. Back issues on specific topics are available from ASE or from EARS.

Ambix, P.O. Box 353, Port Ludlow, WA 98365.
   Alcohol fuels education and publications; newsletter, videotapes, seminars, speakers. See Mandeville, Michael. *Solar Alcohol in BIOMASS: ALCOHOL FUELS.*

American Association for the Advancement of Science, 1515 Massachusetts Ave. NW, Washington, DC 20005. *Science Magazine.* Weekly, $60.00/yr.; membership rates.

Major articles on energy and all scientific disciplines, and reports of recent research. Catalog lists books, tapes, periodicals, and reprints.

American Friends Service Committee, Inc., 1501 Cherry St., Philadelphia, PA 19102.

The Friends advocate non-violent action for social change, and their programs are concerned with disarmament, conversion from military to social production, simple living, alternative energy, opposition to nuclear power and weapons, and worldwide humanitarian activities. Branches in most large cities.

American Friends Service Committee, Nuclear Transportation Project. P.O. Box 2234, High Point, NC 27261.

Bibliography and materials on the transportation of radioactive materials. S.A.S.E.

American Indian Environmental Council. 3105 Campus, NE, Albuquerque, NM 87106.

Organizes against uranium mining. Information on the Church Rock radioactive tailings spill into the Rio Puerco.

American Institute of Architects, 1735 New York Ave., NW, Washington, DC 20006. *AIA Energy Notebook.* $90.00/yr.

A continuing information service on energy and the artificial environment. Other publications on energy conservation and solar energy building design.

American Nuclear Society. 555 N. Kensington Ave., La Grange Park, IL 60525.

Publications of interest to the nuclear industry. Periodicals include *Nuclear News, Nuclear Technology, Nuclear Science and Engineering.* Books include texts on all aspects of nuclear technology in the U.S. and Europe, and are described in the *Publications and Services Catalog.* Large maps of U.S. and world nuclear reactors are updated annually and free upon request. See *AUDIO-VISUAL MATERIALS: MAPS.*

American Public Power Association. *Public Power.* American Public Power Association, 2600 Virginia Ave., NW, Washington, DC 20037.

A review of energy development and regulations as it affects publicly owned utilities.

American Wind Energy Association, 54468 CR 31, Bristol, IN 46507. *Wind Power Digest,* Quarterly, $6.00, including the *Wind Power Access Catalog.*

Other publications include the *AWEA Newsletter,* and *Wind Technology Journal.* AWEA is dedicated to the education of the government, industry, and the public in the enormous potential of small-scale wind systems.

Anti-Nuclear Legal Project. 120 Boylston St., Rm 1011, Boston, MA 02116.

A clearinghouse providing advice to anti-nuclear legal workers all over the country, and bringing civil suits and injunctions to halt nuclear facilties.

Association of Home Appliance Manufacturers, Office of Consumer Affairs, 20 N. Wacker Dr., Chicago, IL 60606.

Information on home appliance energy use.

Atomic Industrial Forum, 7101 Wisconsin Ave., NW, Washington, DC 20014. *Nuclear Industry,* monthly. *AIF Nuclear INFO,* monthly.

This trade organization studies problems of all phases of the nuclear fuel cycle, health and safety, and legislation. Audio-visual materials.

Bio-Energy Council. 1625 Eye St. NW, Suite 825A, Washington, DC 20006.
Coordinates research and conferences, and promotes the commercial development of bio-energy technologies. Publications, grants.

Biomass Energy Institute, Inc. P.O. Box 129, Postal Station C, Winnipeg, Manitoba, Canada R3M 3S7.
Publication, bibliographies, and bulletins on solar energy, anaerobic digestion, methane, and renewable energy.

Bio Sources Digest. Neus, Inc. Box 1979, Santa Monica, CA 90406. Quarterly, $10.00/yr.
Information exchange in biomass utilization.

Black Hills Alliance, P.O. Box 2508, Rapid City, SD 57709.
Monthly tabloid, $5.00/yr., reporting on news of uranium mining and energy development in this "National Sacrifice Area," and actions of this alliance of Indians and white farmers.

Bulletin of the Atomic Scientists. 1020-24 East 58th St., Chicago, IL 60637. 10 issues/yr., $19.50.
Authoritative information on nuclear power, nuclear proliferation and the arms race, and alternative sources of energy. It is concerned with the social implications of the advances of science and technology.

Campaign for Political Rights. 201 Massachusetts Ave. NE, Rm. 112, Washington, DC 20002.
Organizing Notes and resources on issues such as the intelligence community, labor, surveillance and harassment of nuclear power opponents. Film. Member, Safe Energy Communication Council.

Center for Advanced Computation, Energy Library, University of Illinois, Urbana, IL 61801. *Energy Research Group Abstract List.*
A listing of abstracts of this group's research on energy supply, energy demand, statistics, policy, economics, transportation, recycling, pollution, consumer issues, planning, and the ecosystem.

Center for the Biology of Natural Systems. Washington University, Box 1126, St. Louis, MO 63130.
Dr. Barry Commoner and others study energy policy, alternative technology, economics, employment, and environmental pollution.

Center for Development Policy. 401 C St. NE, Washington, DC 20002.
Information on international nuclear economics.

Center for Energy Policy and Research. New York Institute of Technology, Old Westbury, NY 11568.
A national information clearinghouse for the Energy Extension Service of the U.S. Department of Energy, and the Energy and Education Action Center of the U.S. Office of Education. Factsheets and audio-visual material.

Center for Neighborhood Technology, 570 Randolph St., Chicago, IL 60606. *The Neighborhood Works.* Bimonthly.
This newsletter is dedicated to self-reliance for low-income neighborhoods, especially in the Chicago area. Reports on nationwide urban renewable energy projects, grant money, and literature reviews.

Center for Renewable Resources. 1001 Connecticut Ave. NW, 5th fl., Washington, DC 20036.

Research, education, and publications in the field of renewable energy, especially solar. Useful materials for educators. Networking, consumer information. Member, Safe Energy Communication Council.

Center for Science in the Public Interest. 1755 S St. NW, Washington, DC 20009. *Nutrition Action* magazine. Monthly, $15.00/yr.

Focus is on food, the food industry, and government regulation of the food industry. Posters.

Center for Study of Responsive Law, P.O. Box 19367, Washington, DC 20036.

Research and publications on legal aspects of the public interest versus government and industry policies, especially in areas such as nuclear power and education.

Cerro Gordo Community Association. P.O. Box 569, Cottage Grove, OR 97424. *Community Report.* Quarterly, $3.00/yr.

A human-centered community based on ecological principles.

Citizen Participation. Tufts University, Medford, MA 02155. Bimonthly, $12.00/yr.

A survey of trends in citizen groups, government public involvement programs, and electoral participation.

Citizen Soldier. 175 Fifth Ave., #1010, New York, NY 10010.

Works on behalf of veterans exposed to radiation in government A-tests or to Agent Orange in Vietnam.

Citizens Energy Council. P.O. Box 285, Allendale, NJ 07401.

Sponsors the Nuclear Hazards Information Center (see below); distributes films on nuclear hazards.

Citizens' Energy Project. 1110 Sixth St., NW, Suite 300, Washington, DC 20001.

Original research and publications on all forms of renewable energy, the hazards of nuclear and fossil fuels, conservation, community self-reliance, and Native American energy problems. Articles, posters, and books, including the *Citizens' Energy Directory.*
(See *ORGANIZATIONS: REFERENCES.*)

Citizens for a Better Environment. 59 East Van Buren, Suite 2610, Chicago, IL 60605; 88 First St., Suite 600, San Francisco, CA 94105. *CBE Environmental Review.* Monthly, $15.00/yr.

Research, publication, and litigation in areas of nuclear safety and economics, pollution control, toxic substances, environmental health, and solar energy.

Citizens for Energy and Freedom. 941 East 17th Ave., Suite 3, Denver, CO 80218.

A pro-nuclear group organized to "distribute positive facts on the production of energy by nuclear, fossil and solar systems."

Clamshell Alliance. 39 Congress St., Portsmouth, NH 03801. *Clamshell Alliance News.* Bi-monthly. $3.00/yr. (or more)

The Clams lead the resistance to the Seabrook, N.H. reactor. The *News* contains the latest information on the anti-nuke movement in the U.S. and abroad, alternative energy, and educational and organizational resources. Of interest to activists everywhere.

Clergy and Laity Concerned (CALC). 198 Broadway, New York, NY 10038. *CALC Report.* Monthly, $15.00/yr.
An action-oriented interfaith peace and justice organization which opposes nuclear weapons, nuclear power, and corporate power, and works for safe, renewable energy, human rights and human needs all over the world.

Coalition for Full Nuclear Insurance. 317 Pennsylvania Ave. SE, Washington, DC 20003.
Organizing on the issue of full nuclear industry accountability and liability, and the reform of the Price-Anderson Act.

Coalition for a New Foreign and Military Policy. 120 Maryland Ave. NE, Washington, DC 20002.
Reports in opposition to nuclear proliferation.

Coalition for a Non-Nuclear World. 236 Massachusetts Ave., NE, 506, Washington, DC 20002.
A broad coalition of major national and regional organizations engaged in education and action to stop nuclear power and weapons, to promote safe energy and full employment, and to honor Native American treaties.

CoEvolution Quarterly. Produced by the staff of the *Whole Earth Catalog,* Stewart Brand, ed. Box 428, Sausalito, CA 94965. $3.50 single copy, $12.00/yr.
An eclectic non-commercial magazine containing innovative and controversial articles, as well as reviews of books and tools for appropriate technology and simple living.

The Collaborators. P.O. Box 5429, Charlottesville, VA 22903.
Publications to assist in planning and funding community projects. See: *CITIZEN ACTION.*

Committee for Nuclear Responsibility, Inc., M.P.O. Box 11207, San Francisco, Ca 94101; P.O. Box 332 Yachats, OR 97498. John W. Gofman, M.D., chairman.
Technical reports, flyers, and books on nuclear hazards and alternative choices.

Colorado Open Space Council, Mining Workshop. 2239 East Colfax Ave., Denver, CO 80206. Newsletter, *Mine Watch,* $5.00/yr.
Research, education, and publication on the impacts of coal, oil shale, and uranium mining in the West.

Community Action Research Group. P.O. Box 1232, Ames, IA 50010. *New Criteria: The Midwest Journal of Appropriate Technology.* Bimonthly, $8.50.
CARG focuses on energy, the environment, utility reform, housing, land use, and alternatives to wasteful energy consumption patterns.

Community Media. P.O. Box 4964, Washington, DC 20008.
Media training center. Consulting and referral services. Member, Safe Energy Communication Council.

Compost Science: Journal of Waste Recycling. Rodale Press, Incl, 33 East Minor St., Emmaus, PA 18049. Bi-monthly, $6.00/yr.
Articles on methane and other resource recovery techniques.

Congressional Quarterly Weekly Report, and *Congressional Quarterly Almanac,* annual volumes. Congressional Quarterly, Inc., 1414 22nd St. NW, Washington, DC

20037.
Complete and unbiased reports on Congressional actions, arranged in subject categories. Also includes roll call charts, Presidential messages, and other information.

Congress Probe. 346 Connecticut Ave. NW, Suite 415 P, Washington, DC 20036.
A weekly investigative newsletter covering Capitol Hill. S.A.S.E.

Conservation Foundation, 1717 Massachusetts Ave. NW, Washington, DC 20036. *Newsletter,* monthly, $10.00/yr.
Research and educational projects on energy, land use, and environmental quality. Publications and films.

Conservation Law Foundation. 3 Joy St., Boston, MA 02108.
Works for the preservation of the environment, for example, opposition to the leasing of oil rights on Georges Bank.

Conservation Report. National Wildlife Federation, 1412 16th St. NW, Washington, DC 20036. Weekly, free.
This is an excellent means of keeping in touch with environmental legislation in Washington, DC.

Consumer Action Now: Council on Environmental Alternatives. 355 Lexington Ave., 16th fl., New York, NY 10017.
Energy information and education, with the promotion of conservation and solar energy.

Consumer Energy Council of America. 1990 M St. NW, Suite 620, Washington, DC 20036.
Supports consumer interest in problems with the energy utilties.

Consumer Federation of America: Energy Policy Task Force. 1012 14th St. NW, Washington, DC 20005.
Publications on energy policy and the consumer.

Council on Economic Priorities. 84 Fifth Ave., New York, NY 10011.
Research and publication of books, studies, testimony, and newsletters on jobs and energy, the corporate conscience, military spending and the international arms race, power plant performance, utilities, mining, and environmental impact.

Countryside. 312 Portland Road, Highway 19 East, Waterloo, WI 53594. Monthly. $9.00/yr.
Dedicated to the education of the agricultural community and the country at large to the liabilities inherent in our current system, and to provide sound and workable alternatives through eco-farming.

The Cousteau Society, 777 Third Ave., New York, NY 10017. *Calypso Log,* Bi-monthly, $15.00/yr., with membership.
Although the primary focus is on the oceans, this society is concerned with many global environmental issues, especially energy. Information on ocean thermal energy conversion.

Critical Mass Energy Project. P.O. Box 1538, Washington,DC 20013.
Concerned with energy developments, nuclear hazards, utilities, government policies, and citizen action. *Critical Mass Journal,* published monthly by Ralph Nader's Public Citizen, Inc., is $7.50/yr., and is an excellent source of information and resources. A publication list describes books,

reprints, information packets, bibliographies, etc. S.A.S.E. Member, Safe Energy Communication Council.

The Data Base Company. 620 S. Fifth St., Louisville, KY 40202. *Data Courier Inc.*
Six different data bases in journal, on-line access, and magnetic tape format provide information in areas such as *Conference Papers Index, Pollution Abstracts,* and *Oceanic Abstracts.*

doing it! - humanizing city life. 3475 Margarita Ave., Oakland, CA 94605. Bimonthly, $10.00/yr.
Discusses appropriate technology, energy, health, and what cities could do now in the way of self-reliant living. Offers practical applications and educational resources.

Earthmind, 5246 Boyer Road, Mariposa, CA 95338.
A non-profit corporation pursuing alternative energy research. Send 50¢ and long self-addressed envelope for list of publications and slide shows.

The Ecologist. Ecosystems Ltd., 73 Molesworth St., Wadebridge, Cornwall PL27 7DS, United Kingdom. 10 issues/yr. $13.00.
Probing and provocative articles on all aspects of ecology, including energy issues, from an international viewpoint.

Ecology Law Quarterly. School of Law, Boalt Hall, University of California, Berkeley, CA 94720. $10.50/yr.
Analysis of court decisions, legislation and environmental law, with in-depth reviews of current publications.

Ecotope Group. 2332 East Madison, Seattle, WA 98112.
Publications, audio-visual materials, and workshops in appropriate technology, renewable energy, conservation, and recycling.

Edison Electric Institute. 90 Park Ave., New York, NY 10017.
Trade association of investor-owned utilities.

Edmond Scientific Company, *Catalog.* 300 Edscorp Bldg., Barrington, NJ 08007. $.50.
Some designs and kits for the utilization of solar and wind power are available, as well as hard-to-find equipment.

Electric Power Research Institute. P.O. Box 1042, Palo Alto, CA 94303.
Industry's research organization, with publications on nuclear power, energy, and the environment.

The Elements. 1747 Connecticut Ave., NW, Washington, DC 20009. 11 issues/yr., $7.00. (Single copies from EARS, $.75). Edited by James Ridgeway.
Reports on who owns the world, and what people are doing to protect their resources, including energy, minerals, land, food, and the environment.

Energy Abstracts for Policy Analysis, U.S. Government Printing Office, Washington, DC. monthly $20.00/yr. (USGPO)
An annual index is also available.

The Energy Daily, 300 National Press Building, Washington, DC 20045. Published Monday through Friday, $475.00/yr.
Comprehensive coverage of all national energy news, legislation, and nuclear industry events.

Energy Economics Newsletter. Stanford Research Institute, Publications Department,

333 Ravenswood Ave., Menlo Park, CA 94025. Free.
News of research in energy economics. An energy research pamphlet and publication list are also available.

Energy Examiner. 398 National Press Building, Washington, DC 20045. $17.00/yr.
Promotes the accelerated development of domestic energy sources, including nuclear power.

Energy House, P.O. Box 5288, Salem, OR 97304. *Energy House Catalog.* 1978 edition, approx. 300 pp. $3.00, refundable with purchase.
Alternative energy and energy conservation products, such as solar components, stoves, pumps, windpower devices, controls, and publications.

Energy Information Abstracts. New York, N.Y.: Environment Information Center, Inc. Bimonthly, from June '76. $185.00/yr.
Monitors major developments in entire field, including scientific, technical, and socio-economic materials, in 21 major categories.

Energy Information Service, University of Texas, Center for Energy Studies, Austin, TX 78712.
Any questions?

Energy Perspectives. Battelle Energy Program, 505 King Ave., Columbus, OH 43201. Monthly. Free.
Current state-of-the-art in various energy fields, and conference calendar.

Energy Policy. IPC Science and Technology Press, Ltd., Surrey, England. Quarterly, $72.80/yr. Order from IPC Business Press Ltd., 205 E. 42nd St., New York, N.Y. 10017.
An international journal on all aspects of energy policy and planning. IPC publications list includes numerous scholarly works in this area.

Energy Policy Information Center. 3 Joy St., Boston, MA 02108.
Citizens' Organizing Packet on Nuclear Waste, $2.50.

Energy Research Reports. Advanced Technology Publications, 385 Elliot St., Newton, MA 02164. 22 issues/yr, $95.00.
Articles, and reviews of new publications.

Energy Review. UPDATA Publications, Inc., 1756 Westwood Blvd., Los Angeles, CA 90024. Bimonthly, $55.00/yr.
Summaries of publications, conferences, and audio-visual materials in all areas of energy.

Energy Sources: An International Interdisciplinary Journal of Science and Technology. Crane, Russak, & Company, Inc., 347 Madison Ave., New York, NY 10017. Quarterly.
Technical articles for the engineer and professional. Book reviews.

Energy Systems and Policy: An International Interdisciplinary Journal. Crane, Russak, & Company, Inc., 347 Madison Ave., New York, NY 10017. Quarterly.
Concerned with large-scale energy problems and their interactions with the economic, social, and political sectors; international relations, developing nations, and energy policy.

Energy Task Force. 156 Fifth Ave., New York, NY 10010.
Technical advice for community and neighborhood organizations.

Energy Today. Trends Publishing, Inc., National Press Building, Washington, DC

20004. Twice monthly, $90.00/yr.

Recent developments in energy technology, economics, and legislation, and data on related publications.

Energy Users Report. The Bureau of National Affairs, Inc., 1231 25th St., NW, Washington, DC 20037. Weekly, $280.00/yr.

Oriented toward business and industry, it includes information on energy policy, alternatives, conservation, and environmental impact, and governmental action.

Environment Magazine. See Scientists Institute for Public Information.

Environmental Action, Suite 731, 1345 Connecticut Avenue, NW, Washington, DC 20036. Monthly. $15.00/yr.

Lively and informative articles and news notes on energy, pollution, and environmental politics.

Environmental Action Foundation, 724 Duport Circle Building, Washington, DC 20036. *The Power Line,* monthly, $15.00.

Research and education pertaining to energy, environment, solid waste management, transportation, and utilities. A variety of publications is available. Member, Safe Energy Communication Council.

Environmental Action Reprint Service (EARS). Box 545, La Veta, CO 81055. *Energy Catalog* and *Nuclear Catalog,* free.

A mail-order service offering carefully selected resources on a wide range of topics including alternative energy, appropriate technology, nuclear power, and energy policy. The catalogs describe available books, articles, plans, posters, bumper stickers, T-shirts, and pins. An associated bookstore is located at 2239 East Colfax, Denver, CO 80206. Their books are marked (EARS) in this FOE Bibliography.

Environmental Defense Fund. 475 Park Ave. South, New York, NY 10016. *Newsletter,* Bimonthly, $15.00/yr. with membership.

EDF conducts legal action on energy, toxic substances, water, air, land use, transportation, and wildlife.

Environmental Law Institute. 1346 Connecticut Ave. NW, Washington, DC 20036.

Energy Conservation Project Report. Monthly. Explores the legal and regulatory means for promoting energy conservation.

Enrionmental Law Reporter. Monthly. A looseleaf legal service covering energy, pollution, resources, land use, wildlife, and related issues, with recent rulings, statutes, and briefs.

Environmental Policy Institute. 317 Pennsylvania Ave. SE, Washington, DC 20003.

Concerned with the impact of energy on the environment, and the implications for government policies. Publications include research reports on energy conservation, stripmining, nuclear hazards, etc. The associated Environmental Policy Center engages in lobbying and education in these areas.

Environmental Policy and Law. International Council of Environmental Law, Adenauerallee 214 D-53, Bonn, Federal Republic of Germany. Subscriptions: Elsevier Sequoia S.A., P.O. Box 851, 1001 Lausanne 1, Switzerland. 4 issues/yr. $20.00 to individuals.

Concerned with the legal policy aspects of environmental protection and conservation of resources. United Nations Environment Programme Actions are reported, as well as other international developments.

Environmental Study Conference. *ESC Weekly Bulletin.* Environmental Study Conference, 3334 House Annex 2, Washington, DC 20515. Pages vary. $150/yr.
The Environmental Study Conference is a bipartisan legislative research organization made up of Representatives and Senators. The *Weekly Bulletin* lists the latest legislative action and general developments on Capitol Hill, from occupational health to nuclear energy, in a concise and well-structured format. Send S.A.S.E. for a publications list including guides to federal solar and energy conservation programs.

Environmentalists for Full Employment, 1536 15th St., NW, 1st fl., Washington, DC 20036.
Seeks to join environmentalists with labor, minority, and other progressive groups to bring about social change. Research on jobs and energy shows that there need be no conflict between socially useful employment, healthful work-places, and clean, natural environments. See *ENERGY: ECONOMICS.*

The Farallones Institute, 15290 Coleman Valley Rd., Occidental, CA 95465; and 1516 Fifth St., Berkeley, CA 94710.
Research, education, and practice in energy conservation and self-sufficient living.

Friends of the Earth. 124 Spear St., San Francisco, CA 94105; 530 Seventh St. SE, Washington, DC 20003; 72 Jane St., New York, NY 10014; 4512 University Way, Seattle, WA 98105. *Not Man Apart,* Monthly, $25.00/yr. incl. membership. *Soft Energy Notes.* Bimonthly, $15.00/$25.00 & up/yr.
FOE is an international organization committed to the preservation, restoration, and rational use of the ecosphere, and engages in education, publication, lobbying, litigation, and legislation toward these ends. Publications include books on energy, the environment, and the earth's wild places. *Not Man Apart* is a thought-provoking source of news and views on energy and the environment. *Soft Energy Notes,* prepared by FOE's International Project for Soft Energy Paths (IPSEP) reports on international developments in renewable energy applications. Member, Safe Energy Communication Council.

Friends Nuclear Hazards Resource and Information Service. P.O. Box 663, East Quogue, NY 11942.
Literature, bibliography, videotape, and button available on the "Spiderwort Strategy"—how a tiny flower can be used to monitor low-level radiation. Send $1.00 and S.A.S.E.

Fuel: The Science and Technology of Fuel and Energy. IPC Science and Technology Press, Ltd., Surrey, England. Quarterly, $88.40/yr. Order from IPC Business Press Ltd., 205 East 42nd St., New York, NY 10017.
Reports on the latest research on fossil fuel technology, including conversion technology, fluidized beds, gasification of coal and oil, oil shales, tar sands, and pollution by fuel products.

Gasohol U.S.A. P.O. Box 9547, Kansas City, MO 64133. Monthly, $12.00/yr. Single copies also available from EARS, $1.50.
Explores gasohol techniques, production, suppliers, legislation, and events.

Geothermal Energy. 18014 Sherman Way, #169, Reseda, CA 91335. Monthly, $45.00/yr.

News related to the utilization of geothermal energy in the United States and abroad.

Grantsmanship Center, 1031 South Grand Ave., Los Angeles, CA 90015. *Grantsmanship Center News.* Bimonthly, $15.00/yr.

Information and assistance for non-profit and public agencies in obtaining grants, fund raising, lobbying, and developing management skills.

Greater Washington Americans for Democratic Action. 1411 K St. NW, Suite 850, Washington, DC 20005.

Send S.A.S.E. for information on how to organize an initiative drive.

Greenpeace. Building E, Fort Mason, San Francisco, CA 94123.

Although best known for their courageous efforts to end the slaughter of whales and baby seals, Greenpeace activists will also be found sailing to protest nuclear bomb tests and the shipment of radioactive wastes. See McTaggart, David. *Greenpeace III: Journey into the Bomb, NUCLEAR ENERGY: THE CONTROVERSY.*

Green Revolution: The School of Living. RD 7, Box 388A, York, PA 17402. Monthly.

Articles on alternative economics, renewable energy technology, and decentralized living.

Health Physics: The Journal of Applied Nuclear Technology. Pergamon Press, Inc., Maxwell House, Fairview Park, Elmsford, NY 10523. 2 vols./yr, $100.00.

Technical articles on radiation effects and management.

High Country News. Box K. Lander, WY 82520. Bi-weekly. $10.00/yr.

An environmentally oriented newspaper covering the Rockies and Northern Plains, with reports on natural history, conservation, energy, and land use.

INFORM. 25 Broad St., New York, NY 10004. *INFORM News.* Bimonthly, $25.00/yr.

Research studies on industry and its relationship to the environment and energy, new technologies, pollution control, land use, and social impacts.

Initiative America. 606 Third St. NW, Washington, DC 20001.

Send S.A.S.E. for information on how to select your initiative issue, researching, drafting, and organizing.

Institute for Ecological Policies. 9208 Christopher St., Fairfax, VA 22031. *People and Energy.* Bimonthly, $15.00/yr. 2408 18th St., NW, Washington, DC 20009.

Research and information about environmentally sound and socially equitable policies, especially those leading to a safe energy future. Action-oriented projects. *People and Energy* reports on renewable energy technologies, utilities, recycling, and nuclear hazards.

Institute for Local Self-Reliance. 1717 18th St. NW, Washington, DC 20009. *Self-Reliance.* Bimonthly, $8.00/yr.

Assists communities in planning their own economic development through new small-scale technologies. Engages in studies, projects, education, and publication on local economic development, waste utilization, urban agriculture, and appropriate technology. Books, articles, packets, and posters available.

Institute for Policy Studies, Inc. 1901 Q St. NW, Washington, DC 20009. *In These Times.* Weekly newspaper, $17.50/yr. P.O. Box 228, Westchester, IL 60153.

Provides in-depth analyses of social policy issues, including energy and the environment. Resource catalog includes books and films, for example, *Paul Jacobs and the Nuclear Gang. In These Times* reports national and international news from an independent socialist viewpoint.

Intermediate Technology, 556 Santa Cruz Ave., Menlo Park, CA 94025. Quarterly, $10.00/yr.

Inspired by E.F. Schumacher, IT works to redirect the course of technology through practical projects.

International Atomic Energy Agency. *INIS Atom Index.* Biweekly, $150/yr. (UNIPUB)

Abstracting and indexing coverage of scientific and technical publications on atomic energy.

International Atomic Energy Agency. *Nuclear Fusion.* 6 issues/yr., $49.00. (UNIPUB)

Original articles, review papers, and conference reports on plasma physics and fusion reactor technology.

International Biomass Institute. 1522 K St., NW, Suite 600, Washington, DC 20005. *Bio-Times Newsletter.*

Concerned with the development of alcohol fuels.

International Journal of Energy Research. John Wiley & Sons, c/o Expediters of the Printed Word, Ltd., 527 Madison Ave., New York, NY 10022. Quarterly, $70.00/yr.

Scholarly reports on all aspects of energy research.

International Project for Soft Energy Paths (IPSEP). Friends of the Earth, 124 Spear St., San Francisco, CA 94105. *Soft Energy Notes.* Bimonthly, $15.00/$25.00 & up/yr.

IPSEP is an information center for the development of soft energy systems: renewable, diverse, efficient, and environmentally benign. Its journal, *Soft Energy Notes,* provides a network of researchers and public interest groups in over 70 countries with technical and economic information on the status of renewable energy systems and research in this field.

International Solar Energy Society, American Section. P.O. Box 1416, Killeen, TX 76541.

Conducts research, holds conferences, meetings, and workshops, and prepares educational materials on the conversion and use of solar energy. Publications include periodicals, proceedings, books, and articles. *Solar Age Magazine.*

Komanoff Energy Associates. 475 Park Ave. South, 32nd fl., New York, NY 10016.

Publication list of research and reports on nuclear power costs and energy economics.

LAND Educational Associates Foundation, Inc. 3368 Oak Ave., Stevens Point, WI 54481. *LAND/LEAF Newsletter,* $5.00/yr.

Research and education on the dangers of radioactive contamination. Publications include pamphlets and books. See Huver, Charles. *Methodologies.* under *NUCLEAR ENERGY: RADIATION.*

League Against Nuclear Dangers, LAND, Inc. Route 1, Rudolph, WI 54475. *LAND/LEAF Newsletter*, $5.00/yr.
Citizen group engaged in research, education and action against nuclear dangers, and for alternative energy use.

League of American Wheelman. P.O. Box 988, Baltimore, MD 21203.
Information on bicycling.

League of Conservation Voters. 317 Pennsylvania Ave. SE, Washington, DC 20003.
Prepares congressional voting records on environmental issues.

League of Women Voters. 1730 M St. NW, Washington, DC 20036. *National Voter.* Quarterly, $20.00/yr with membership; also local newsletters.
Study, education, and action on socially significant national issues, including energy and the environment. Publications include a series of articles and booklets on energy.

Massachusetts Public Interest Research Group (MassPIRG). 233 N. Pleasant St., Amherst, MA 01002.
Pamphlets and posters on energy and other issues.

Media Access Project. 1609 Connecticut Ave. NW, Washington, DC 20009.
Legal counsel to citizen groups on Fairness Doctrine. Member, Safe Energy Communication Council.

MHB Technical Associates. 1723 Hamilton Ave., Suite K, San Jose, CA 95125.
Technical consultants on energy and the environment.

Mobilization for Survival. 3601 Locust Walk, Philadelphia, PA 19104. The *Mobilizer,* bimonthly, $10.00/yr.
A coalition to mobilize individuals and organizations against nuclear weapons, nuclear power, and the arms race, and for the funding of human needs. The *Mobilizer* provides news and resources. Resource packet, $6; Audio-visual guide, $2.; other literature and paraphernalia. Bureau of prominent speakers.

The Mother Earth News. 105 Stoney Mountain Road, Hendersonville, NC 28739. Bi-monthly, $12.00/yr.
The magazine of self-sufficient living, with many articles and resources on alternative energy sources, and what is happening at the grass roots level.

Musicians United For Safe Energy, MUSE. 72 Fifth Ave., New York, NY 10011.
Raises funds through concerts, records, and films for distribution to grass-roots energy groups. Published a 52-page magazine on nuclear and solar issues; $2.00.

National Academy of Sciences. 2101 Constitution Ave. NW, Washington, DC 20418.
Research and publications on energy and other scientific issues of public concern.

National Aeronautics and Space Administration. *Energy: A Continuing Bibliography with Indexes.* NTISUB/026. Quarterly, $40.00/yr. (NTIS)
A journal covering regional, national, and international energy systems, research and development, energy conversion, and energy storage.

National Alcohol Fuels Producers Association. 2444 B St., Lincoln, NE 68502.
Newsletter, manual, workshops, and other resources. Workshop center at

Colby County College, P.O. Box 686, Colby, KS 67701.

National Association of Atomic Veterans. 1109 Franklin St., Burlington, IA 52601.
Works to obtain compensation from the government for soldiers exposed to radiation during bomb-testing and at Hiroshima and Nagasaki, and now suffering from radiation-induced illnesses.

National Association of Home Builders, NAHB Research Foundation, Inc., P.O. Box 1627, Rockville, MD 20850.
Information on the use of solar energy in buildings.

National Audubon Society. 950 Third Ave., New York, NY 10022. *Audubon.* Bimonthly, $13.00/yr.
Audubon's goals include the conservation of wildlife and life-support systems, the promotion of energy conservation and renewable energy sources, and protection from pollution, radiation, and toxic substances. Educational materials.

National Campaign for Radioactive Waste Safety. 1822 Lomas Ave. NE, Albuquerque, NM 87106.
A non-profit research and action organization associated with the Southwest Research and Information Center; acts as a watchdog on government and industry programs for nuclear waste disposal. with special focus on the Waste Isolation Pilot Plant planned for New Mexico, and the development of better solutions to the problems of the transportation and disposal of radioactive waste.

National Climatic Center. Federal Building, Ashville, NC 28011.
Local solar and climate data are tabulated by the National Oceanic and Atmospheric Administration, in state-by-state records on temperature, cloud cover, rain, snow, wind, and, in some cases, solar radiation. Tables are $.15 for each state.

National Committee Against Repressive Legislation. c/o Frank Wilkinson, 1250 Wilshire Blvd., Suite 501, Los Angeles, CA 90017.
In pursuit of First Ammendment rights, this group opposes repressive laws such as SB 1722 (Kennedy, 96th Congress) which could make participants in energy project protests and anti-nuclear demonstrations subject to prosecution for federal crimes.

National Conference of State Legislatures. 1405 Curtis St., 23rd fl., Denver, CO 80202. *Energy Report to the States.* Biweekly, $15.00/yr.
Reports on state energy legislation.

National Consumer Law Center. 11 Beacon St., Boston, MA 02108.
Legal assistance for nuclear power challenges.

National Council of Churches of Christ Energy Project. 475 Riverside Dr., New York, NY 10027.
Has called for a moratorium on the commercial use of plutonium, and made studies on the ethical implications of energy use. *Energy Packet,* $6.00, includes books and pamphlets on the ethics and social costs of energy.

National Indian Youth Council. 201 Hermosa NE, Albuquerque, NM 87108. *Americans Before Columbus,* Monthly, $8.00/yr.
Education and action on the impact of energy development on Native Americans, especially uranium mining and radioactive waste disposal in New

Mexico, dams, and appropriate technology.

National Land for People. 2348 N. Cornelia, Fresno, CA 93711. *National Land for People*, Monthly, $10.00/yr.
Works for democratic rural land control, and is concerned with land use, water rights, small farmers vs. agribusiness, and related government policies.

National League of Cities and Conference of Mayors. 1620 Eye St. NW, Washington, DC 20005.
Conferences, lobbying, and publications on community planning, with emphasis on energy conservation.

National Recreation and Parks Association, 1601 N. Kent St., Arlington, VA 22209.
Free *Energy Directory* and other publications.

National Solar Energy Education Campaign. 10762 Tucker St., Beltsville, MD 20705. *Solar Energy Books*. 1977. 120 pp. $4.50.
This catalog lists most of the solar books on the market, in categories, which can be ordered from this company.

National Wildlife Federation. 1412 16th St. NW, Washington, DC 20036. *National Wildlife*. Bimonthly, $8.50/yr.
Other publications include *Conservation Report*, weekly during Congressional sessions, and *Conservation News*, biweekly. The *Conservation Directory describes national organizations, and is updated annually. The Catalog* lists inexpensive educators' materials, including a pamphlet on energy.

Natural Resources Defense Council. 25 Kearny St., San Francisco, CA 94108; 1725 I St., NW, Washington, DC 20006; 122 E. 42nd St., New York, NY 10017. *Amicus*. Quarterly, $15.00/yr.
The newly enlarged journal brings news and articles on nuclear hazards, toxic substances, pollution, and environmental protection, and NRDC's legal efforts in these areas. Publications include research reports and testimony before courts and governmental bodies.

New Alchemy Institute. P.O. Box 47, Woods Hole, MA 02543. *Journal of the New Alchemists*. $15.00/yr.
Research, publications, and a film demonstrate practical applications of alternative energy and appropriate technology.

New Criteria: The Midwest Journal of Appropriate Technology. See Community Action Research Group. Box 1232, Ames, IA 50010.

New Directions, 2021 "L" St., NW, Washington, DC 20036. *Citizen Force*, bimonthly, with $25.00 membership.
Political action programs toward a safe energy future, controlling the arms race, and meeting basic human needs. National and international in viewpoint.

New England Solar Energy Association. P.O. Box 541, Brattleboro, VT 05301. *Newsletter*. Bimonthly.
Promotes the utilization of renewable energy sources. Books and bookstore.

New Roots: Notes on Appropriate Technology and Community Self-Reliance for the Northeast. New Roots, Rm A25, Graduate Research Center, University of Massachusetts, Amherst, MA 01003. Bimonthly, $8.00/yr.

Concerned with energy alternatives and resources for regional self-reliance for New England and New York State.

New Scientist, King's Research Tower, Stamford, St., London SEI 9LS, England. U.S.A.: Publications Expediting Inc., 200 Meacham Ave., Elmont, NY 11003. Weekly, $53.95, airfreight.
International news briefs and in-depth articles for the general reader with broad interests. Covers all aspects of science, with emphasis on the social and human dimensions.

New York Public Interest Research Group (NYPIRG). 5 Beekman St., New York, NY 10038.
Citizen action on energy, health, and consumer issues. Inexpensive pamphlets on nuclear and other issues are available for general distribution.

New York Times. 229 West 23rd St., New York, NY 10036. Daily and Sunday, $150/yr.
This newspaper is one of the best places to find comprehensive articles on the latest energy developments, energy policy, publications, and government reports.

No Nuclear News Collective, c/o Boston Clamshell, 595 Massachusetts Ave., Cambridge, MA 02139. *No Nuclear News*, monthly, $12.00/yr including special issues.
News clippings and graphics are received from all over the world and arranged in categories such as mining, health, wastes, etc.; accident scoreboard; references.

Nuclear Hazards Information Center. Box 619, Woodstock, NY 12498. Sponsored by the Citizens Energy Council, P.O. Box 285, Allendale, NJ 07401. Monthly newsletter, $10.00/yr.
Inexpensive leaflets are available on nuclear power, radiation, radioactive waste, and occupational hazards in nuclear facilities.

Nuclear Information and Resource Service. 1536 16th St. NW, Washington, DC 20005. Toll-free phone: (800) 424-2477, M-F, 1-5 pm, EST. *Groundswell*, monthly, $12.00/yr.
Groundswell is an invaluable reference for all concerned with nuclear issues, often providing an in-depth "Resource Guide" on one particular topic, such as radiation, as well as current news and reviews. The *Distribution Service* offers publications for sale, such as government studies, research reports, testimony, articles, bibliographies, and resource guides. Information is available on all aspects of the nuclear fuel cycle, occupational hazards, legislation, initiatives, audio-visual materials, etc., as well as an excellent summary of the nuclear question. Member, Safe Energy Communication Council.

Nucleonics Week. McGraw-Hill, Inc., 1221 Avenue of the Americas, New York, NY 10020. Weekly, $465/yr.
Much valuable information is contained in this comprehensive and condensed bulletin of worldwide developments in the nuclear industry and related governmental actions. It may be located in university libraries.

Oil, Chemical, and Atomic Workers International Union. P.O. Box 2812, Denver, CO 80201.
Anthony Mazzocci and friends fight for worker safety and against the hazards of radiation and toxic substances.

Pacifica Foundation, FM Radio. Program Service, 5316 Venice Blvd., Los Angeles, CA 90019; KPFA, 2207 Shattuck Ave., Berkeley, CA 94704; KFCF, P.O. Box 881, Fresno, CA 93714; KPFK. 3729 Cahuenga Blvd., North Hollywood, CA 91604; KPFT, 419 Lovett Blvd., Houston, TX 77006; WPFW, 700 H St., NW, Washington, DC 20001; WBAI, 505 8th Ave., New York, NY 10018.

Listener-sponsored radio provides excellent news coverage, programs on energy and the environment, and free media access to individuals and citizen groups.

Paul H. Douglas Consumer Research Center, 1012 14th St. NW, #910, Washington, DC 20005.

Newsletter, resource list of national organizations, and consumer information; associated with the Consumer Federation of America.

People and Energy Magazine. See Institute for Ecological Policies.

Physicians for Social Responsibility. P.O. Box 295, Cambridge, MA 02238; 944 Market St., Rm. 808, San Francisco, CA 94102.

Dr. Helen Caldicott and other professionals seek to educate health care providers and the general public regarding the dangers of radiation.

Public Citizen. P.O. Box 19404, Washington, DC 20036. Newspaper, *Public Citizen,* 3 issues/yr, with $15.00 membership.

A Nader organization, with groups acting on many consumer, environmental, and energy issues, including tax reform, public health and safety, and legislation. Numerous publications are available.

Public Citizen Congress Watch. P.O. Box 19404, Washington, DC 20036.

Educates and lobbies on citizen and consumer rights, corporate activities, energy, and the environment. The annual *Congressional Voting Index* analyzes votes and trends in major issues.

Public Interest Economics Foundation. 1714 Massachusetts Ave. NW, Washington, DC 20036. Provides information on nuclear and solar economics, jobs and energy, utility rate challenges, and legal intervention.

Public Interest Research Group, P.O. Box 19312, Washington, DC 20036.

An organization for public policy research, including nuclear power and energy alternatives. Organizes community action through numerous university branches. Publication list available. Safe Energy Communication Council.

Rain Magazine. 2700 NW Irving, Portland, OR 97210. Monthly, $15.00/yr.

Features down-to-earth articles and resources on appropriate technology, with news of people, groups, events, and publications concerned with living lightly on the earth. *Rainbook.* Ecotopia posters.

Rand Corporation. *A Bibliography of Selected Rand Publications: Energy.* The Rand Corporation, 1700 Main St., Santa Monica, CA 90406.

This independent reserach organization lists books and reports on energy policy, alternatives, technology, economics, conservation, utility rate structures, national security, and public welfare. Bibliographies on other subjects available.

Re-Source, Inc. P.O. Box 127, Astor Station, Boston, MA 02123.

A free catalog lists resources for nuclear activists, including books, literature, posters, buttons, bumper-stickers, recordings, and the *Clamshell*

News in bulk.

Resources for the Future, 1775 Massachusetts Ave., NW, Washington, DC 20036.
Research and publications on resources, supplies, and options.

Roby, John. *Energy-Related Literature.* List E-200. John Roby, 3703 Nassau Dr., San Diego, CA 92115. 1978. 73 pp. $1.00.
A catalog listing over 1600 current and out-of-print publications in the field of energy which may be ordered. Other lists available.

Rural America. 1346 Connecticut Ave. NW, Washington, DC 20036. *ruralamerica.* Monthly, $10.00/yr.
Reports on problems of inflation, land speculation, farming, agribusiness, health, energy impact, and government policies.

Safe Energy Communication Council. 1536 16th St. NW, Washington, DC 20036.
A coalition of safe energy organizations who are combining resources to counter industry's media campaign to boost nuclear power. Member groups include Campaign for Political Rights, Center for Renewable Resources, Community Media, Critical Mass Energy Project, Environmental Action Foundation, Friends of the Earth, Media Access Project, Public Interest Research Group, Nuclear Information and Resource Service, Solar Lobby, and Union of Concerned Scientists.

SANE. 514 C St. NE, Washington, DC 20002. *Sane World.* Monthly newsletter, $4.00. *Conversion Planner.* Bimonthly, $5.00.
Education and action against nuclear power and weapons, and for safe energy; attempts to redirect the economy from war and toward social needs.

Science for the People. 897 Main St., Cambridge, MA 02139. Bimonthly, $6.00/yr, or with $15.00 membership.
Criticizes, challenges, and proposes alternatives to the present uses of science and technology, and endeavors to develop political strategies to ally the progressive forces in society.

Scientists Institute for Public Information. 355 Lexington Ave., New York, NY 10017. *Environment Magazine* (with the Helen Dwight Reid Educational Foundation). 4000 Albemarle St. NW, Washington, DC 20016. 10 issues/yr, $12.75/yr.
Concerned with all environmental issues, energy impacts upon the environment, and related governmental policies. Research reports on synthetic fuels, nuclear power, energy conservation, pollution, etc.

Seriatim: An Ecotopian Journal of Research and Innovation. 122 Carmel, El Cerrito, CA 94530. Quarterly. $2.50 single copy, or $9.00/yr, in the Northwest. $12.00/yr. elsewhere.
Contains accounts of research, strategies, and ideas relevant to the evolution of the stable-state society. Includes appropriate technology, forestry, agriculture, shelter, wilderness, and related concerns.

Sierra Club, 530 Bush St., San Francisco, CA 94108. *Sierra,* The Sierra Club Bulletin, 10 issues/yr., with $20.00 membership. *National News Report.* 35 issues/yr. during Congressional sessions, $10.00/yr. by first class mail.
This national conservation organization publishes studies and books on environmental issues. and engages in educational, legal, and political action.

Sierra Club Atlantic Chapter Waste Campaign, Box 64, Station G, Buffalo, NY 14213. *The Waste Paper*, published quarterly.
This newspaper is devoted to fighting waste disposal projects in New York, and includes international news on this problem.

Solar Age. Solar Vision, Inc., Church Hill, Harrisville, NH 03450. Monthly, $20.00/yr.
The official magazine of the International Solar Energy Society, American Section, is of interest to both the professional and general reader. It covers applications of solar energy, photovoltaics, ocean thermal electricity, wind energy, bioconversion, and conservation. Also features a buyer's guide, and news of legislation, industry, and energy events.

Solar Energy Digest. P.O. Box 17776, San Diego, CA 92117. Monthly, $30.50/yr.
Reports on all aspects of solar energy utilization, both in the U.S. and abroad. It is aimed at a broad readership. A calendar of events is included.

Solar Energy Industries Association. 1001 Connecticut Ave. NW, Suite 800, Washington, DC 20036.
A trade organization for manufacturers, distributors, and designers of solar energy equipment; publishes a newsletter and directories.

Solar Energy Institute of North America. 1110 Sixth St. NW, Washington, DC 20001. *Newsletter.* $15.00/yr.
An organization of solar professionals, educators, and consumers dedicated to making economical solar systems a reality. Programs include speakers, educational materials, and legislative assistance.

Solar Energy Intelligence Report. Business Publishers, Inc., P.O. Box 1067, Silver Spring, MD 20910. Bi-weekly, $90.00/yr.
News of developments, government programs, markets, and meetings of interest to the solar energy industry.

Solar Engineering. Solar Engineering Publishers, Inc., 8435 N. Stemmons Freeway, Suite 880, Dallas, TX 75247. Monthly, $15.00/yr.
Short descriptions of devlopments in the private sector of the U.S. solar energy industry.

Solar Greenhouse Digest. P.O. Box 3218, Kingman, AZ 86401. Bimonthly, $10.00/yr.
Greenhouse news, plans, articles, resources, and information on legislation.

Solar Heating and Cooling. Gordon Publications, P.O. Box 2126-R, Morristown, NJ 07960. Bi-monthly, $6.00/yr.
Short articles on solar heating and cooling developments and equipment. Primarily of interest to manufacturers and builders.

Solar Lobby. 1001 Connecticut Ave. NW, 5th fl., Washington, DC 20036. *Sun Times.* Monthly, $15.00/yr.
A national legislative lobbying organization which grew out of SUN DAY 1978. Publications on solar programs and citizen action are useful for the grassroots solar energy movement. "Sundries" department offers bumper-stickers, T-shirts, etc. Member, Safe Energy Communication Council.

Solar Times. 901 Bridgeport Ave., Shelton, CT 06484. Monthly, $12.50/yr.
A journal for professionals, researchers, architects, manufacturers, and officials, reporting on new developments and organizations in all areas of renewable energy.

Solar Usage Now, Inc. P.O. Box 306, Bascom, OH 44809. *S.U.N. Catalog*, $2.00. Updated annually.

A mail order company offering a complete selection of solar equipment, books, and educational materials.

Solar Utilization News. Alternative Energy Institute, P.O. Box 3100, Estes Park, CO 80517. Monthly, $8.00/yr.

This periodical is of use to individuals, schools, and business. It includes latest developments in technology and reviews of publications.

Southwest Research and Information Center. P.O. Box 4524, Albuquerque, NM 87106. *The Workbook: Access to Information.* 7 issues/yr., $10.00.

Helps people to gain access to information and control over their own lives. Interests include solar energy, uranium mining, radioactive waste disposal, land use, and consumer concerns. Publishes books on solar energy; a newsletter on WIPP, the government's Waste Isolation Pilot Plant planned for New Mexico; produces slide shows; and holds workshops on renewable energy.

Stop Uranium Mining, Inc. c/o Malvine Cole, R.D. #1, Jamaica, VT 05343.

Works for a legislative ban on all uranium development in Vermonth, through public education on the health and environmental effects of mining.

Sun Up: Energy News Digest. Drawer S, Yucca Valley, CA 92284. Monthly, $6.50/yr.

Practical applications of solar and energy conservation techniques of interest to homeowners, educators, architects, builders, and industry.

Supporters of Silkwood. 14th & Shepherd Sts., NE, Washington, DC 20017.

Civil liberties, worker safety, and low-level radiation are among the issues pursued by the defense committee for the late Karen Silkwood, the worker who was killed while investigating safety at the Kerr McGee plutonium plant.

Survival Rights: A Journal of Environmental Debate. P.O. Box 60961. Sacramento, CA 95860. Quarterly, $4.00.

Airs the controversies over energy and the ecology in the nation and in the world.

Task Force Against Nuclear Pollution, P.O. Box 1817, Washington, DC 20013. *Progress Report.* Quarterly.

Continues to circulate the nation-wide *Clean Energy Petition,* urging Congress to phase out nuclear and promote solar energy. Other legislative actions.

Technology Review. Massachusetts Institute of Technology. Subscriptions, P.O. Box 700, Whitinsville, MA 01588. 8 issues/yr, $15.00.

Scientists and engineers report the latest developments in energy, materials, computers, anthropology, and many diverse fields of science and technology.

Total Environmental Action, Inc. *Catalog.* 24 Church Hill, Harrisville, NH 03450. Free. (TEA)

Describes solar and wind energy materials available through this organization, including books, slides, charts, and plans. Courses, research, and consulting services are also offered.

Transnational Network for Appropriate/Alternative Technologies (TRANET). P.O. Box 567, Rangeley, ME 04970. Quarterly, $15.00/yr & up.

This newsletter-directory is an excellent source of current information regarding individuals, organizations, projects, and publications from around the world.

Union of Concerned Scientists, 1384 Massachusetts Ave., Cambridge, MA 02238.
Publishes reports on research, and intervenes in regulatory hearings on the environmental impact of technology, especially nuclear. Studies include the Browns Ferry fire, the nuclear fuel cycle, and the NRC's reactor safety studies. Member, Safe Energy Communication Council.

UNIPUB, 345 Park Ave., South, New York, NY 10010.
Publishers of United Nations scientific studies, and also the work of other international information services, such as the IAEA, International Atomic Energy Agency. Publication lists describe books, bibliographies, directories, periodicals, and maps on energy, environment, and many other topics.

U.S. Department of Energy. *Energy Research Abstracts.* Washington, DC. Bi-weekly, $184.00/yr. (USGPO)
Current reports, plus an annual index.

U.S. Department of Energy. *Energy Conservation Update.* Monthly, $27.50/yr. (NTIS)
Abstracts of current scientific and technical reports from many countries.

U.S. Department of Energy. *Fossil Energy Update.* Monthly, $27.50/yr. (NTIS)
Abstracting and indexing coverage of current scientific and technical publications on fossil energy.

U.S. Department of Energy. *Fusion Energy Update.* Monthly, $27.50/yr. (NTIS)
A journal of abstracts relating to controlled thermonuclear research.

U.S. Department of Energy, *Geothermal Energy Update.* Monthly, $27.50/yr. (NTIS)
Abstracting and indexing coverage of current scientific and technical publications on the exploration and development of geothermal resources.

U.S. Department of Energy. *Solar Energy Update.* Monthly, $27.50/yr. (NTIS)
Abstracting and indexing coverage of current scientific and technical publications on the utilization of solar, tidal, and wind energy.

U.S. Department of Energy. *Weekly Government Abstracts: Energy.* Springfield, Va.: National Technical Information Service. $75.00/yr. (NTIS)
Reviews of the latest government research publications.

U.S. Department of Energy, Office of Consumer Affairs. *Energy Consumer.* U.S. DOE, Office of Consumer Affairs, 8G031 Forrestal, Washington, DC 20585.
Information on federal programs in energy conservation, solar and renewable energy, low-income assistance, conferences, and resources. The 40page January 1980 issue is devoted to alcohol fuels.

U.S. Department of Energy, Office of Public Affairs. *Energy Reporter.* U.S. DOE, Office of Public Affairs, Washington, DC 20585. Bi-monthly, free.
News notes on energy developments, government programs, and publications.

U.S. Department of Energy/Technical Information Center. *Nuclear Safety.* Prepared for the Nuclear Regulatory Commission by the Nuclear Safety Information Center at Oak Ridge National Laboratory. Washington, DC. Bimonthly, $14.00/yr. (USGPO)
Articles and reports on nuclear safety, "safety-related occurrences", environmental effects, and status of power plants undergoing licensing

review.

Uranium Information Network, Colorado Open Space Council. c/o C.O.S.C., 2239 East Colfax Ave., Denver, CO 80206.

A Uranium Mining and Milling Information Packet is available for a $5.00 donation. It covers nuclear economics, uranium mining and milling methods, radioactive decay, and the environmental and health effects of uranium development.

Uranium Resource and Action Network. Paul Robinson, P.O. Box 4524, Albuquerque, NM 87106.

A coalition of national and local organizations providing information and support to the opposition to uranium development and to minimize its impact.

Volunteers in Technical Assistance. 3706 Rhode Island Ave., Mt. Rainier, MD 20822.

VITA publishes books and pamphlets on energy, the environment, appropriate technology, and self-reliance.

Wall Street Journal. 22 Cortlandt St., New York, NY 10007; Subscriptions, 200 Burnett Rd., Chicopee, MA 1020. Daily, $63/yr.

Don't overlook this excellent source of current information on the energy industry, economics, government policy, and important publications.

War Resisters League. 339 Lafayette St., New York, NY 10012. *WRL News,* Bimonthly, $15.00/yr. *WIN Magazine.* 503 Atlantic Ave., 5th fl., Brooklyn, NY 11217. 36 pp. Biweekly, $15.00/yr.

Non-violent resistance against war, fascism, and human exploitation; concerned with the arms race, nuclear power, and social justice. Anti-nuclear packet, $2.00, includes 17" x 22" map of "Nuclear America".

Wind Energy Report. P.O. Box 14, Rockville Center, NY 11571. Monthly, $75.00/yr. Information on political, economic, and technical trends in wind power.

Woodburning Quarterly and Home Energy Digest. Division of Investment Rarities, Inc., 8009 34th Ave., South Minneapolis, MN. 55420. Quarterly, $6.00/yr.

Information on energy use in the home, wood stoves, and fireplaces.

Wood Energy Institute. P.O. Box 800, Camden, ME 04843. *Wood n' Energy.* 6 issues/yr, $5.00.

Promotes the use of fiber and wood resources through public information programs.

World Citizen Assembly. 312 Sutter St., Rm 608, San Francisco, CA 94108. *World Citizen.* 3 issues/yr, with $25.00 membership.

Goals are to stop the arms race, meet basic human needs, preserve the environment, and educate for world citizenship. Also opposes nuclear power and favors the development of alternative energy sources.

World Information Service on Energy, WISE. 2e Weteringplantsoen 9, 1017 ZD, Amsterdam, Netherlands; WISE, c/o Kitty Tucker, 520 Butternut St. NW, Washington, DC 20012. Six issues, $7.50.

WISE acts as a switchboard for the world-wide transnational anti-nuclear and soft-energy movement, exchanging information and facilitating effective action.

Worldwatch Institute, 1776 Massachusetts Ave., NW, Washington, DC 20036. Research and education. Publications include excellent monographs on global issues such as energy, environment, conservation, population, and social justice. These are presently available from FOE.

Wyoming Outdoor Council. P.O. Box 1184, Cheyenne, WY 82001. *Crossroads Monitor.* $15.00/yr.
Reviews siting applications for energy projects; intervenes and organizes.

Youth Project/Native Self-Sufficiency Tribal Sovereignty Program. P.O. Box 1040, Guerneville, CA 95446. *Native Self-Sufficiency.* Every six weeks, $6.00/yr.
Information on energy, natural resources, land and water rights, food production, and tribal government for self-sufficiency.

Zero Population Growth, 1346 Connecticut Ave., NW, Washington, DC 20036.
Committed to sustaining the quality of life by reducing per capita consumption of resources and energy, and by stabilizing population. Educational materials available.

ORGANIZATIONS AND PERIODICALS BY CATEGORY

Descriptions will be found in the preceding section of *ORGANIZATIONS—Alphabetical*.
Some organizations are listed in more than one category.

Alternative Energy, Appropriate Technology, Community Self-Reliance

Alternate Architecture: The Energy Management Journal

Alternative Energy Collective, Inc.

Alternative Energy Resource Organization

Alternatives: Perspectives on Society and the Environment

Alternative Sources of Energy Magazine

Center for Neighborhood Technology

Cerro Gordo Community Association

Citizens' Energy Project

CoEvolution Quarterly

Community Action Research Group: *New Criteria*

Compost Science: Journal of Waste Recycling

Countryside

doing it! humanizing city life

Earthmind

Ecotope Group

Energy Task Force

Farallones Institute

Green Revolution: The Art of Living

Institute for Local Self-Reliance

Intermediate Technology

International Project for Soft Energy Paths

Mother Earth News

National Land for People

New Alchemy Institute

New Roots: Notes on Appropriate Technology

People and Energy

Rain Magazine

Rural America

Seriatim: An Ecotopian Journal

Southwest Research and Information Center

Survival Rights

TRANET: Transnational Network for Appropriate/Alternative Technologies

Volunteers in Technical Assistance

Biomass; Alcohol Fuels

Alcohol Renewable Resource Center News

Ambix

Bio-Energy Council

Biomass Energy Institute, Inc., Canada

Bio-Sources Digest

Gasohol U.S.A. Journal

International Biomass Institute

National Alcohol Fuel Producers Association

Citizen Action; Consumer Groups

Citizen Participation

The Collaborators

Community Media

Consumer Action Now: Council on Environmental Alternatives

Consumer Federation of America, Energy Policy Task Force

Grantsmanship Center

Greater Washington Americans for Democratic Action

Initiative America

Massachusetts Public Interest Research Group

Media Access Project

National Consumer Law Center

New York Public Interest Research Group

Oil, Chemical, and Atomic Workers International Union

Paul H. Douglas Consumer Research Center

Public Citizen

Public Citizen Congress Watch

Public Interest Research Group

Wyoming Outdoor Council

Energy Conservation

Alliance to Save Energy

Association of Home Appliance Manufacturers

Environmental Action Foundation

League of American Wheelman

National Association of Home Builders

National League of Cities and Conference of Mayors

U.S. Department of Energy. *Energy Conservation Update*

Energy Education: See main section, *ENERGY EDUCATION: REFERENCES* and *RESOURCES FOR TEACHERS*

Energy Information; Periodicals

American Association for the Advancement of Science: *Science*

Center for Energy Policy and Research

Data Courier

Energy Abstracts for Policy Analysis

Energy Daily

Energy Economics Newsletter

Energy Information Abstracts

Energy Information Service. University of Texas

Energy Perspectives. Battelle

Energy Policy

Energy Research Reports

Energy Review

Energy Sources: An International Interdisciplinary Journal

Energy Systems and Policy: An International Interdisciplinary Journal

Energy Today

Energy Users' Report

International Journal of Energy Research

, MHB Technical Associates

National Aeronautics and Space Administration. *Energy*

National Climatic Center

Technology Review

U.S. Department of Energy. *Energy Consumer*

U.S. Department of Energy. *Energy Reporter*

U.S. Department of Energy. *Energy Research Abstracts*

U.S. Department of Energy. *Weekly Government Abstracts: Energy*

Environmental and Broad Interest Groups

American Friends Service Committee

Center for Science in the Public Interest

Citizens for a Better Environment

Clergy and Laity Concerned

Conservation Foundation

Conservation Report

Cousteau Society

The Ecologist

The Elements

Environmental Action

Environmental Action Foundation

Environmental Defense Fund

Friends of the Earth. *Not Man Apart*

Greenpeace

High Country News

Mobilization for Survival

National Academy of Sciences

National Audubon Society

National Council of Churches of Christ

National Recreation and Parks Association

National Wildlife Federation

Natural Resources Defense Council

New Scientist

SANE

Sierra Club

Scientists Instiute for Public Information. *Environment Magazine*

Science for the People

War Resisters League

World Citizens Assembly

Zero Population Growth

Fossil Energy

Citizens' Energy Project

Colorado Open Space Council

Fuel: Science and Technology of Fuel and Energy

Komanoff Energy Associates

U.S. Department of Energy. *Fossil Energy Update*

Geothermal Energy

Geothermal Energy

U.S. Department of Energy. *Geothermal Energy Update*

Native Americans

Akwesasne Notes

American Indian Environmental Council

National Indian Youth Council

The Youth Project/Native Self-Sufficiency

Nuclear Energy

American Friends Service Committee Nuclear Transportation Project

Anti-Nuclear Legal Project

Black Hills Alliance

Bulletin of the Atomic Scientists

Campaign for Political Rights

Center for Development Policy

Citizen Soldier

Citizens' Energy Council

Citizens' Energy Project

Clamshell Alliance

Clergy and Laity Concerned

Coalition for Full Nuclear Insurance

Coalition for a New Foreign and Military Policy

Coalition for a Non-Nuclear World

Committee for Nuclear Responsibility

Critical Mass Energy Project

Energy Policy Information Center

Friends of the Earth

Friends Nuclear Hazards Resource and Information Service

Greenpeace

Health Physics: The Journal of Applied Nuclear Technology

International Atomic Energy Agency. *Atom Index*

International Atomic Energy Agency. *Nuclear Fusion*

LAND Educational Associates Foundation, Inc.

League Against Nuclear Dangers, LAND, Inc.

Mobilization for Survival

Musicians United for Safe Energy, MUSE

National Association of Atomic Veterans

National Campaign for Radioactive Waste Safety

National Consumer Law Center

No Nuclear News

Nuclear Hazards Information Center

Nuclear Information and Resource Service

Nucleonics Week

Physicians for Social Responsibility

Re-Source, Inc.

Safe Energy Communication Council

SANE

Sierra Club

Sierra Club Atlantic Chapter Waste Campaign

Southwest Research and Information Center

Stop Uranium Mining, Inc.

Supporters of Silkwood

Task Force Against Nuclear Pollution

Union of Concerned Scientists

U.S. Department of Energy. *Fusion Energy Update*

U.S. Department of Energy. *Nuclear Safety*

Uranium Information Network

Uranium Resource and Action Network

War Resisters League

World Information Service on Energy

Pro-Nuclear Groups

American Nuclear Society

Atomic Industrial Forum

Citizens for Energy and Freedom

Energy Examiner

Policy, Legislation, and Economics

Congressional Quarterly Weekly Report

Congress Probe

Conservation Law Foundation

Council on Economic Priorities

Ecology Law Quarterly

Environmental Law Institute

Environmental Policy Institute

Environmental Policy and Law

Environmental Study Conference (Congress)

Environmentalists for Full Employment

Institute for Ecological Policies. *People and Energy*

Institute for Policy Studies, Inc. *In These Times*

League of Conservation Voters

League of Women Voters

National Committee Against Repressive Legislation

National Conference of State Legislatures

New Directions

New York Times

Public Citizen Congress Watch

Wall Street Journal

Research Organizations

American Institute of Architects

Center for Advanced Computation

Center for the Biology of Natural Systems

Center for Study of Responsive Law

Electric Power Research Institute
INFORM
Komanoff Energy Associates
Rand Corporation
Resources for the Future
Worldwatch Institute

Solar Energy

Center for Renewable Resources
Citizens' Energy Project
International Solar Energy Society, American Section
National Solar Energy Education Campaign
New England Solar Energy Association
Solar Age Magazine
Solar Energy Digest
Solar Energy Industries Association
Solar Energy Institute of America
Solar Energy Intelligence Report
Solar Engineering
Solar Greenhouse Digest
Solar Heating and Cooling
Solar Lobby
Solar Times
Solar Usage Now
Solar Utilization News
Southwest Research and Information Center
Sun Up: Energy News Digest
Total Environmental Action
U.S. Department of Energy. *Solar Energy Update*

Solid Waste and Recycling

Environmental Action Foundation
Institute for Local Self-Reliance

Utilities

American Public Power Assocation

Consumer Energy Council of America

Edison Electric Institute

Environmental Action Foundation

Public Interest Economics Foundation

Wind Energy

American Wind Energy Association. *Wind Power Digest*

Wind Energy Report

Wood Energy

Woodburning Quarterly

Wood Energy Institute. *Wood 'n Energy*

Catalogs

Many of the commercial publishing houses will send catalogs; Garden Way, Rodale, Ann Arbor, and others contain much material of interest. Too numerous to list here, their addresses may be found in the publishers' section of *Books in Print* at your library reference desk. The following addresses are listed under *ORGANIZATIONS*.

Edmond Scientific Co.

Energy House Catalog

Environmental Action Reprint Service

National Solar Energy Education Campaign. *Solar Energy Books*

Re-Source, Inc.

Roby, John. *Energy-Related Literature*

Solar Usage Now, Inc. *S.U.N. Catalog.*

Total Environmental Action

UNIPUB

Book-length catalogs are also listed as *REFERENCES* in other sections of this bibliography.

Catalogs or publication lists are available from many government agencies; See *U.S. GOVERNMENT ENERGY-RELATED AGENCIES*.

Alternative Energy Groups

Only a few of the hundreds of citizen groups are listed here. Addresses are subject to frequent change. To locate other groups, see organizations in *REFERENCES*.

References

Under *ORGANIZATIONS: REFERENCES* see Citizens' Energy Project and U.S. DOE Solar Energy Research Institute.

ANTI-NUCLEAR GROUP list which follows; your nearest Friends of the Earth branch.

ORGANIZATIONS: major national groups such as Solar Lobby: *People and Energy Magazine;* Friends of the Earth, San Francisco.

U.S. GOVERNMENT: National Center for Appropriate Technology; National Solar Heating and Cooling Information Center.

State Energy Offices; University Energy Centers.

Local branches of the American Friends Service Committee and League of Women Voters.

Groups

AL: Solar Energy Center, University of Alabama, P.O. Box 1247, Huntsville, AL 35807.

AK: Fairbanks Environmental Center, 431 Steese, Fairbanks, AK 99701. FOE, Margie Gibson, 1069 W. Sixth Ave., Anchorage, AK 99501.

AZ: Arizona Solar Energy Assocation, College of Architecture, Arizona State University, Tempe, AZ 85281.

AR: Arkansas Community Organizations for Reform Now (ACORN), 523 W. 15th St., Little Rock, AR 72202.

CA: Solar Utilization Now for Resources and Employment (SUNRAE), P.O. Box 915. Goleta, CA 93017.
Mid-Peninsula Conversion Project, 867 W. Dana, #203, Mountain View, CA 94041.
FOE, Betty Warren, 124 Spear St., San Francisco, CA 94105.

CO: Coalition for Full Employment, 2239 East Colfax, Denver, CO 80206.

CT: Citizen Action Group, P.O. Box G, 130 Washington St., Hartford, CT 06106.

DE: Delawareans for Energy Conservation, 111 Rodney Rd., Dover, DE 19901.

DC: Citizens Energy Project, 1110 Sixth St. NW #300, Washington, DC 20001.
FOE, Rafe Pomerance, 530 Seventh St. SE, Washington, DC 20003.

FL: Environmental Information Center, 935 Orange Ave., Winter Park, FL 32789.

GA: Georgia Solar Coalition, 3110 Maple Dr., NE, #403A, Atlanta, GA 30305.

HI: Energy Education Project, University of Hawaii, 1776 University Ave., Honolulu, HI 96822.

ID: Alternative Energy Association, P.O. Box 7963, Boise, ID 83707.

IL: Human Environmental Planning Program, Governor's State University. Park Forest South, IL 60466.

IN: Citizens Action Coalition, 3620 N. Meridian St., Indianapolis, IN 46208.

IA: Community Action Research Group, P.O. Box 1232, Ames, IA 50010.

KS: Kansas Sun Day, P.O. Box 979. Lawrence, KS 66044.
KY: Environmental Alternatives, 818 E. Chestnut St., #A303, Louisville, KY 40204.
LA: Ecology Center of Louisiana, P.O. Box 19344, New Orleans, LA 70179.
ME: Maine Audubon Alternative Energy Network, 118 U.S. Rt. 1, Falmouth, ME 04105.
FOE, LaRue Spiker, P.O. Box 625, Southwest Harbor, ME 04679.
MD: Solar Action of Maryland, 346 Glebe Rd., Easton, MD 21601.
MA: Massachusetts Public Interest Research Group, 120 Boyleston St., Boston, MA 02116.
FOE, Mark Weber, 3 Joy St., Boston, MA 02108.
MI: Michigan Solar Energy Association, 201 E. Liberty St. #2, Ann Arbor, MI 48104.
MN: Minnesota Public Interest Research Group, 3036 University Ave. SE, Minneapolis, MN 55414.
MS: Mississippi Solar Council, 887 Briarwood Dr., Jackson, MS 39211.
MO: Coalition for the Environment, 6267 Delmar Blvd., St. Louis, MO 63130.
FOE Midwest, Don Pierce, 29 Bearfield Rd., Columbia, MO 65201.
MT: Alternative Energy Resources Organization (AERO), 435 Stapleton Bldg., Billings, MT 59101.
FOE, Edward Dobson, P.O. Box 882, Billings, MT 59103.
NE: Midwest Energy Alternatives, 2444 B St., Lincoln, NE 68501.
NV: Nevada Solar Energy Association, Clark City Community College, 3200 E. Cheyenne Ave., North Las Vegas, NV 89030.
NH: Total Environmental Action, 24 Church Hill, Harrisville, NH 03450.
NJ: New Jersey Solar Coalition, 32 W. Lafayette St., Trenton, NJ 08608.
NM: Southwest Research and Information Center, P.O. Box 4524, Albuquerque, NM 87103.
NY: Consumer Action NOW, 355 Lexington Ave., 16th fl., New York, NY 10017.
FOE, Lorna Salzman, 72 Jane St., New York, NY 10014.
NC: North Carolina Coalition for Renewable Energy Resources, P.O. Box 10564, Raleigh, NC 27605.
ND: North Dakota Energy Office, 1533 N. 12th St., Bismark, ND 58501.
OH: Natural P.O.W.W.E.R., 6031 St. Clair Ave., Cleveland, OH 44103.
OK: Oklahoma Sun Day, 3115 Harvey Parkway, Oklahoma City, OK 73118.
OR: Center for Environmental Action, P.O. Box 188, Cottage Grove, OR 97424.
PA: Pennsylvania Solar Power Advocates, 615 Hedgerow Lane, Lancaster, PA 17601.
FOE, Kathleen O'Leary, 757 N. Croskey St., Philadelphia, PA 19130.
RI: Rhode Island Solar Energy Association, 195 Waterman St., #3, Providence, RI 02906.
SC: South Carolina Energy Task Force, P.O. Box 11781, Columbia, SC 29211.
SD: FOE, Ann Kunze, Alpena, SD 57312.
TN: Tennessee Environmental Council and Solar Coalition, P.O. Box 1422, Nashville, TN 37202.
TX: Texas Solar Energy Society, 1007 S. Congress, #348, Austin, TX 78704.

NOTE: If you have additions or corrections to this list, please write to Betty Warren, Friends of the Earth, 124 Spear St., San Francisco, CA 94105. Many thanks!

Anti-Nuclear/Safe Energy Groups

Only a few of the hundreds of citizen groups are listed here. Addresses are subject to frequent change. To locate other groups, see organizations in *REFERENCES.*

References

Under *ORGANIZATIONS: REFERENCES* see Citizens' Energy Project.

ALTERNATIVE ENERGY GROUP list (preceding); your nearest Friends of the Earth branch.

ORGANIZATIONS: major national groups, such as Coalition for a Non-Nuclear World, Critical Mass Energy Project, Clamshell Alliance (New England), Nuclear Information and Resource Service, Public Interest Research Group, and Friends of the Earth, San Francisco.

Local branches of the American Friends Service Committee, League of Women Voters, and Mobilization for Survival.

Groups

AR: Arkansans for Safe Power, 1805 Bradley Lane Russelville, AR 72801.
CA: Abalone Alliance, 944 Market St. #307, San Francisco, CA 94102.
Alliance for Survival, 712 S. Grand View St., Los Angeles, CA 90057.
FOE, Betty Warren, 124 Spear St., San Francisco, CA 94105.
CO: Rocky Flats Action Group, 1432 Lafayette, Denver, CO 80218.
FOE, Kevin Markey, 2239 East Colfax, Denver, CO 80206.
CT: Hartford Clam, P.O. Box 6346, Hartford, CT 06106.
DE: Coalition for Nuclear Power Plant Postponement, 810 West 25th St., Wilmington, DE 19802.
DC: Potomac Alliance, P.O. Box 9306, Washington, DC 20005.
Nuclear Information and Resource Service, 1536 16th St. NW, Washington, DC 20005.
FOE, Rafe Pomerance, 530 Seventh St. SE, Washington, DC 20003.
FL: Catfish Alliance, P.O. Box 20049, Tallahassee, FL 32304.
GA: Georgians Against Nuclear Energy, P.O. Box 8574, Station F, Atlanta, GA 30306.
HI: Life of the Land, 404 Piikoi St., Honolulu, HI 96814.
ID: Groundwater Alliance, Ketchum, ID 83340.
IL: Bailly Alliance, 711 S. Dearborn, #548, Chicago, IL 60605.
Citizens for a Better Environment, 59 E. Van Buren St. #2610, Chicago, IL 60605.
IN: Paddlewheel Alliance, P.O. Box 194, New Albany, IN 47150.
IA: Citizens United for Responsible Energy, 1342 30th St., Des Moines, IA 50311.
KS: Kansans for Sensible Energy, 1340 N. Hillside, Wichita, KS 67208.
KY: Paddlewheel Alliance, 1426 Highland Ave., Louisville, KY 40204.
LA: Oystershell Alliance, 1808 Robert St., New Orleans, LA 70115.
ME: Nuclear Reaction, c/o Mary Snell, 54 Eastern Promenade #2, Portland, ME 04101.
FOE, La Rue Spiker, P.O. Box 625, Southwest Harbor, 04679.
MD: Chesapeake Energy Alliance, c/o Joel Kilgore, 3549 Green Mount Ave., Baltimore, MD 21218.
MA: Boston Clamshell, 595 Massachusetts Ave., Cambridge, MA 02139.
FOE, Mark Weber, 3 Joy St., Boston, MA 02108.
MI: Detroit Safe Energy Coalition, 691 Seward #E-1, Detoirt, MI 48202.
MN: Northern Sun Alliance, 1573 E. Franklin Ave., MN 55404.
MS: Catfish Alliance, c/o Ron Lewis, 1305 Madison Ave., Oxford, MS 38655.
MO: Missourians for Safe Energy, 811 Cherry St. #319, Columbia, MO 65201.
FOE Midwest, Don Pierce, 29 Bearfield Rd., Columbia, MO 65201.
MT: Alternative Energy Resource Organization, 435 Stapleton Bldg., Billings, MT 59101.
FOE, Edward Dobson, P.O. Box 882, Billings, MT 59103.
NE: Nebraskans for Peace, 430 S. 16th St., Lincoln, NE 68501.
NV: Citizen Alert, P.O. Box 5731, Reno, NV 89513.
NH: Clamshell Alliance, 39 Congress St., Portsmouth, NH 03801.
NJ: Citizens Energy Council, P.O. Box 285, Allendale, NJ 07401.
NM: Southwest Research and Information Center, P.O. Box 4524, Albuquerque, NM 87103.
FOE, Sally Rodgers, Rt. 7, Box 131, Santa Fe, NM 87501.

NY: Syracuse Peace Council, 924 Burnet Ave., Syracuse, NY 13203.
Long Island Safe Energy Coalition, P.O. Box 972, Smithtown, NY 11787.
FOE, Lorna Salzman, 72 Jane St., New York, NY 10014.
NC: Carolinians for Safe Energy, P.O. Box 8165, Asheville, NC 28804.
ND: See SD: Black Hills Alliance, P.O. Box 2508, Rapid City, SD 57701.
OH: Ohioans for Utility Reform, P.O. Box 10006, Columbus, OH 43201.
OK: Citizens' Action for Safe Energy, P.O. Box 924, Claremore, OK 74017.
OR: Trojan Decommissioning Alliance, 215 SE 9th Ave., Portland, OR 97214.
PA: Mobilization for Survival, 3601 Locust Walk, Philadelphia, PA 19104.
Susquehanna Valley Alliance, 114 Kloss Dr., Lancaster, PA 17603.
FOE, Kathleen O'Leary, 757 N. Croskey St., Philadelphia, PA 19130.
RI: Rhode Island Clam, c/o AFSC, 2 Stimson Ave., Providence, RI 02906.
SC: Palmetto Alliance, 18 Bluff Rd., Columbia, SC 29201.
SD: Black Hills Alliance, P.O. Box 2508, Rapid City, SD 57701.
FOE, Ann Kunze, Alpena, SD 57312.
TN: Catfish Alliance, 362 Binkley Dr., Nashville, TN 37415.
TX: Armadillo Coalition, P.O. Box 15556, Fort Worth, TX 76116.
UT: FOE, Gordon Anderson, P.O. Box 820, Moab, UT 84532.
VT: Central Vermont Safe Energy Coalition, P.O. Box 1117, Montpelier, VT 05602.
New England Coalition on Nuclear Pollution, P.O. Box 637, Brattleboro, VT 05301.
FOE, George Longenecker, P.O. Box 285, Burlington, VT 05402.
VA: North Anna Environmental Coalition, P.O. Box 3951, Charlottesville, VA 22903.
WA: Crabshell Alliance, 1114 34th Ave., Seattle, WA 98122.
FOE Northwest, Dale Jones, 4512 University Way NE, Seattle, WA 98105.
WV: West Virginia Alliance, c/o Isabelle Umpleby, 17 Gallatin St., Ravenswood, WV 26164.
WI: League Against Nuclear Dangers, RR 1, Rudolph, WI 54475.
FOE, Chris Kalka, P.O. Box 224, Holcombe, WI 54745.
WY: Wyoming Outdoor Council, P.O. Box 1184, Cheyenne, WY 82001.
FOE, Howie Wolke, P.O. Box 2671, Jackson, WY 83001.
CANADA: Friends of the Earth/Les Amis de la Terre, 54-53 Queen St., Ottawa, Ontario, K1P 5C5.

NOTE: If you have additions or corrections to this list, please write to Betty Warren, Friends of the Earth, 124 Spear St., San Francisco, CA 94105. Many thanks!

Paraphernalia

Bumper-stickers, buttons, T-shirts etc.

Border Crossings, P.O. Box 146, Turners Falls, MA 01376. Smiling Sun buttons & stickers, the international safe energy symbol.

Donnelly/Colt. Box 271, New Vernon, NJ 07976.

Environmental Action Reprint Service (EARS). Box 545, La Veta, CO 81055. Literature also.

Larry Fox. Box M, Valley Stream, NY 11582.

Mellow Crafts, RFD 2, Newmarket, NH 03857. T-shirts, canvas shoulder bags, pillows.

Mobilization for Survival. 3601 Locust Walk, Philadelphia, PA 19104. Literature also.

No Nukes. Box 30, Montague, MA 01351.

Pacific Alliance. P.O. Box 1738, San Luis Obispo, CA 93406.

Re-Source, Inc. P.O. Box 127, Astor Station, Boston, MA 02123. Literature also.

Sky Designs. P.O. Box 2610, Santa Cruz, CA 95062.

Solar Future. P.O. Box 19177, Sacramento, CA 95819.

Sundries. 1001 Connecticut Ave. NW, 5th fl., Washington, DC 20036.

Vereniging Milieudefensie—FOE/Netherlands. 2e Weteringplantsoen 9, 1017 ZD Amsterdam, Netherlands. The Action Sun buttons, stickers, and T-shirts.

AUTHOR/EDITOR INDEX

Organizations and government agencies are listed here only if specified as authors of publications. Producers of audio-visual materials are not included.

-A-

Abalone Alliance. 91
Abbotts, J. 89
Abelson, P.H. 35
Abrecht, P. 86
Acton, J.P. 135
Adams, A. 40
Adams, G. 86
Adams, R.W. 117
Adzema, R. 153
Ahern, W.R. 73
Ahmed, S.B. 85
Aitken, D. 109
Albright, R. 38
Alderson, G. 143
Aldridge, R.C. 95
Alexander, M.Y. 148
Alexander, S.S. 24
Alterman, J. 12
Alternative Energy Resources
    Organization. 153
Alternative Sources of
    Energy. 59
Alves, R. 59
American Bar Foundation. 116
American Inst. of Architects. 41, 117
American Nuclear Society. 85, 161
American Physical Society. 122
Ames, M.E. 9
Ametek. 122
Anderson, B. 118, 121
Anderson, J.M. 143
Anderson, L.K. 66
Andrassy, S. 111
Ann Arbor Science Task Group. 109
Anthropology Resource Center. 27
Argue, R. 111
Armstead, H.C. 80
Armstrong, J.E. 35
Aronowitz, S. 9
Ashley, H. 9
ASHRAE: see Jordan, 125
Asian Productivity Organization. 30

Askin, A.B. 24
Auerbach, L. 63
Augustyn, J. 115, 154
Ayres, R.U. 131

-B-

Backus, C.E. 123
Baer, S. 111
Bailey, J.E. 9
Bailey, R.L. 123
Bainbridge, D.A. 109, 118
Baker, B. 38
Baker, J.M. 73
Baldwin, J. 51
Banks. F.E. 24
Barkas, J.L. 170
Barling, J. 154
Barnaby, C.S. 118
Barney, G.O. 9
Barnouw, D.B. 7
Barton, J.H. 96
Bass, S.C. 148
Baylon, D. 63
Beacon Press. 146
Beckman, W. 123
Beedell, S. 139
Behrens, W.W. III. 33
Behrman, D. 111
Bell. 63
Bell, F.A. 27
Bello, W. 85
Bendavid-Val, A. 52
Bender, T. 41,52
Bendixson, T. 131
Bennett, R. 123
Benson, J. 47
Benson, J.W. 24
Bereny, J. 109
Berger, J. 85
Berger, M. 154
Bergaust, E. 154
Bergman, E. 9
Berkowitz, N. 76

Dye, L. 73

Metos, T.H. 155
Metz, W.D. 14, 114
Metzger, N. 17
Metzger, H.P. 89
Meyer, L.A. 100
Meyers, P. 47
Meyers, R.A. 77
Meynell, P.J. 64
MHB Technical Associates. 102
Michaelis, D. 97
Michigan Assn. of School
    Administrators. 150
Mid-Peninsula Conversion Project.
    114
Miernyk, W.A. 26
Milgram, J.H. 73
Miller, A.S. 117
Miller, G.T. 17
Miller, R.L. 26
Miller, S. 94
Milligan, C. 59
Milora, S.L. 81
Mindell, H.L. 48
Minnesota Environmental Sciences
    Foundation. 150
Mitchell, E.J. 25
Mitchell, B. 135
Mitchell, J. 14
Mitsui, A. 64
Mobilization for Survival. 157
Montefiore, H. 95
Montgomery, R.H. 120
Moran, T.H. 71
Morell, D. 92
Morgan, K.Z. 88
Morgan, M. 77
Morgan, M.G. 17
Morgan, R. 17
Morgan, R. 94
Morresi, A.C. 66
Morris, D. 47, 149
Moss, E. 77
Mostert, N. 74
Mother Earth News. 60
Mountain Community Union.
    79
Murdock, S.H. 29
Murphy, J.A. 40
Murphy, K. 35
Murray, R.B. 17
Murray, F.X. 78
Myers, D. III. 89
Myers, J.G. 49

-N-

Naar, J. 61
Nader, R. 89
Nadis, S.J. 105, 113
Naill, R.F. 18
Nakamura, L. 49
Nash, H. 33
National Academy of Sciences. 18,
    57, 67, 71, 78, 108, 132
National Assn. of Independent
    Schools. 150
National Audubon Society. 150
National Consumer Information
    Center. 135
National Council of Churches. 29
National 4-H Council. 146
National League of Cities. 42
National No-Nukes Strategy
    Conference. 92
National Recreation & Park Assn.
    151, 152, 171
National Referral Center. 165, 168
National Science Foundation. 126,
    141
National Science Teachers Assn. 151
National Solar Energy Education
    Campaign. 110
National Wildlife Federation. 131,
    151, 171
Nealey, S. 89
Nearing, H. 130
Nearing, S. 130
Nelkin, D. 92
Nelson, L. 55, 118
Nelson, P.A. 80
Nero, A. 89
New Alchemists. 55
New England Congressional Caucus.
    60
Newkirk, R.T. 135
Newland, K. 26
Newman, D.K. 29
New Mexico Solar Energy Assn. 146
Nichols, C. 39
Nicholls, R. 130
Nicholson, N. 120
NIRS. 100, 108, 145, 157
Noll, E.M. 140
Norman, C. 18, 131
Norton, T.W. 151
Novick, S. 92

RESOURCES FROM
FRIENDS OF THE EARTH

Soft Energy Paths
Toward a Durable Peace

By Amory B. Lovins, introduction by Barbara Ward

Soft Energy Paths crowns the critical work of Amory Lovins and FOE with a new program for energy sanity. This is an epoch-making book, the most important Friends of the Earth has published.

Lovin's soft path can take us around nuclear power, free industrial nations of dependence on unreliable sources of oil and the need to seek it in fragile environments, and at the same time enable modern societies to grow without damaging the earth or making their people less free.

Soft Energy Paths provides a conceptual and technical basis for more efficient energy use, the application of appropriate alternative technologies, and the clean and careful use of fossil fuels while soft technologies are put in place.

Harper & Row/Colophon edition
231 pages
$3.95

Pathway to Energy Sufficiency
The 2050 Study

By John Steinhart

Pathway to Energy Sufficiency is a hardheaded, hopeful look at an American society seventy years in the future. The authors draw a picture of what it would be like to live along a soft energy path, using 36 percent of the energy we used in 1975. They tell how this would affect our houses, travel, countryside, factories, gardens, and public institutions. They find this low energy society decentralized, more rural, less hurried, and healthier.

"The benefits that will accrue to a society that accepts the low-energy scenario could be most attractive. If people want a world in which people restrain their numbers and appetites, people can achieve it—and will prefer it to the grim alternatives."
David R. Brower

96 pages, illustrated
$4.95

Frozen Fire:
Where Will It Happen Next?
By Lee Niedringhaus Davis

An LNG accident could be as bad as a reactor meltdown, and the major exporters of liquefied natural gas are OPEC countries.

But the gas industry wants to make it common, building terminals on most American coasts, Europe and Japan, bringing 125,000-cubic-meter shiploads of it in from the Middle East, Indonesia, and Alaska.

US trade in LNG is insignificant now, and world trade is small compared to industry plans. So there is still time to avert the dangers. If we do not, recent horrors with liquefied gases in Spain, Mexico, England, Abu Dhabi, and Staten Island may be the harbingers of a fearful future.

Lee Davis's book is the first major study of LNG prepared for the general reader. It tells everything you should know about the stuff before they try to put it in your town.

"The scope and logic of *Frozen Fire* should make it the Bible of anti-LNG groups throughout the world. It could even make converts of government agencies and the gas industry, preventing the inevitable LNG holocaust."
—Gene and Edwina Cosgriff
B.L.A.S.T.

"An impressive and powerful compendium of information on the dangers of another chemical threat to the so-called civilized world."
—John G. Fuller

256 pages
Paperback: $6.95

The Whale Manual
By Friends of the Earth Staff

The Whale Manual lays out the latest facts and figures about the great whales. Population estimates, habitats, and how quickly they are being killed, by whom, for what, and how—and what could be used as alternatives to whale products.

A special section outlines Friends of the Earth's controversial program to preserve the endangered Bowhead, with the help of the Eskimos who hunt it.

The Whale Manual is an invaluable source for readers committed to saving our planet's largest creatures.

168 pages
$4.95

Progress
As If Survival Mattered
Edited by Hugh Nash

The environmental book of 1978, *Progress As If Survival Mattered* presents Friends of the Earth's comprehensive and realistic program to take America away from energy crises and resource shortages . . . and charts the way to an abundant, healthy, and free future. This "Handbook for a Conserver Society" includes the thinking of our finest writers on energy, environment, and society.

"Here is a book undoubtedly headed for fame . . . an important anthology of long articles on issues which are critical . . . a guidebook for citizen action . . . an all-around introduction to the ills and successes of our planet, it should find its way into the homes of almost anyone who reads more than the Sunday comics. . . . Highly recommended."

—Library Journal

320 pages
$6.95

SUN!
A Handbook For the Solar Decade
Edited by Stephen Lyons

The Sun's rays inspired life on earth and stocked the planet with the fuel we've nearly exhausted. It's time we acknowledge the Sun's importance to our future.

By relying on the energy of the Sun, we can put an end to the costly and dangerous nuclear experiment. The solar future will be cleaner and freer, more equitable and enjoyable than the present.

Sun! is the official book of the International Sun Day movement.

"Here you have the thoughts of an extraordinary range of minds attending the solar nexus: Brower, Lovins, Bookchin, Illich, Goodman, Mumford, Grossman, Hayes, Long, Commoner, Georgescu-Roegen, von Arx, H. Odum, Inglis, Lyons, Stein, Shurcliff (especially), Reis, Goldman, Mills, Harding."

—CoEvolution Quarterly

". . . This is an overview of the social, economic, and technical advantages of solar energy. There is an extensive bibliography and a listing of organizations active in this field. Recommended. . . ."

—Library Journal

". . . a crusading, provocative, and prophetic work."

—Los Angeles Times

364 pages
$2.95

To: Friends of the Earth
124 Spear Street
San Francisco, CA 94105

Please Join Us.

☐ Please enroll me for one year in the category checked, entitling me to *Not Man Apart* and discounts on selected FOE books.
(*Contributions to FOE are not tax-deductible.*)

☐ Regular = $25   ☐ Spouse = add $5
☐ Supporting = $35*   ☐ Life = $1000***
☐ Contributing = $60**   ☐ Patron = $5000***
☐ Sponsor = $100**   ☐ Retired = $12
☐ Sustaining = $250**   ☐ Student/Low Income = $12

*Will receive free a paperback volume from our *Celebrating the Earth* Series.

**Will receive free a volume from our *Earth's Wild Places* Series.

***Will receive free a copy of *Headlands* (our award-winning, gallery-format book).

☐ Check here if you do not wish to receive your bonus book.

☐ Please accept my *deductible* contribution of $ _____ to Friends of the Earth Foundation (*checks must be made to FOE Foundation*).

Please send me the following FOE Books:

Number	Title, price (*members' price*)	Cost
_____	*Frozen Fire* at $12.50 ($10.00)	_____
_____	paperback *Frozen Fire* at $6.95 ($5.95)	_____
_____	*Energy Controversy* at $12.50 ($10.00)	_____
_____	paperback *Energy Controversy* at $6.95 ($5.95)	_____
_____	*Progress As If Survival Mattered* at $6.95 (5.75)	_____
_____	*SUN! A Handbook for the Solar Decade* at $2.95 ($2.25)	_____
_____	*Soft Energy Paths*, H&R ed. at $3.95 ($3.25)	_____
_____	*The Whale Manual* at $4.95 ($3.95)	_____
	Other FOE Titles:	

_____   _____
_____   _____
_____   _____

                                    Subtotal _____
                     6% tax on Calif. delivery _____
                 Plus 5% for shipping/handling _____

☐ Send full FOE Books catalogue.   TOTAL _____
☐ VISA   ☐ Mastercharge
Number _____ Expiration date _____
Signature _____
Name _____
Address _____
City _____ State _____ Zip _____ .

228

The Energy and Environment Checklist

An Annotated Bibliography of Resources

The Checklist is an annotated guide to more than 1600 sources of information for doing everything from fighting a nuclear plant to building a roof-top solar collector.

The Checklist is a valuable tool for students, teachers, activists, researchers or citizens who want the information to understand—and do something about—today's headlines, gas lines, and power-plant controversies.

Energy and The Environment
Energy Conservation
Appropriate Technology
Alternative Sources of Energy
Biomass
Fossil Fuels
Geothermal Energy
Hydrogen and Fuel Cells
Nuclear Energy
Solar Energy
Transportation
Utilities
Water Power
Wind Energy
Citizen Action
Energy Education
Audio-Visual Materials
United States Government
Organizations

Friends of the Earth

ISBN: 0-913890-37-5
$5.95